Addressing Conflict, COVID-19, and Climate Change

Praise for this book

A major challenge in common for all in WASH and emergency response is their intersectoral nature and the apparent ineffectiveness of the usual siloed approaches. This book, a compilation of authoritative and practical analyses and recommendations, is a valuable resource for all working within humanitarian and developmental contexts. The case studies and lessons learnt provide valuable evidence on which to build short-term effectiveness and long-term resilience and sustainability.

Sally Sutton, Consultant and Practitioner in rural water supply,
SWL Consultants

It is hard to do WASH well, especially in humanitarian crises that have significant aspects of insecurity, conflict, fragility, and environmental and public health dimensions. To do so in ways that also acknowledge and address the multiple needs of affected populations is even harder. In this book, the authors tackle these various and simultaneous challenges head-on, in an attempt to draw learning from existing case studies and so inform better practices in future. Readers will find a wealth of insight and analysis in this book, all focused on bringing together the sectors and actors that together can more effectively address the needs of those caught up in humanitarian crises.

Richard Carter, Researcher and Consultant in water and sanitation,
groundwater development and agricultural water management

Addressing Conflict, COVID-19, and Climate Change

A multisectoral approach to integrated WASH programming

Edited by
Mariëlle Snel and Nikolas Sorensen

Practical Action Publishing Ltd
25 Albert Street, Rugby,
Warwickshire, CV21 2SD, UK
www.practicalactionpublishing.com

© Mariëlle Snel, Nikolas Sorensen and the contributors, 2023

The moral right of the editors to be identified as editors of the work has been asserted under sections 77 and 78 of the Copyright Design and Patents Act 1988.

All rights reserved. No part of this publication may be reprinted or reproduced or utilized in any form or by any electronic, mechanical, or other means, now known or hereafter invented, including photocopying and recording, or in any information storage or retrieval system, without the written permission of the publishers.

Product or corporate names may be trademarks or registered trademarks, and are used only for identification and explanation without intent to infringe.

A catalogue record for this book is available from the British Library.
A catalogue record for this book has been requested from the Library of Congress.

ISBN 978-1-78853-222-8 Paperback
ISBN 978-1-78853-227-3 Hardback
ISBN 978-1-78853-223-5 Electronic book

Citation: Snel, M., Sorensen, N. (2023) *Addressing conflict, COVID-19, and climate change: A multisectoral approach to integrated WASH programming*, Rugby, UK: Practical Action Publishing <http://doi.org/10.3362/9781788532235>.

Since 1974, Practical Action Publishing has been publishing and disseminating books and information in support of international development work throughout the world. Practical Action Publishing is a trading name of Practical Action Publishing Ltd (Company Reg. No. 1159018), the wholly owned publishing company of Practical Action. Practical Action Publishing trades only in support of its parent charity objectives and any profits are covenanted back to Practical Action (Charity Reg. No. 247257, Group VAT Registration No. 880 9924 76).

The views and opinions in this publication are those of the editors and do not represent those of Practical Action Publishing Ltd or its parent charity Practical Action. Reasonable efforts have been made to publish reliable data and information, but the editors and publisher cannot assume responsibility for the validity of all materials or for the consequences of their use.

Cover design by Katarzyna Markowska, Practical Action Publishing.
Typeset by vPrompt eServices, India

Contents

List of abbreviations	vii
Introduction	ix
Marïelle Snel and Nikolas Sorensen	
Chapter 1: Integrated WASH narrative literature review: the 3Cs and intersectoral coordination *Marley P. Gibbons, Cristina Mena-Lander, and Syed Yasir Ahmad Khan*	1
Chapter 2: A WASH framework to address conflict, COVID-19, and climate change: leveraging the humanitarian–development–peace nexus *Tim Grieve*	33
Chapter 3: Integrating WASH with health in humanitarian settings *Nikolas Sorensen and Marïelle Snel*	67
Chapter 4: WASH–nutrition integration: for vulnerable populations affected by conflict, climate change, and the COVID-19 pandemic *Jovana Dodos and Bram Riems*	85
Chapter 5: Integrated WASH and shelter *Susannah Webb*	109
Chapter 6: Integrated WASH and education *Anne Corwith and Erin Sorensen*	135
Chapter 7: Child protection and WASH integration *Allison Jeffery*	153
Chapter 8: Focusing on the future: integration of WASH around conflict, COVID-19, and climate change *Marïelle Snel and Nikolas Sorensen*	175
Index	187

List of abbreviations

IDP	internally displaced person
GBV	gender-based violence
CCA	Common Country Assessment
GWC	Global WASH Cluster
JIAF	Joint Intersectoral Assessment Framework
HCT	Humanitarian Country Team
HNO	Humanitarian Needs Overview
HRP	Humanitarian Response Plan
IFI	International Financing Institution
JOF	Joint Operational Framework
NWOW	New Way of Working
RRP	Refugee Response Plan
RC/HC	UN Resident Coordinator/Humanitarian Coordinator
SDG	Sustainable Development Goal
SWA	Sanitation and Water for All
WASH	Water, sanitation, and hygiene
UNCT	United Nations Country Team
UNSDCF	United Nations Sustainable Development Cooperation Framework

Introduction

Marïelle Snel[1] *and Nikolas Sorensen*

Humanitarian contexts globally are increasing in number, length, and complexity. Given ongoing geopolitical conflicts, water wars[2] continue to increase, creating greater stress on the global humanitarian and development water, sanitation, and hygiene (WASH) community. Our intent here is to argue the need for multisectoral, integrated approaches to humanitarian responses. However, with each new crisis, the difficulty of such approaches increases as scarce humanitarian funding, workers, and other critical resources get spread out to meet ever-growing new needs. However, notwithstanding these difficulties, we argue that multisectoral humanitarian responses are even more vital as the humanitarian and development sectors face new crises, remember and attend to old ones, and advocate for more resources to meet the needs of those most impacted by the effects of conflict, COVID-19[3], and climate change.

In 2021 we published our book *Bridging the WASH Humanitarian–development Divide: Building a Sustainable Reality*, in which we began our discussion of what integrated WASH programming could look like and how humanitarian/development actors can improve ongoing integrated cooperation (Snel and Sorensen, 2021). Within the context of this publication, integrated WASH programming refers to a multisectoral, 'integrated' response to humanitarian and development problems as a more effective and innovative way of solving problems. This entails a focus on WASH from both an immediate and long-term prevention-and-control perspective, which includes connecting WASH services to other critical humanitarian and development priorities, like improving health, reducing poverty, and progressing socio-economic development, as well as responding to global emergencies, disease outbreaks, epidemics, and pandemics.

As conflicts and crises become more protracted, a long-term development vision in a short-term humanitarian context is needed to increase the ability of aid organizations to save lives and reduce suffering. Integration, therefore, becomes essential to bridging the humanitarian–development–peace (or triple) nexus. Integration in this context refers both to the bridging of the humanitarian–development divide, which was the primary focus of our last book (Snel and Sorensen, 2021), and to multisectoral integration between sectors, which is the primary focus of this publication. However, to truly succeed at bridging the humanitarian–development divide, integration between subsectors like WASH, health, nutrition, shelter, education, and child protection, to name the primary topics of this publication, is essential regardless of humanitarian or development context. This is not easy and requires humanitarian and development workers to rethink siloed approaches and systems, and look for new, innovative solutions in increasingly complex situations.

This publication focuses on how governments, funders, and other international non-government organizations (INGOs) can better integrate services in humanitarian settings. A strong systems approach is required to manage the needs of various stakeholders and ensure WASH services are sustainable (GWC, 2022; SWA, 2020). Building sustainable systems is a gradual process, especially in humanitarian settings, and takes buy-in from all levels of system development and maintenance. The International Water and Sanitation Centre has developed a systematic approach that allows longer-term WASH services to scale up, and learning and adaptation to filter down as needs change (IRC, 2017).

However, systems for change also require a framework for understanding the intricacies of relationships between stakeholders, institutions, and other empowering or limiting factors. One such framework is the sustainable WASH model, which highlights the intersectionality of institutional, social, technical, financial, and environmental issues in providing sustainable WASH services (WASH Alliance International, 2021). However, many of the institutions and organizations that take part in the design and implementation of WASH programming have an inherently top-down perspective of WASH programming. As is always the case, a bottom-up perspective is vital to the successful implementation and uptake of WASH services, integrated or not. Some of the most successful humanitarian and development interventions utilized community-led programming, which creates community buy-in and helps ensure the long-term success and impact of services. In the WASH sector, one example is the Community-Led Total Sanitation (CLTS) approach, which, while facing some controversy, gives benefitting communities ownership over sanitation programming and impact (The Sanitation Learning Hub, n.d.). Systems approaches and community-led programming in humanitarian contexts can help to immediately begin the process of shifting short-term humanitarian thinking into longer-term integrative development.

To date, there is a knowledge gap specifically regarding the integration potential of WASH programming from a multisectoral perspective. This volume was conceptualized as an opportunity to bring together experts from across various humanitarian and development fields with the purpose of addressing WASH services and the potential of integration across the humanitarian–development–peace nexus and with subsectors like health, nutrition, shelter, education, and child protection. The contributions specifically look more closely at ways each subfield could better integrate with WASH programming. We recognize that neither we nor our contributors can provide a one-size-fits-all solution to an integrated humanitarian–development response. However, we aim to provide deeper insights into the 'how' question underlying integrated WASH programming. To achieve this, most contributors have used case studies that highlight avenues of integration between their field and WASH, looking specifically at conflict, COVID-19, and climate change, or what we call the '3Cs'.

The question that may arise is: why focus on the 3Cs in each of these chapters? As the global statistics are proving, the convergence of conflict, COVID-19, and climate crisis is jeopardizing global humanitarian as well as long-term development goals. As directly cited from the UNHCR (Harper and Vinke, 2020):

- One-third of the world's internally displaced live in the ten countries most at risk from COVID-19. They now face a health crisis, a socio-economic crisis, and a protection crisis against the backdrop of an ever-growing climate crisis.
- COVID-19 adds an additional layer of vulnerability to displaced persons in environmentally fragile areas and in regions heavily impacted by the effects of climate change, which are often further impacted by poverty, conflict, and weak health systems.
- Those who are displaced suddenly because of disasters will face increasing health risks as it may not be possible to respect hygiene and social distancing measures in these contexts. Displaced populations often have precarious livelihoods, and reduced or no access to social safety nets and health services. These vulnerabilities are exacerbated for those in 'climate hotspots', or where livelihoods are already at risk due to climate change and environmental degradation.
- Humanitarian access during the COVID-19 pandemic will remain constrained, and the forcibly displaced and other vulnerable populations will be hit the hardest by the crisis.

From the perspective of long-term WASH development, the United Nations 2022 report on progress toward the Sustainable Development Goals (SDGs) notes that 'the convergence of increased fighting, the continuing COVID-19 pandemic, and the long-term climate crisis, could push an additional 75 to 95 million people into extreme poverty this year – compared with pre-pandemic projections – and jeopardize the SDG blueprint for more resilient, peaceful and equal societies' (United Nations, 2022). In other words, the 3Cs reflect the most significant crises facing the humanitarian and development sectors today and in the future, and therefore represent vital issues to address in each chapter.

The primary audience for this publication is professionals working in the humanitarian and development WASH sector. However, we hope it will also interest others working in the humanitarian, development, and peace sectors, ranging from government officials to managers working directly or indirectly around WASH. It is possible to dip into specific chapters without reading the full publication, although reading the first two chapters and the last one is recommended. This book focuses heavily on humanitarian–development practitioners and organizations' willingness to bridge sectors and divides, and to increase effectiveness and impact on the lives of those served.

How is this book structured?

A multisectoral approach to humanitarian responses requires the voices and experience of experts from diverse backgrounds to come together under a shared vision. As such, the structure of this publication aims to bring together a handful of voices with expertise in key humanitarian and development sectors to discuss the integration between their focus areas and WASH. We acknowledge that a vital component of any humanitarian response is local contextualization, which requires input from those receiving humanitarian aid. However, despite abundant local input, success is still dependent on uniting numerous competing organizations, funders, and national governments under a shared vision of success.

In chapter 1, Gibbons, Mena-Lander, and Khan provide a literature review of intersectoral collaboration in connection with the 2020-2025 road map (GWC, 2020). Specifically, they take a deeper look at the integration of WASH programming with other sectors like health, nutrition, and emergency response, highlighting both the successes and barriers to impactful integration.

In chapter 2, Grieve discusses the role frameworks have in operationalizing the global humanitarian–development–peace nexus in the context of WASH. This triple nexus plays a vital role in understanding the current ongoing debate around the humanitarian and development WASH crisis and how to align these three subsectors. Grieve also touches on the impact of the 3Cs on WASH programming, and the role the triple nexus can play in addressing current and future needs with the aid of frameworks. This chapter highlights 'a global call to address the needs, risks, and vulnerabilities of affected populations in crisis and to lay the foundation for advancing sustainable development' by operationalizing a global humanitarian–development–peace nexus policy in the context of WASH through a Joint Operational Framework (JOF).

In chapter 3, N. Sorensen and Snel focus on integrating WASH programming with health services. The importance of key non-household settings is briefly discussed. A heavy focus is placed on the impact of COVID-19 in humanitarian contexts. A case study is provided from Nigeria, Africa, looking at the integration of WASH services to improve the ability of health care facilities to serve refugee and communities of internally displaced persons (IDPs) safely.

In chapter 4, Dodos and Riems consider integrated WASH linked to nutrition for vulnerable populations affected by the 3Cs. A case study from Nigeria, Africa, highlights the direct effects proper WASH practices have on decreasing the prevalence of diarrhoea and improving child nutrition. They conclude with a strategic framework for the integration of WASH with nutrition.

In chapter 5, Webb discusses integrated WASH linked to adequate housing and shelter, with a focus on the importance of integrated, multisector approaches for shelter and WASH outcomes to succeed. An in-depth look at shelter and WASH linked to the 3Cs is provided. Two compelling case studies – one based in Malawi, Africa, and the other in Northwest Syria, the Middle East – highlight the challenges of successfully integrating WASH and shelter programming, and the safety and dignity successful integration can bring to the daily lives of those served.

In chapter 6, Corwith and E. Sorensen focus on integrated WASH linked to education, and what this means in line with the 3Cs. They emphasize the role of linking WASH and education in bridging the humanitarian–development and peace divide, focusing on monitoring, evaluation, long-term indicators, training, and the role of the community and children in contributing to WASH and education outcomes. Each thematic area provides several case studies from Bangladesh, Nepal, and Syria.

In chapter 7, Jeffery discusses child protection linked to integrated WASH, focusing on understanding what integrated child protection linked to WASH means. A list of suggested actions for integrating child protection and WASH is provided, followed by a brief overview of WASH and child protection in schools. Child protection links to the 3Cs are then reflected upon. A spotlight is on child protection linked to schools, with a case study from Northwest Syria in the Middle East. The final section focuses on child safeguarding and suggested ways for integrating child protection and WASH.

Finally, in chapter 8, the editors briefly discuss critical themes and barriers identified by the many contributors. Even though our contributors bring diverse backgrounds and experiences, they all provide a shared vision of the possibilities for the future. Hence, as acknowledged earlier, we cannot provide a one-size-fits-all solution to the complicated process of integration. Instead, we aim to present a few practical steps forward.

Notes

1. Marïelle Snel is the senior global humanitarian WASH advisor for Save the Children International. However, the opinions addressed in this chapter are expressly her own and do not represent Save the Children in any way.
2. Water conflicts of the future include five hotspots in areas of the Nile, Ganges-Brahmoputra, Indus, Tigris-Euphrates, and Colorado rivers (Ratner 2018).
3. By COVID-19 we not only reference the ongoing pandemic, but the potential for epidemics/pandemics in the future that must be anticipated and prepared for.

References

Global Wash Cluster (GWC). 2020. 'Delivering humanitarian WASH at scale, anywhere and any time: road map for 2020–2025'. Geneva: UNICEF. <http://www.washroadmap.org/uploads/1/3/8/8/138810292/road_map_2025_english_1.pdf>

GWC. 2022. 'Strategic plan 2022-2025'. Geneva: UNICEF. <https://www.washcluster.net/sites/gwc.com/files/inline-files/Global_WASH_Cluster_Strategic%20Plan_2022_2025_FINAL_lowres.pdf>

Harper, A. and K. Vinke. 2020. 'COVID-19, displacement and climate change.' UNHCR. <https://www.unhcr.org/2020-unhcr-annual-consultations-with-ngos/COVID-19_Displacement_Climate-Change-Factsheet-June-2020.pdf>

IRC. 2017. 'IRC's systems approach: key resources.' 13 June. <https://www.ircwash.org/news/irc%E2%80%99s-systems-approach-key-resources>

Ratner, P. 2018. 'Where the water wars of the future will be fought.' Big Think [blog post]. 18 October. <https://bigthink.com/the-present/where-the-water-wars-will-be-fought>

Sanitation and Water for All (SWA). 2020. 'The SWA framework.' 30 January. <https://www.sanitationandwaterforall.org/about/our-work/priority-areas>

Snel, M. and N. Sorensen. 2021. *Bridging the WASH Humanitarian–Development Divide: Building a Sustainable Reality*. Rugby UK: Practical Action Publishing.

The Sanitation Learning Hub. n.d. 'The community-led total sanitation approach.' <https://sanitationlearninghub.org/practical-support/the-community-led-total-sanitation-approacprogramh>

United Nations. 2022. 'Convergence of conflicts, covid and climate crises, jeopardize global goals.' *UN News*. 7 July. <https://news.un.org/en/story/2022/07/1122112>

WASH Alliance International. 2021. 'Welcome to the FIETS sustainability portal.' 29 January. <https://wash-alliance.org/our-approach/sustainability>

CHAPTER 1
Integrated WASH narrative literature review: the 3Cs and intersectoral coordination

Marley P. Gibbons, Cristina Mena-Lander, and Syed Yasir Ahmad Khan

Introduction

The goal of this chapter is to provide documentation of what has worked in intersectoral collaboration (ISC) and what has not by providing a literature review that focuses on coordination mechanisms. We chose coordination mechanisms because they are the focus of one of the initiatives under the WASH road map[1], which aimed to systematically integrate the WASH sector into public health and emergency responses, specifically looking at engagement with, and commitment from, the health and nutrition sectors. It became apparent that existing coordination mechanisms translate into the day-to-day operations of those working toward improving conditions for affected populations. It is our belief that coordination mechanisms represent an operational route to affecting the most change in the shortest time possible.

We begin with a broad overview of the 3Cs in relation to the need for integrated WASH. We then look at the barriers to ISC, as challenges tend to be present across most emergency response activities. Next, we discuss the enablers for ISC, and then finish by focusing on entry points.

Intersectoral collaboration and the 3Cs

The 3Cs (climate, COVID-19, and conflict) are a way of re-labelling some of the reasons why better integration of WASH into public health systems and humanitarian response is so critical.

- Climate: as the cause of many natural disasters that trigger the response of the cluster system, climate draws particular attention to water scarcity, malnutrition, undernutrition, and other food insecurity challenges that stem from it, requiring response from the WASH, nutrition, health, and food security clusters. The human-caused climate crisis continues to render swaths of our planet uninhabitable, expediting human migration to crowded urban centres, exacerbating familiar and new public health

challenges there, while opening new opportunities for the localization of solving those problems.
- Conflict: some of the most extreme famines, public health emergencies, and humanitarian crises of our time (Yemen, Ethiopia, and Ukraine, to name a few) are the result of political unrest arising from the challenges of development following colonial rule, the surge of right-wing extremism, or some combination of these factors. These factors and the events stemming from them have given rise to the concept of a 'complex emergency' defined by the Inter-Agency Standing Committee (IASC) as, 'a situation where there is a total or considerable breakdown of authority resulting from civil conflict and/or foreign aggression; a humanitarian crisis which requires international response which goes beyond the mandate or capacity of any single agency' (IASC, 1994). Because active conflict zones present an increased risk for the entry of non-national humanitarian workers, they underscore the urgent need to support solutions initiated locally, led by affected communities. Our literature review returned very limited results on this topic, but we were able to include case studies and examples about the Yemen response, perhaps because Yemen is one of the longest-standing conflicts.
- COVID-19: this is the most glaring reminder of the humanitarian community's enduring work, specifically in coordination and emergency preparedness. Considering the importance of WASH access for COVID-19 infection prevention and control (IPC) and the devastation brought by the pandemic to communities without access to it, we find here some of the strongest arguments for better integration of WASH. The pandemic accentuates existing inequalities in communities globally, and it exacerbates the effects of climate change and conflict. However, COVID-19 represents an opportunity for the WASH sector to redefine its incorrectly limited identity as a service provider and lead the call to action for better preparation and a less reactive approach to humanitarian response.

The crux of the humanitarian–development divide – the humanitarian community's approach leaning toward rapid response (often without enough time to consider process and analysis) versus that of development aiming to advance similar goals but along a longer-term timeline – and the need to work toward shared goals across the humanitarian–development–peace nexus are timely arguments calling for improved integration of the WASH sector, and successful coordination between WASH, health, nutrition, and the other sectors who must contribute if these challenges are to be addressed.

The 3Cs emphasize the importance of supporting initiatives at the national and local level if the Sphere core humanitarian standards and the sustainable development goals (SDGs) are ever to be met. All of the challenges that humanitarian response aims to address – especially in the context of the 3Cs – meet the coordination principles developed by Kritz and Batsa, who documented

ISC strategies to address a public health problem in their 2020 piece about a latrine installation project located in the informal urban settlement Old Fadama in Accra, Ghana (more on the coordination principles in the next section). In Kritz and Batsa's definition, a problem that requires cross-sector collaboration is a challenge so big and complex that one sector cannot respond to it alone, and therefore parties with different strengths must work together to address it. So, while the themes of climate, COVID-19, and conflict are not a direct output of the literature review, they are a focus of this chapter.

Background

The UN Office for the Coordination of Humanitarian Affairs (OCHA) relies on the cluster system to coordinate the way a multitude of agencies respond to humanitarian crises. The cluster system is currently 'triggered' by 'complex emergencies,' which can be any combination of the following:

- Natural disasters (increasingly the result of climate change)
- Conflict or political unrest (often directly or indirectly the result of climate change)
- Global health crises, such as COVID-19 (heavily linked to climate and conflict)

While comprised of organizations with the best of intentions, (i.e. actors with missions to overcome the inequalities at the root of these crises), humanitarian responses tend to suffer from competing interests, meaning that humanitarian actors have differing strategies for prioritizing the needs of underserved populations, who often have the least say in how those needs are addressed. The SDGs are an attempt to reach consensus around which needs and solutions to prioritize. The 17th SDG acknowledges that partnership and inclusion are vital to attaining all of the goals, stating that we should 'strengthen the means of implementation and revitalize the global partnership for sustainable development' (UN, 2015).

As one of eleven clusters within the system,[2] WASH is meant to address some of the most basic human needs and rights:

- Sustenance (hydration)
- Relief (known in high-resource settings as using the restroom)
- A place and the means to personally sanitize after defecation, after changing diapers, before preparing food, and before eating

In its comparatively short existence, the WASH cluster has gained a reputation as one that merely provides these three things. Indeed, the provision of clean drinking water, a clean and safe space to defecate, and the systematic separation of these two requires individuals with a specific skill set (usually the input of a water engineer). More specifically, implicit in all three scenarios above is the need to separate clean drinking and cooking water from water containing faeces or the runoff from sanitizing.

However, the WASH cluster is much more than a service provider. The social determinants of health[3] are examples of the systemic environmental forces that impact whether WASH interventions – such as the provision of latrines in a displaced community – positively impact the people they are meant to help. If the WASH sector's work is executed according to the lofty humanitarian missions and goals, factors such as the social determinants of health should influence the integration and approach of the WASH cluster going forward. All of these factors and influences are important to understanding WASH's role in humanitarian response well before the 3C forces that trigger the cluster coordination system even come into focus.

In its own words, the GWC is tasked with providing 'timely, predictable and high-quality WASH outcomes that are inclusive and equitable, for the people most affected by and vulnerable to crises', supplying leadership and accountability at the high level, and supporting national coordination platforms at the national level (GWC, 2022). The GWC's mission emphasizes, as the cluster system acknowledges by its very existence, that this cannot, and will not, happen without successful coordination both among WASH-specific actors and organizations and those outside of the sector, within the humanitarian world. The GWC's road map 2021–2025 includes initiatives (some still in progress, many completed) that focus on moving forward the three strategic priorities of coordination, localization and collaboration (GWC, 2022).

In terms of coordination, Kritz and Batsa describe how they employed community- and participant-led research methods to address the spread of communicable diseases in a community lacking access to WASH. They reflect on coordination principles that establish what types of challenges qualify for the enormous effort of cross-sector collaboration. The starting point is that the problem is larger than one sector can address on its own; thus, the solution requires the collaboration of many sectors with differing abilities (Kritz and Batsa, 2020). They also identify the following additional aspects of a problem that call for ISC:

- Those attempting to address the problem often do not agree on neither the cause nor the solution to said problem.
- Given the above, discussing potential solutions requires a 'neutral' person or party to mediate the conversation, based not on stakeholders' needs, and to coax consensus by finding similarities of interests and goals. This should lead to an agreement on the definition of the problem.
- Actors who have attempted to address said problem either from the top down (government-driven) or bottom up (community-driven) were ill-suited or unsuccessful.
- Parties such as NGOs fill gaps in defining problems and build a bridge by providing a middle path toward a solution, especially in low-resource and socioeconomic environments.
- In working toward a solution, stakeholders (in many of the contexts we will discuss, this translates to affected populations) must lead strategic

decisions at every stage – from problem definition to the design of an intervention and solution.
- Stakeholder buy-in, as opposed to monetary incentives, compensation, or the basic provision of aid by 'developed' countries or actors based in the global north, is critical (Kritz and Batsa, 2020).

Methods

We conducted the literature review within two different types of sources: the first type included over 300 reports, tools, templates, and guidelines produced by organizations playing lead, participant, and contributing roles to initiative 3.3 of the GWC's road map 2021–2025 implementation plan. This type will be henceforth referred to as 'grey literature'. The grey literature was catalogued and organized by theme; sources relevant to the focus on coordination mechanisms were highlighted and eventually sent to the source screening programme, Covidence. The second type of source, peer-reviewed journal articles, was identified using a search string that was entered into various academic search engines and EMBASE, ReliefWeb, and the Emergency Nutrition Network (ENN.net). After creation of the inclusion and exclusion criteria, we screened the sources in several rounds, narrowing the number of included sources from almost 3,000 down to approximately 40 (see Appendix I).

Framework

We used two major frameworks for guidance throughout the review and for determining which of the 40 sources would be cited here: the multisectoral preparedness coordination framework (WHO, 2020) and the 6+1 core functions noted in the IASC's reference module for cluster coordination at country level (IASC, 2015). The Accountability and Quality Assurance Initiative (AQA), nested within the Accountability to Affected Populations and the Core Humanitarian Standard (CHS) on quality and accountability frameworks (CHS Alliance, 2014), was also influential. We also noted similar themes around the expectations for ISC that included accountability to affected populations and the provision of emergency response services that are reliable, effective, inclusive, and respectful of the humanitarian principles.

Successful humanitarian response is measured and driven by 'results' that ought to be delivered to populations in need, but frameworks often represent ideal situations that are not easily translated into practical, measurable, and replicable actions. Indeed, throughout the sources reviewed, there was an emphasis on principles and concepts over practice, making it challenging to document examples that would be useful to move the understanding of successful ISC forward in a substantive way. Friel et al noted this in their

2015 article 'Health in all policies approaches: pearls from the western Pacific region'. In Levin's 2019 examination of an intersectoral effort between western Kenya's health and agriculture sectors, the authors called for more 'empirical estimates' examining ISC.

Yet, frameworks are still important because they represent a standard by which we can understand success – 'what is working' in the context of mechanisms improving ISC in humanitarian response efforts. IASC's Reference Module for Cluster Coordination recognized that under their transformative agenda, the cluster approach had become 'overly process driven and … perceived to potentially undermine rather than enable delivery', validating the choice to focus this chapter on coordination mechanisms and the evaluation of them (2015).

Results

ISC mechanisms

According to some of the grey literature, an ISC mechanism is meant to support or enhance coordination within humanitarian response, regardless of which clusters are involved (IASC, 2015 and OCHA, 2016). The Joint Operational Framework (JOF) 'Improving coordinated and integrated multi-sector cholera preparedness and response within humanitarian crises' specifies inter-cluster and humanitarian country teams ('humanitarian architecture'), incident management systems, emergency operations centres, and cholera task forces as examples of ISC mechanisms. It also specifies that too many coordination mechanisms cause gaps in response, time lags, and confusion (GWC and GHC, 2020). In other words, based on the author's perspective, the sources selected in this literature review clearly give different answers to the question of 'what is an ISC mechanism?'. We agreed that a successful ISC mechanism furthers the goals of integrated programming, meaning two or more disparate sectors or groups working in coordination to meet shared goals. It is the aspiration that the case studies throughout this chapter will further the collective understanding of these mechanisms and why they are so important to successful ISC overall.

Barriers to successful ISC

The challenges of, and barriers to, ISC are certainly known both in the ivory tower of academia and the world of humanitarian response within the cluster system. As opposed to other review themes explored in later sections, we found that challenges in emergency response tend to be present across varied contexts and countries, which is why we chose to start with them.

Ambiguity around roles and resources
The following examples are case studies of ISC in sectors other than WASH. The health and nutrition sectors are some of the most accomplished in ISC,

so there are lessons to be learned for the WASH sector, which is nascent in comparison.

- Levin, 2019: one of the only sources to explore the cost of ISC across sectors, this study noted that the health and nutrition sectors documented the cost of coordination scale-up and lamented the paucity of literature about the costs and benefits resulting from integration across multiple sectors.
    - Intervention basics: the Mama SASHA project 'integrated agriculture and nutrition interventions into existing Ministry of Health (MOH) antenatal care (ANC) services, with the aim of maximising the benefits of orange-fleshed sweet potato (OFSP) on the health status of mothers and children <2 years of age.' In addition to receiving nutrition education at ANC visits, beneficiaries were given vouchers for OFSP vines to encourage at-home cultivation; agriculture experts came to beneficiaries homes for follow -up support.
    - Relevant finding: an impact assessment revealed that the intervention led to increased utilization of ANCs, improved diet diversity and increased knowledge of nutrient-rich food for the target population. The intervention's largest costs were tied to joint training, monitoring activities, coordination, and feedback meetings. The authors concluded that cost estimates and breakdowns across sectors are crucial to informing the 'design, planning and implementation of multi-sectoral programmes. Knowing costs by components enables thoughtful examination of where cost savings can be made with the goal of achieving the same level of impact'.
- Cole, 2016: this intervention, aimed at integrating agricultural and health programming to improve nutrition outcomes, revealed that time is a very important resource for successful ISC.
    - Intervention basics: planning the evaluation of the Programme on Appropriate Technology for Health (PATH), which also involved ANC promoting OFSP growth to attending mothers.
    - Relevant finding: The extensive effort and resources it took to plan a truly multisectoral project like this one, notably: the cost, the awareness work with community leaders, the organisational support at different levels of jurisdiction, and time, 'years versus the actual months allocated by most funders'.
- Tappis, 2020: looked at the delivery of reproductive, new-born and child health services in Yemen and found that the relationship between UN-agencies, the WHO and the government in Yemen is complex and often confusing for national-level workers. The authors observed that, 'although some UN staff noted the ability to rapidly mobilize funds when needed, other respondents noted earmarking of funds as a barrier to effective humanitarian assistance.'

- While it seems as though fulfilling one of the 6+1 core functions of working alongside government is being upheld in the third example, sometimes the needs of affected populations were not met in a timely manner, which violates a principle of those core functions.

A potential solution to role and resource ambiguity
While the JOF did not appear in the sources of this literature review, we believe it represents an example of overcoming some of the issues described above, particularly because it was created after analysis and evaluations found themes of unclear understanding around roles and responsibilities (GWS & GHC, 2020).

The JOF clearly defines the role of humanitarian clusters in relation to government actors in countries, stating that cluster engagement should vary depending on national capacity to respond. It recommends a multisector cholera prevention and response plan, aligned with a national cholera plan (NCP), and advocates for 'common messaging and community engagement strategies' and consensus around which parties are responsible for which activities to minimize duplication. For example, in each phase (prevention, preparedness, and response), responsibilities are organized into levels. The first level, leadership and multisector coordination, is meant to create an enabling environment for the second level of actors to function effectively. This clearly defines the responsibilities and roles of those with more power and stakeholders on a more local level who are responsible for facilitating ISC.

Whether the use of the JOF substantively improves cholera prevention and response globally is difficult to measure. However, the fact that two clusters recognized their responses to a particular disease as siloed and collaborated to create a framework that both could use to overcome issues in a specific, targeted and data-informed way, is successful ISC in action. Under GWC's road map initiative 3.3, the WASH, nutrition, and health sectors will create another JOF to help define the roles of stakeholders in response to undernutrition crises.

Challenges to information sharing and measurement
OCHA's 2016 overview of coordination mechanisms found that 'the sharing of core information products between the clusters such as cluster strategies (55%) and cluster workplans (35%) is quite low'. Authors looking at Ethiopia's national nutrition program (NNP) I and NNP II noted a hesitancy to share data across the health, nutrition and agriculture sectors and the lack of a common mechanism with which to measure outcomes (Bach, 2020). The inability to 'compare notes' presents a major barrier to successful ISC within the WASH sector and the partnerships that can, and should be, strengthened through ISC mechanisms.

Sectors also collect data at different scales:

- The Global Trachoma Mapping Project (GTMAP), which has been collecting primary data on WASH and disease-related indicators, ran into issues with 'aligning scales'. Generally, WASH-related data is collected at the national level (or rarely below the district level), whereas data about neglected tropical diseases (NTDs) is collected at the national, district, and local levels (Waite, 2016).

- WASH-NTD indicators have been developed, and there continue to be promising developments. However, there is an important gap in the way that monitoring and evaluation are conducted within the WASH sector. In measuring the efficacy of WASH interventions, counting points of access is prioritized instead of understanding whether existing facilities adequately serve populations, and, in the context of preventing or reducing the prevalence of certain NTDs, whether they adequately prevent the spread of them (Campbell, 2018).
- Missing from the monitoring and evaluation of these interventions is whether an accompanying behaviour change in the population is present (Campbell, 2018). Campbell calls for 'more appropriate' indicators to be created, 'to record programmatic interventions and to define strategic priorities more effectively'.
- OCHA published a short document with guidelines and specific examples of how to set collective outcomes, to operationalize their 'New Way of Working' (NWOW) initiative, which could serve as a helpful resource in overcoming these challenges (OCHA, 2018).
- Ouedraogo et al (2020) developed a scoring system to evaluate how integrated nutrition was in Burkina Faso's multisectoral nutrition strategic plan (MNSP) and other relevant national policy documents of non-nutrition sectors. The scoring system measured:

    a. the extent to which nutrition was established as a problem in the policy;
    b. whether strategic interventions had been 'included in the policy compared with the total number of nutrition interventions'.

    When reviewing a policy, if the answer for questions a and b was 'yes', the policy received a coding of 25–75 per cent, and if the answer was 'no,' the policy received a 0 per cent coding.

    – Of the 22 documents, seven received nutrition integration scores between 50 and 75 per cent, while other sector policies (WASH included) received integration scores between 25 and 50 per cent.
    – The authors concluded that nutrition integration had improved in other sector policies since 2000 and that Burkina Faso had embraced a policy reform process that enabled all relevant sectors to contribute to stunting reduction.

This type of scoring system, if adapted for other sectors, could be helpful in forthcoming reviews relating to ISC coordination mechanisms.

Ouedraogo et al also interviewed national-level stakeholders from the involved sectors that focused on lessons learned and challenges, and the best ways to operationalize the MNSP.

- The government-led planning process constantly fed analysis findings back to stakeholders. These ongoing conversations created an awareness and understanding that sectors other than nutrition were responsible

for addressing malnutrition (previously been considered a health-specific issue).
- A WASH actor said, 'contrary to what I thought before participating in this planning process, with its restitutions, I understood that nutrition is not just a matter of food and that we can have food but be malnourished; also, the question of the fight against malnutrition is not only the responsibility of the Ministry of Health; each sector has a significant role to play. The development of the analyses on the coverage of the interventions made it possible to see all that is carried out in the field of nutrition, whether it is by public structures or by NGO partners.'

This type of contextualization of 'self' as representative of a sector in action and the realization of common goals that require coordination with other sectors seem to be an important catalyst to successful ISC.

While the process described by Ouedraogo et al might seem complex and labour-intensive, the key summary that emerged truly emphasized the importance of successful ISC beyond verbal acknowledgement. Creating a scoring system in the Burkina Faso MNSP was an investment in the systematic evaluation of integration itself. Burkina Faso's MNSP took three years to plan, which is consistent with similar efforts in Uganda and Nepal, and it still met common challenges mentioned earlier in this section. While a line for nutrition was created in the MoH budget, the authors concluded that 'it will be important to create additional nutrition budget lines in other relevant sectors to support the nutrition-sensitive interventions included in sectoral policies and plans'. Thus, at the time of writing, funding and coordination goals were not accomplished (Ouedraogo, 2020). Similar cross-sectoral stakeholder interviews are under way that will inform the creation of the WASH, nutrition and health JOF as part of the GWC's road map initiative 3.3.

ISC enablers ('The conspicuous helpers')

What follows are examples of 'drivers' that contributed to successful ISC between WASH and other sectors and ISC lessons outside of WASH that emerged from this literature review. These are tweaks actors can make to their role in, and contribution to, the mechanics of the coordination system itself to improve ISC.

Building on what is already in place

Given the extensive resources required to plan and execute successful ISC, some of the key remaining entry points involve comparatively little work, because they build on existing systems, infrastructure and resources. For example, in piloting a toolkit for integrating menstrual hygiene management (MHM) into emergency responses, Sommer et al (2018) found that, after introductory and co-planning workshops, the health sector was able to add an MHM screening question to the questionnaire they were already administering to patients, allowing them to track key MHM-related data in their monthly metrics. This highlighted that 'MHM can harmoniously be integrated into existing programming if carefully framed and well designed' (Sommer, 2018). Sommer et al's approach also speaks to the importance of first helping actors working in other sectors to see their role in contributing toward the solution of a problem that requires coordination, and then to define their role in accomplishing this goal. The fact that the *Compendium of Hygiene Promotion in Emergencies*, by the GCW and other partners, contains a section on MHM is a testament to the impact of this work (Gensch et al, 2022).

The Mama SASHA project, which integrated the promotion of OFSP consumption to ANC, relied on training personnel within existing, well-established antenatal clinics in the region to ensure that nutrition and agriculture were 'explicitly integrated' (Levin, 2019). The authors noted that the costs and outputs of the project declined over the three-year project life, perhaps because patients' trust of ANC clinics had already been established. Building on this existing infrastructure and the trust-based network of patients may have contributed to the project's cost reduction over time.

One of the key elements of the multisectoral preparedness coordination framework is mapping existing resources to minimize duplication of efforts and resources (WHO, 2020). Many case studies and examples that follow rely on this principle of first taking stock of what is already working and building upon that, instead of starting anew. It could be helpful to produce evidence that the commitment of additional time and resources at the outset of an ISC project leads to lower costs and effort in the long term.

A champion in every sector

The need for the presence of a champion/champions for a multisectoral cause within each sector came up throughout the literature review. Often this champion was an NGO or a community-based organization (CBO) – part of, but not entrenched within the formal humanitarian system – with the mobility to pivot and support the needs of a multifaceted ISC coordination effort. The IASC's 2016 coordination mechanism overview found that '42% of cluster/sectors have an NGO in a co-facilitation role at National level. For activated clusters alone, the result is 50% have an NGO in a co-facilitation role' (OCHA, 2016).

In looking at the implementation of NNP I and NNP II, which specifically intended to increase multisectoral linkages in Ethiopia, Bach (2020) noted that a major contributor to the operational success was the establishment of programme delivery units (PDUs). These groups usually consist of a health manager, a multisectoral programme manager, a programme analyst, a communication adviser and WASH and agricultural managers. They were placed in federal and regional offices to achieve political commitment to nutrition activities and assure accountability. The PDUs were a key aspect of the overall project, for which, after a nutrition resource mapping project conducted by the Ethiopian MoH, funding increased from $181 million (2013/14) to $455 million (2015/16), with a significant funding increase for nutrition-sensitive programmes (Bach, 2020).

Aside from the participatory nature of the planning process, other factors contributing to the success were the mobilisation and support provided by scaling up nutrition (SUN) (Ouedraogo, 2020). SUN was an external, yet integrated, advocate, continuously providing non-nutrition sectors with best practice information and content to maintain their engagement. This facilitation role could only be accomplished by an NGO, given the high turnover of government personnel (Ouedraogo, 2020). The ENN extensively documented the importance of their own role as information managers and coordinators to the SUN movement (Bush, 2020). In addition to the technical support and the 'home' ENN provided to partners for documenting best practices, it hosted meetings for stakeholders to define their knowledge management needs (Bush, 2020).

To achieve successful ISC, these additional resources, personnel, and funds must be well planned and budgeted for, given their significant costs.

Allowing actors to define their role

The siloed nature of various sectors and the existence of the humanitarian–development divide have often been discussed and acknowledged. A means of overcoming these challenges, which seem to be caused by old habits and stagnant operations, lies in facilitating a change in outlook, approach, or just how actors see themselves. This applies to actors in sectors involved in both humanitarian response and development at the national level. Earlier we quoted a WASH actor in Ouedraogo's evaluation of nutrition integration in the planning of Burkina Faso's MNSP, who confirmed that training and introductory exercises helped him see his sector's role in addressing malnutrition nationally. The WHO publication 'Improving nutrition outcomes with better water, sanitation and hygiene: practical solutions for policies and programs' (2015) is an example of implementation strategies targeted at those in the nutrition sector who want to integrate WASH-informed activities into their practices.

The results of the literature review focus strongly on sectors outside of WASH, mainly the health and agriculture sectors. This highlights the need for more documentation of lessons learned in WASH, but, in the meantime, we felt the following examples emphasize the importance of actors recognizing their own role toward successful ISC:

- Hemrich and Topouzis (2000): the authors began by placing HIV/AIDs on meeting agendas of other sectors, with the goal of drawing the attention of teams implementing rural development and agricultural programming in Tanzania (non-health actors) to the cross-cutting issue

of HIV/AIDS and its implications on non-health programmes. Next, a regional AIDS project hosted a number of workshops. Eventually, a local AIDS working group stepped in to prepare and conduct meetings. The authors stated that managerial support was critical to the success of the HIV/AIDS programme. This case shows that it begins with a simple step of making it onto an agenda, but as with any worthwhile change, maintenance is a key ingredient to success.
- Sommer et al (2018): in an account of piloting an MHM toolkit designed for emergency response actors, the authors concluded that the following activities allowed non-health actors to define their part in integrating MHM into their work:
  - mapping out training opportunities for integration of MHM response into existing programming;
  - discussing 'novel approaches' to MHM integration for WASH and non-WASH stakeholders;
  - engaging with WASH actors to address facility improvements, especially where operations had previously overlapped.

Campbell et al (2018) summarized this need well when they said, 'The key will be to identify mutual benefits. Countries will need to be supported to incrementally achieve WASH goals themselves'.

In moments of initiating ISC partnership, all of these authors show the importance of facilitating the ability of other sector partners to think about how they will approach ISC work 'on their own', when there is no time for ISC meetings to take place or the funding to support more formal ISC efforts runs out. Beyond actors from each sector conceptualising their own roles, multiple sources stated the importance of setting aside actual time and space to facilitate collaboration and, over time, solidify collaboration as a facet of continuing operations.

Investing in face-to-face meetings

As important as self-determination is constant feedback and communications about the roles of cross-sectoral partners engaged in ISC. The Mama SASHA integrated agriculture and health programme invested in travel for in-person meetings to resolve coordination challenges. They used a 'partnership check-up tool', which allowed participating actors to appraise partnership functionality, and facilitators shared check-up results throughout. Participants felt that this allowed issues to be addressed before they became problems (Cole, 2016).

Waite's 2016 study looking at mechanisms that support improved WASH integration identified three key in-person meeting events that improved communications between the WASH and NTD communities and required actors from both sectors to agree on priority areas to work on ahead of, and following, these meetings. Workstreams for both WASH and NTD actors were aligned thanks to the organization of these meetings (Waite, 2016). The existence of the meeting itself requires allocating time, thought, and effort toward ISC when, as is evident, this does not occur organically.

Of course, preparation and follow up from in-person meetings are not a silver bullet for successful ISC. Reflecting on lessons learned and the work required to further integrate programmes addressing malnutrition across many sectors, Bach et al (2020) commented on the continued nutrition challenge in Ethiopia. The government's priorities at the time (shaped by political or financial factors) dictated whether the health or agricultural ministries took responsibility for the nutrition issue, a dynamic that changed often and thus presented clear challenges to ISC. The authors recommended the involvement of boundary-spanning actors or coordinating parties who could hold multiple government bodies accountable to set priorities, to clarify roles and responsibilities, and to institutionalize nutrition 'in all relevant sectors'. This point reinforces the importance of the role of CBOs and NGOs in this system.

ISC entry points

This section contains our thematically organized case studies on entry points for ISC. In the case of nutrition and NTDs, we can learn from successful documentation of ISC, but more needs to be done toward adapting for WASH integration. The 3Cs are themes that arise in increasingly more complex and protracted emergencies, and show how sorely needed improved ISC is.

Nutrition

The connection between proper WASH and the reduction of nutrition-related issues is well established. Improved access to WASH:

- could avoid over 400,000 child deaths by 2030 (Lucas, 2019);
- prevent diarrhoea, which is a huge cause of death in low- and middle-income countries (LMICs) and the spread of soil-transmitted infections (Cumming, 2016);
- prevent environmental enteric dysfunction (EED), which causes inflammation in the small intestines and negatively affects their ability to absorb nutrients from food. It is also thought to cause stunting in children (Cumming, 2016).

The ISC mechanisms and frameworks employed to integrate the work of WASH and nutrition clusters are extensive. Below is a summary of them; please refer to Appendix III for a more in-depth look.

- The Link NCA (nutritional causal analysis) methodology: an approach or framework with the goal of expanding generic nutritional interventions by understanding context-specific determinants that cause

undernutrition, using a mixed-methods approach and community-led surveys (Dodos, 2017).
- Looking at the connection between WASH and nutrition from a social and economic perspective: improving access to WASH decreases security threats and financial strain for vulnerable populations (Cumming, 2016).

Analysis of government policies and documents and institutional mapping to meaningfully measure government commitment to ISC (Momberg, 2020), coupled with a scoring system such as Ouedraogo's, could also contribute to the ongoing process of documenting what is still needed for improved ISC. Reviews, interviews, and a conference following the analysis also still called for more proof of the link between WASH and nutritional status in children.

The nutrition sector has thus far made a commendable effort to engage other sectors to work together toward reducing stunting, malnutrition, and so on, but there is still much to be done.

Neglected tropical diseases (NTDs)

The review revealed a multitude of scientific proof about the connection between the prevention of NTDs and improved access to WASH, which is essential to IPC. NTD prevention rarely – if ever – is a consideration in humanitarian emergency response efforts, but the established need for IPC within NTDs surely represents a gateway to increased integration of WASH in health sector efforts.

WASH service ladders, which use a straightforward colour-coded diagram to indicate which aspects of water, sanitation, and hygiene are 'improved' according to international standards, have been adapted and applied to address the transmission of soil-transmitted helminths, also known as hookworm (Campbell, 2018). This provides a clear example of overcoming some of the challenges associated with different measurement styles and uses of indicators across sectors to prevent the spread of public health threats.

Providing the type of scientific proof for the need for WASH integration to address NTDs that is typically expected by the academic and scientific communities (such as randomized control trials) is difficult for ethical and logistical reasons, but it is vital to continue the forward momentum of WASH integration here. If we are to improve NTD prevention efforts, which currently rely too heavily on drug administration, we need more evidence on the impact of improved WASH coverage at the community and school level (most of the currently published research is at the household level), and health experts need to provide the WASH sector with details that will better inform behaviour change programming (Campbell, 2018). Again, the gaps are vast, but the work ahead has been clearly articulated.

Adding to the momentum is the support for ISC between these two sectors by relevant SDGs, specifically the goals of establishing 'good health and well-being' for all and providing access to clean water to all humans (UN, 2015). Essentially, investment in the integration of WASH into NTD prevention will augment preventive medication distribution and move us closer toward WHO goals (Campbell, 2018). This shared goal-setting represents the future of humanitarian response and public health efforts if we are to have any success.

Conflict

The importance of actors who can quickly respond to changing circumstances is apparent in times of unprecedented challenges and conflict. This is especially true for situations in which the cluster system cannot or will not be activated because the conditions required for cluster activation are not met, but ISC work is still very much needed.

The multi-level response to the Ebola outbreak in the West African countries Guinea, Sierra Leone, and Liberia is a good example of this. The outbreak, which occurred in the context of civil and political unrest, was considered an ISC success. While it could be argued that this success was due to the outbreak's unique and unprecedented nature, there are lessons to be learned. In their overview of how INGOs, NGOs and CBOs responded to the outbreak, Mobula et al (2018) noted some key characteristics: the ability to pivot (flexibility) and consistent and constant communication, followed by adjustment (as needed) according to that feedback and communication.

Studies also found that 'traditional development actors,' such as locally based NGOs, were important contributors, working within the unfamiliar humanitarian ecosystem without coordination support from the health and other clusters (IASC, 2015; Mobula, 2018). This shows the importance of letting organizations who have established trust within local communities lead. Partners typically dedicated to development activities such as health systems strengthening pivoted their operations to offer IPC training in health facilities (Mobula, 2018). It should also be noted that the USAID's Bureau for Humanitarian Assistance (BHA; formerly the Office of US Foreign Disaster Assistance) provided major financial support (over $809 million) to actors responding across three countries, including WASH, as well as operational support, including IPC and contact tracing for health care workers (Mobula, 2018). Thus, in the absence of leadership from the health cluster, the BHA took the lead in coordination. This example could represent an instance of top-down leadership contributing to successful ISC across the humanitarian–development divide.

The complex emergency involving civil conflict and dire humanitarian conditions taking place since Saudi Arabia's 2015 intervention in Yemen's civil unrest is another example of required multisectoral collaboration due to the sheer magnitude of the affected population. In their content analysis and key informant interviews, which looked at the delivery of reproductive, maternal, new-born, child, and adolescent health and nutrition (RMNCAH+N) services,

Tappis et al (2020) found familiar barriers to the successful delivery of care and ISC. One of the most notable challenges was the many and different manifestations of leadership (government or otherwise), depending on which Yemeni governorate (geographic entities somewhat like states in Western territories) response took place. The authors also pointed out the issue of competing priorities, with technical priority being given to cholera outbreaks and nutrition-related concerns, which led to a deprioritization of routine health care services, including reproductive ones.

Access to preventative treatment or even WASH services, for example, are key issues that tend to fall through the cracks in these contexts. The recommendation for addressing the many barriers in-need populations face to accessing care is to invest in community-based service delivery and mobile clinics (Tappis, 2020). For example, the NGO Yemen Relief and Reconstruction Foundation (YRRF), in partnership with other local Aden and Sana'a-based NGOs, has been able to successfully deliver aid to populations in need, including food supplies and distribution of 1,200 water filters (Kimball and Jumaan, 2020). Kimball and Jumaan explained that the deep ties and trust they had established with local communities enabled them to access such difficult-to-reach populations in war-torn Yemen.

Climate change

Climate change and the multitude of problems caused by its effects, such as water scarcity, undernutrition, malnutrition, food security challenges, and stunting, to name but a few, typically elicit responses from actors in the nutrition, health, food security, and WASH clusters. But the line separating the work or responsibility between these actors is unclear at best. In real time, this lack of clarity can mean that two actors (or even clusters) dedicate precious time and resources toward addressing the same issue, through possibly in different or even competing strategies, as part of the same emergency response. This is frustrating, wasteful, and possibly dangerous for people caught in the crosshairs of conflicting information or approaches, and further emphasizes the need for improved ISC in this area.

The following examples may touch on themes from other sections of this chapter but fall under the umbrella of environmental interventions:

- Amalima: an intervention from the agriculture and WASH sectors supporting the creation of community health clubs (CHCs), which trained people in income-generating activities to increase village savings and lending. This included productive resources creation (i.e. rehabilitated or new irrigation schemes) and the increase of disaster risk reduction activities.
    - Results: 59 per cent of CHCs that participated in these activities were able to build latrines in their villages, versus 32 per cent who did not participate (Ncube-Murakwani, n.d.). Through the community-led trainings, villages in Zimbabwe saw a 7.3 per cent reduction in stunting in children under five and a 8.9 per cent reduction in

households with moderate to severe hunger. Also, 18,997 households experienced improved access to water for productive use and agriculture, all at the population level (CNFA, 2020).
- A research project under the Global Task Force on Cholera Control (GTFCC, n.d.) called OVERCOME (digital innovation in climate hazard early warning and related disease prevention for community capacity building and resilience) established a multi-national, multidisciplinary expertise for collaborative research across sectors using traditional epidemiological strategies, artificial intelligence, and climate and weather forecasting to strengthen the collective ability to predict cholera and other water-related disease outbreaks (GTFCC, 2020).
- An UN-Water policy brief (2019) called for increased coordination across sectors to reduce the impact of climate-related weather events (floods, droughts, and so on) and to decrease greenhouse gas emissions by making the supply of water to global communities more sustainable by installing energy-efficient water pumps, as an example.

Migration due to climate change

Significant portions of populations all over the world are moving from rural to urban settings, many as a result of climate change, even if climate change is not consciously understood or stated as the reason. Less than three per cent of respondents to a cross-sectional survey of homes across deltas in India, Ghana, and Bangladesh said that 'environmental stress' was the reason for their relocation, instead citing economic opportunities and generally improved living conditions (de Campos, 2020). However, Bangladesh is known as a climate-change hotspot (Vidal, 2017).

The historically relied upon 'camp model', in which INGOs construct and operate sprawling temporary dwellings for displaced populations, migrants, and refugees, is no longer working given today's environmental challenges and the changing needs of displaced people. As of 2012, Jordan's already limited fresh water supply was further strained by an influx of refugees from Syria settling at the Zaatari refugee camp (Aldroubi, 2019). As of 2021, just three in every ten refugees were living in camps (Laub, n.d). The UN High Commissioner for Refugees (UNHCR) has provided extensive guidance, such as the section of their standardized expanded nutrition survey (SENS) providing guidance for refugee populations and the needs assessment for refugee emergencies (NARE), but more research is needed, both demographically and in assessing population needs in these parts of the world.

Kritz and Batsa documented the use of ISC strategies to address cholera outbreaks in their study of a latrine installation project in Old Fadama, in Accra, Ghana, using participatory action research[4] to set priorities and meet goals (2020). The project worked in three phases:

1. Interviews: each stakeholder was interviewed upon joining the project. The conversation identified the location, barriers to success,

and organizational strengths, and educated stakeholders about the principles of cross-sectoral collaboration. The initial interviewees identified a dire public health situation in the Fadama slum,[5] including the lack of WASH infrastructure. Community members had been disposing of collected waste in a nearby river, causing stilting in the local water source. Later, to create more space for building shelter, residents filled the lagoon with sawdust, refuse, and car chassis, which caused a spread of faecal matter into the local food market, flooding, and frequent cholera outbreaks. Fadama met the conditions of a WHO cholera hotspot.
2. Focus group discussions: these brought in more stakeholders identified by the interview participants. The discussion highlighted both community (Fadama resident) and local government (Accra Metropolitan Assembly – AMA) priorities, in addition to strategies to address increased sanitation and the details of the latrine installation project.
3. Community survey: this involved more stakeholders and increased community participation, and 'introduced a democratic component into latrine management' by measuring opinions and asking open-ended questions. Survey responses added more detail and colour to important concepts of the latrine project design.

The study not only bore out the collaboration principles, but also provided a blueprint for overcoming a public health challenge by employing participant or community-led research methods to generate knowledge as well as organizational action and change (Kritz and Batsa, 2020). The first participants included Catholic sisters (selected for their trusted role in the community) and representatives of the AMA, who suggested more stakeholders to be brought in as project momentum grew. While the original contingency awaited permits for the Fadama slum (which they were able to obtain thanks to buy-in from the AMA representatives included in the process), they shared project details with other sanitation specialists in the city, who then started latrine projects with other Fadama community members and residents throughout the city. The project resulted in coordination between actors at the community level (Fadama residents) and the government level (AMA members), who reached consensus under the guidance of neutral parties: the Catholic sisters and study organizers.

In documenting the decision-making process by building consensus, Kritz and Batsa proved that intersectoral coordination yields public value, and that listening to public concerns articulated over time by many interviewees, and using focus group discussions and the community survey to understand how to best go about solving the problem, provided a community-built solution to a public health concern (frequent cholera outbreaks). The authors also applied what are commonly seen as principles of ISC that work in 'developed' contexts in a low-resource setting. While the results of this particular study were specific to the Ghanan context, the participatory research process was well documented and is repeatable.

COVID-19

A strong example of the importance of connecting WASH and other key sectors involved in emergency response, especially regarding investment in both access to WASH and behaviour change, is the recent COVID-19 pandemic. Much of the IPC guidance is focused on individuals and households, but IPC challenges extend beyond that, to institutions. Institutional coordination mechanisms that improve IPC and thus health care outcomes are an impetus for improved WASH infrastructure and access at the community and individual levels. However, the inability of institutions and facilities to meet WASH standards negatively impacts community-level health promotion (Abu, 2021). Individuals often have their first experience with, and an understanding of the importance of, improved WASH at health care facilities and clinics, such as maternal wards.

Schools represent an institutional setting that has seen progress in improving WASH awareness, behaviour change, and access to facilities over many years. Their three-star approach (see Appendix IV) is a combined checklist-and-rating system to ensure that 'healthy habits are taught, practised and integrated into daily school routines' (UNICEF and GIZ, 2013). While the three-star approach does not include ISC guidance for the WASH and education clusters, it is still an example of a mechanism that has been proven to reach beyond the immediate population (students) and positively influence community attitudes and behaviours. Improving WASH access in schools, where support from government leadership, established protocols, and systems already exist, is the first step in implementing WASH access links for larger populations. Children who bring home knowledge and messaging from schools (institutions their families trust) can be the gateway to improved WASH access for often ignored communities.

The clean clinic approach, which relies on collaboration between implementors in health care facilities and national MoHs, provides a simple, ten-step, low-cost strategy for protecting at-risk populations from contracting COVID-19 in institutions (e.g. schools, religious gathering places, markets) in low-resource settings (Lopez, 2020; see also Appendix IV). While Lopez's study was not conducted in the COVID-19 context, the clean clinic approach represents an ISC mechanism that improved coordination between the health and WASH sectors, and can be adapted to the humanitarian context. Related is the issue of health care waste from institutions, an existing problem exacerbated by the COVID-19 pandemic, which led to an approximately tenfold increase in the amount of hazardous health care waste (WHO, 2022).

COVID-19 in urban settings

The billions of people living in densely populated urban settlements (often referred to as 'slums') face unique constraints following COVID-19 IPC. Residents with limited access to water and WASH-related services must pay higher prices to have it transported to them, latrines are shared if available at all, and excrement, often dumped in shared spaces, creates biohazard risks, including COVID-19 exposure, especially for waste collectors and people who rely on income from what is known in more privileged communities as 'frontline work' (Wilkinson, 2020). All of these factors make following IPC guidelines like handwashing and social distancing 'all but impossible' (Wilkinson, 2020).

Before discussing interventions that could address these constraints, Wilkinson emphasizes the importance of contextualizing the historical treatment of people living in slums, who find it ironic that they are only being given protective equipment now (during COVID-19), even though 'the health threat of their work extends to people beyond them' and always has (Wilkinson, 2020; Johari, 2020). To achieve successful ISC work and WASH integration in these contexts, it is imperative to partner with CBOs that provide necessary services when government and municipal actors do not, and know how to tailor COVID-19 communications, responses, and interventions to the communities who already trust them.

COVID represents an opportunity to move ISC forward. However, for this to happen, the humanitarian response and development communities must listen, and remain accountable, to affected communities. Inclusion, localization, and representation are of critical importance, and the *IASC's Guidance on Strengthening Participation, Representation and Leadership of Local and National Actors in IASC Humanitarian Coordination Mechanisms* (2021) provides extensive advice, particularly on documentation and evaluation of these exact priorities.

Conclusion

Given the evidence encountered in this literature review, there is arguably no longer as much of a need to prove the causal connection between WASH and the prevention of large public health issues in order to justify the resources and commitment needed to ensure successful ISC.

However, the powers that govern, or at least regulate, humanitarian response agree that the status quo is insufficient if we are to address the world's complex challenges, and doing so will take more than the efforts of one sector. The way humanitarian actors, governed by the cluster system, operate is too reactionary and does not address root causes (social and economic determinants) or sufficiently tackle preparedness for tomorrow's emergencies (IASC, 2020). Furthermore, funding for humanitarian response is typically given for six- (sometimes twelve-) month periods, leaving no time to properly transition efforts to entities informed or run by local communities that can support, sustain, and flourish in the long term.[6] By championing the concept of collective outcomes, coordination between the humanitarian and development WASH sectors is being encouraged (see also Snel and Sorensen, 2022). In addition, there is now ongoing discussion around bridging the activities of humanitarian and development actors. This humanitarian–development–peace, or triple, nexus is discussed more in the next chapter.

The percentage of inter-cluster coordination groups 'linking with development coordination mechanisms is reported at 60%', indicating an ongoing coordination gap that must be closed (OCHA, 2016). Prioritizing the triple nexus is a fundamental step in the right direction in terms of addressing the 3Cs. However, the challenges falling within these categories go beyond Kritz and Batsa's coordination principles. The tripel nexus linked to WASH and ISC is not a technical problem that can be solved by one sector, observers, and/or world powers. Currently peace, humanitarian, and development actors take different approaches to similar challenges and hence could learn best practices from each other.

However, humanitarian actors will not be able to meet their responsibilities to the triple nexus if they do not make progress on improving ISC within the cluster system. Employing and building on existing resources, clearly documenting successes and failures, using established language and indicators, and following up through wide dissemination all matter if we are to empower the triple nexus, achieve collective outcomes, and meet the SDGs. In this world of increasingly complex emergencies and protracted crises, the focus must be on improving ISC within humanitarian sectors and on the longer-term solutions and collaborations that come through focusing on the HDPN and prioritizing collective outcomes.

Appendix I A more detailed account of the search process and literature review

One of the authors, Marley Gibbons, completed the literature review as a consultant for this project.

Some of the grey literature was also located via SCOPUS and Google Scholar databases, and some version of the following search string was entered for the search:

> (((WASH or "water sanitation hygiene") AND Nutrition) OR (WASH AND Health) OR (Nutrition AND Health)) AND (intersector* OR "shared indicator*" OR "shared outcome*" OR "coordination") AND ("public health" OR "public health"[mesh])

We entered the search string into PubMed, PAIS Index, Web of Science and EBSCO for a total of 2,762 potential sources (search results). We then drafted a set of inclusion and exclusion criteria for screening the grey literature and results returned by database searches into Covidence, an online platform that hosted the screening process. Covidence automatically removed a total of 358 duplicate sources.

After meeting with stakeholders and advisors, we determined that additional searches would be performed in EMBASE, ReliefWeb and on the ENN website (ENN.net). Simplified versions of the above search string were used in some cases, as search capabilities on some websites were relatively more limited compared to larger databases.

The screening criteria were also edited according to the Cochrane guidelines and in consultation with Lauren D'Mello Guyett, a fellow at the London School of Hygiene and Tropical Medicine overseeing research-related initiatives of the GWC road map 2021–2025, in order to further narrow down the pool of potential sources.

We then manually screened the titles and abstracts via Covidence over two months, narrowing the accepted sources to 118 in total. We reviewed the full text of those remaining 118 sources using the same general screening criteria, and 40 sources were left. Finally, we created an annotated bibliography with those 40 sources and reworked the initial outline for this narrative review accordingly.

Appendix II An in-depth look at ISC between nutrition and WASH

Our review yielded many examples of the nutrition sector implementing and documenting successful ISC. The nutrition sector has created practical documents that assist actors in other sectors with understanding their role in nutrition-focused efforts that require the input of other sectors, such as eliminating stunting. Examples from the grey literature include:

- the 'IYCF-E policy and programme review template 2020' (with IYCF-E signifying infant & young child feeding in emergencies) by Save the Children and the Nutrition Technical Rapid Response Team (Tech RRT), with the support of the members of the Infant Feeding in Emergencies (IFE) core group;
- the WHO's 'Planning guide for national implementation of the global strategy for infant and young child feeding', which translates international approaches (the SDGs) to national-level strategies.

Nutrition represents an entry point for the successful integration of WASH. A 2011 study of demographic data from 70 LMICs reported that stunting in children under five was reduced when their access to, and use of, improved water sources increased (Fink, 2011). These connections have been endorsed by UNICEF, starting in 1990, and two series on the subject published in the *Lancet* journal, one in 2008 and another in 2013. The results of a more recent analysis employing integrated models to project the effect achieving certain SDGs related to the environment (access to WASH and energy, or fuel, improved nutrition, and protection from malaria) could have on global child mortality showed that achievement of the targets 'would avoid 433 thousand child deaths by 2030' (Lucas, 2019).

Cumming and Cairncross (2016) provide a well-sourced exploration of the potential for WASH to prevent childhood stunting, which includes several examples of how improved WASH access accomplishes ISC, addressing both the biological links and social and economic mechanisms that cause them. For the biological links, aside from the prevention of repeated bouts of diarrhoea for children and the spread of soil-transmitted infections (see the ISC entry points nutrition section above), Cumming and Cairncross also note that, 'although more research is needed, it has been argued that EED [environmental enteric dysfunction], and not diarrhoea, may be the primary causal mechanism linking WASH to child growth'. The authors cite several studies that further the epidemiological evidence of WASH having an impact on stunting. However, there is work to be done in quantifying, monitoring, and evaluating the behavioural and long-term outcomes of WASH interventions on stunting, but the beginnings of proof of this connection are in place.

Under Action Against Hunger, a leader in ISC between the WASH and nutrition sectors, Dodos et al (2017) performed a participatory analysis on the causal link between the three main causes of undernutrition (insufficient food intake, infectious disease, and poor care practices) and inadequate access to WASH, looking at the results from 12 studies conducted between 2014 and 2016. This mechanism, known as Link NCA, aims to strengthen both the conceptual base on which stunting and undernutrition reduction interventions are based and to 'go beyond generic interventions by identifying context-specific determinants of nutritional status in order to propose adequate and sustainable solutions'.

This context-specific approach is accomplished using mixed methods; quantitative surveys to understand the prevalence of known risk factors for nutrition; and qualitative, community-led data collection (surveys, focus group discussions and so on) to understand details (the what and how) of underlying causes of undernutrition. The approach breaks nutrition risk factors into categories (food security, mental health and care practices, health WASH and other) to assess which category contributes the most to undernutrition. Next, a participatory process is used to triangulate the mixed methods data collection results and to reach a consensus on the causality of undernutrition. Once identified, this hopefully informs the design of a targeted, customized intervention (Dodos, 2017). Analysis of Link NCA-informed interventions concluded that inadequate WASH contributes to undernutrition in populations. It also found that different causal categories were more prominent triggers of undernutrition, depending on where in the world the undernutrition occurred; in Africa, water-associated risk factors had a higher presence (40 per cent) than they did in south and south-east Asia (31.3 per cent), where sanitation associated risk factors dominated. Personal hygiene was more influential in the eight African studies compared to the four Asian ones.

Looking at the relationship between WASH and stunting prevention through the lens of economic and social mechanisms also illuminates the incredible loss of energy and nutritional implications for (often) women and children who are responsible for fetching and carrying household water over long distances. This lens is also informative for understanding the difficulties of the growing proportion of the global population living in informal urban settlements, of whom the poorest pay the highest prices for clean water due to transportation costs (Cumming, 2016). There are also security concerns about the risks that vulnerable populations, such as women and children, are exposed to when trekking to and from water sources.

The concept of health promotion has evolved from solely focusing on nutrition-specific interventions (exclusive of breastfeeding, nutrition education, and supplementation) to incorporate nutrition-sensitive interventions, including WASH interventions (Bach et al, 2020). Indeed, one of the changes from NNP I to NNP II was the inclusion of a WASH manager on the PDU teams (Bach et al, 2020). This harkens back to the concept of allowing actors in other sectors to define their own roles in multisectoral efforts, as these stakeholders tend to create more sustainable strategies and outcomes for themselves in the long term.

While Momberg et al's 2020 analysis is focused on undernutrition in children below the age of five in South Africa, their approach to the analysis of governmental policies and documents, institutional mapping, and interviews with stakeholders (the selection of whom was informed by the policy review) provides a model for what we should be looking for in ISC – beyond commitment from government – when we evaluate how successful ISC is. The results of the institutional mapping were unique to the South African context, but the lessons learned are applicable to documenting the successful integration of WASH with other sectors.

Momberg et al (2020) reviewed six national policies, three of which mentioned WASH, nutrition, and children; 'however, none explicitly linked WASH to nutritional status in children'. Among the documents that mentioned those three keywords, a national sanitation policy gave responsibility for coordination to another department, and the food and nutrition policy stated the importance of ISC, integration into existing policies, and involvement of community-based and non-governmental organizations, and suggested a 'comprehensive Food and Nutrition Security and Vulnerability analysis, which would serve as a national data set including health, nutritional status and sanitation' (Momberg et al, 2020). The third document, an integrated early childhood development policy, which specifically aimed 'to provide an overarching multisectoral enabling framework of early childhood development services, inclusive of national, provincial and local spheres of government', specified which areas needed priority attention, acknowledged the importance of 'mutually dependent partnerships', and even designated accountability and responsibility to specific government agencies (Momberg et al, 2020). The mention of WASH in a policy document is a start but does not by any means guarantee successful ISC. This, coupled with a scoring system like the one discussed in Ouedraogo and mutually established cross-sectoral indicators, would contribute to the next step of documenting what is still missing.

The themes that resulted from the reviews, interviews, and a consensus development conference held with stakeholders called for 'articulation of the link between the various WASH components and nutritional status in children', as well as 'coordinated and complementary indicators across clinical and service provision sectors' and improved operationalization of communication between sectors within government bodies (Momberg et al, 2020). Momberg et al also recommended 'localising the SDG indicators' to synchronize targets, while scaling them down from an international to local level. This would also address competing priorities of different governmental departments, and seems to work toward overcoming the challenges of measurement, evaluation, and a lack of common indicators mentioned in previous sections. Nutrition has a great ISC track record and has made an effort to engage other sectors to work toward national and international goals of preventing malnutrition and stunting in line with the SDGs, but there is more work to be done toward improved ISC with the WASH sector in particular.

Appendix II references

Bach, A. and E. Gregor, S. Sridhar, H. Fekadu, W. Fawzi. 2020. 'Multisectoral integration of nutrition, health, and agriculture: implementation lessons from Ethiopia'. *Food Nutr Bull* 41(2): 275–292. <https://doi.10.1177/0379572119895097

Cumming, O. and S. Cairncross. 2016. 'Can water, sanitation and hygiene help eliminate stunting? Current evidence and policy implications: water, sanitation and hygiene, and stunting'. *Maternal & Child Nutrition* 12: 91–105.

Dodos, J. and B. Mattern, J. Lapegue, M. Altmann, M.A. Aissa. 2017. 'Relationship between water, sanitation, hygiene, and nutrition: what do link NCA nutrition causal analyses say?' *Waterlines* 36: 284–304. <https://practicalactionpublishing.com/article/2420/relationship-between-water-sanitation-hygiene-and-nutrition-what-do-link-nca-nutrition-causal-analyses-say>

Fink, G. and I. Günther, K. Hill. 2011. The effect of water and sanitation on child health: evidence from the demographic and health surveys 1986–2007. *International Journal of Epidemiology* 40(5): 1196–1204.

Lucas, P. and H.B.M. Hilderink, P.H.M. Janssen, S. KC, D.P. van Vuuren, L. Niessen. 2019. 'Future impacts of environmental factors on achieving the SDG target on child mortality-A synergistic assessment'. *Global Environmental Change* 57: 101. <https://www.sciencedirect.com/science/article/pii/S0959378018301262>

Momberg, D.J. and P. Mahlangu, B.C. Ngandu, J. May, S.A. Norris, R. Said-Mohamed. 2020. 'Intersectoral (in)activity: towards an understanding of public sector department links between water, sanitation and hygiene (WASH) and childhood undernutrition in South Africa'. *Health Policy and Planning* 35(7): 829–841. <https://doi.org/10.1093/heapol/czaa028>

Appendix III Mechanisms for the coordination of institutional WASH: the clean clinic and three-star approach

Explanation and evaluation of the clean clinic approach

Considering the multiple levels of the socioecological model on which COVID-19 has impacted, the challenges extend beyond the individual and household. Few sources returned in this review looked at WASH at the institutional level. However, an assessment of the implementation of the clean clinic approach, and how or whether it contributed to IPC efforts, as documented by Lopez et al (2020) in Guatemala, provides an example of a low-cost intersectoral coordination mechanism that was effective in improving ISC between the health and WASH sectors. USAID and partners designed the clean clinic approach, which consists of ten steps that implement WASH provisions incrementally in health care facilities, relying on close collaboration between implementers and national ministries of health to develop criteria and rating systems by which to evaluate WASH implementations and then working alongside health care facilities staff to improve their score (Lopez, 2020).

The approach aims to 'empower HCF [health care facilities] staff and health systems to implement simple, low-cost, and effective WASH improvements that are proven to help protect patients and staff from infection' (Lopez, 2020). The study found that, '[o]verall, HCFs improved their mean clean clinic approach assessment scores by more than 40%'. While this look at implementation was not in a COVID-19 context, the findings, particularly in terms of the low cost and marked IPC improvements in a short period, have positive implications for protecting at-risk populations from contracting COVID-19 in institutions (schools, religious gathering places, markets) in low-resource settings.

Characteristics of the three-star approach to WASH in schools

The three-star approach to WASH in schools is a combined checklist-and-rating system designed to assure that 'healthy habits are taught, practised and integrated into daily school routines' to 'address the bottlenecks that block the effectiveness and expansion of current WASH in school programs' (UNICEF and GIZ, 2015). Three-star-approach documents include guidance around ensuring the inclusion of, and support from, the community, government, and external partners, monitoring and evaluation, and detailed benchmarks and requirements schools must meet to obtain and maintain status as a one-, two- or three-star WASH institution. There is no guidance, however, around coordination with the education cluster for those working in or for the WASH cluster.

Appendix III references

Lopez, J. and S.T. Sierra, A.M. Rodas Cardona, S. Sara. 2020. 'Implementing the clean clinic approach improves water, sanitation, and hygiene quality in health facilities in the western highlands of Guatemala'. *Global Health: Science and Practice* 8(2): 256–269. <https://doi.org/10.9745/GHSP-D-19-00413>

UNICEF and GIZ. 2013. 'Field guide: the three star approach for WASH in schools'. UNICEF Programme Division/WASH. <https://www.unicef.org/kyrgyzstan/reports/field-guide-three-star-approach-wash-schools>

Notes

1. As the WASH Road Map is no longer led by the GWC. You can view the Global WASH cluster strategy here: https://www.washcluster.net/sites/gwc.com/files/inline-files/Global_WASH_Cluster_Strategic%20Plan_2022_2025_FINAL_lowres.pdf
2. At the time of writing (2022), there are 11 clusters, but there could soon be 12.
3. Examples of social determinants of health include, but are not limited to the following: one's gender assigned at birth and the significant security threats women and other vulnerable populations face as they fetch water for their families,; the socioeconomic status of the family or community one is born into; and whether one's community can afford a modern sewage systems.
4. The participatory action research is part of some of the key work done at the Institute for Development Studies (IDS), University of Sussex, focusing on various participatory methodologies including the controversial community-led total sanitation (CLTS). The IDS department that previously focused mainly on development WASH is now also focusing on links to humanitarian WASH using some of these key participatory tools.
5. The authors recognize that the term 'slum' can be intended as derogatory in some contexts. We would like to clarify that it is not intended as such here; it is referenced merely because some readers may be more familiar with this term over others such as 'informal urban settlements.'
6. Having stated that, humanitarian response efforts are often extended to build some initial bridging of sustainable WASH services.

References

Abu, T.Z. and S.J. Elliott, D. Karanja. 2021. '"When you preach water and you drink wine": WASH in healthcare facilities in Kenya'. *Journal of Water Sanitation and Hygiene for Development*. 11(4): 558–569.

Aldroubi, M. 2019. '"The water comes to us": Zaatari camp residents enjoy new luxury'. *The National News*. 21 March. <https://www.thenationalnews.com/world/mena/the-water-comes-to-us-zaatari-camp-residents-enjoy-new-luxury-1.839945>

Bach, A. and E. Gregor, S. Sridhar, H. Fekadu, W. Fawzi. 2020. 'Multisectoral integration of nutrition, health, and agriculture: implementation lessons from Ethiopia'. *Food and Nutrition Bulletin* 41(2): 275–292. <https://doi.10.1177/0379572119895097>

Bush, A. 2020. 'Story of change: ENN's role in knowledge management related to the SUN movement'. Emergency Nutrition Network (ENN). <https://www.ennonline.net/storyofchangesunkm>

Campbell, S.J. and N.K. Biritwum, G. Woods, Y. Velleman, F. Fleming, J. Russell Stothard. 2018. 'Tailoring water, sanitation, and hygiene (WASH) targets for soil-transmitted helminthiasis and schistosomiasis control'. *Trends Parasitol* 34(1): 53–63.

Cole, D.C. and C. Levin, C. Loechl, G. Thiele, F. Grant, A.W. Girard, K. Sindi, J. Low. 2016. 'Planning an integrated agriculture and health program and designing its evaluation: experience from western Kenya'. *Evaluation and Program Planning* 56: 11–22.

Core Humanitarian Standard Alliance. 2014. 'Core humanitarian standard on quality and accountability'. <https://corehumanitarianstandard.org/language-versions>

Cultivating New Frontiers in Agriculture, USAID. (2015). 'Zimbabwe: Amalima' [webpage]. <https://www.cnfa.org/program/amalima>

Cumming, O. and S. Cairncross (2016). 'Can water, sanitation and hygiene help eliminate stunting? Current evidence and policy implications: Water, sanitation and hygiene, and stunting'. *Maternal & Child Nutrition* 12: 91–105.

de Campos, R.S. and S.N.A. Codjoe, W.N. Adger, C. Mortreux, S. Hazra, T. Siddiqui, S. Das. 2020. 'Where people live and move in deltas'. In R.J. Nicholls, W.N. Adger, C.W. Hutton, S.E. Hanson (eds) *Deltas in the Anthropocene*. Palgrave Macmillan. <https://doi.org/10.1007/978-3-030-23517-8>

Dodos, J. and B. Mattern, J. Lapegue, M. Altmann, M.A. Aissa. 2017. 'Relationship between water, sanitation, hygiene, and nutrition: what do Link NCA nutrition causal analyses say?' *Waterlines* 36: 284–304. <https://practicalactionpublishing.com/article/2420/relationship-between-water-sanitation-hygiene-and-nutrition-what-do-link-nca-nutrition-causal-analyses-say>

Friel, S. and P. Harris, S. Simpson, A. Bhushan, B. Baer. 2015. 'Health in all policies approaches: pearls from the western Pacific region'. *Asia and the Pacific Policy Studies* 2: 324–337.

Gensch, R. and S. Ferron, P. Sandison (eds) (2022). 'Compendium of hygiene promotion in emergencies'. WASH Netzwerk. <https://www.washnet.de/wp-content/uploads/2022/04/GWN_Emergency-Hygiene-Compendium_2022.pdf>

GWC. 2022. 'About us' [webpage]. <https://www.washcluster.net/about-us>

GWC and Global Health Cluster. 2020. 'Joint operational framework improving coordinated and integrated multi-sector cholera preparedness and response within humanitarian crises'. World Health Organization. <https://healthcluster.who.int/publications/m/item/joint-operational-framework-improving-coordinated-and-integrated-multi-sector-cholera-preparedness-and-response-within-humanitarian-crises>

GTFCC. n.d. 'OVERCOME – digital innovation in climate hazard early warning and related disease prevention for community capacity building and resilience: project summary' [webpage]. <https://www.gtfcc.org/research/overcome-digital-innovation-in-climate-hazard-early-warning-and-related-disease-prevention-for-community-capacity-building-and-resilience>

Hemrich, G. and D. Topouzis. 2000. 'Multi-sectoral responses to HIV|AIDS: constraints and opportunities for technical co-operation'. *Journal of International Development* 12: 85–99.

IASC. 2021. 'Guidance on strengthening participation, representation and leadership of local and national actors in IASC humanitarian coordination mechanisms'. Inter-Agency Standing Committee. <https://interagencystandingcommittee.org/operational-response/iasc-guidance-strengthening-participation-representation-and-leadership-local-and-national-actors>

IASC. 2020. 'UN-IASC light guidance on collective outcomes'. 29 June. Inter-Agency Standing Committee. <https://interagencystandingcommittee.org/inter-agency-standing-committee/un-iasc-light-guidance-collective-outcomes>

———. 2015. 'IASC reference module for cluster coordination at country level'. Inter-Agency Standing Committee. <https://interagencystanding-committee.org/iasc-transformative-agenda/iasc-reference-module-cluster-coordination-country-level-revised-july-2015>

———. 1994 'Definition of complex emergencies'. 30 November. <https://inter-agencystandingcommittee.org/content/definition-complex-emergency>

Johari, A. 2020. 'Coronavirus: they cannot work from home. Or follow social distancing. Here is why'. *Scroll.in*. <https://scroll.in/article/956385/corona-virus-they-cannot-work-from-home-or-follow-social-distancing-here-is-why>

Kimball, A. and A. Jumaan. 2020. 'Yemen: the challenge of delivering aid in an active conflict zone'. *Global Security: Health, Science and Policy* 5: 65–70.

Kritz, J. and P. Batsa. 2020. 'Building cross-sector collaboration to improve community health'. *Journal of Health and Human Services Administration* 42(4): 428–460.

Laub, Z. n.d. 'No refuge – why the world's swelling refugee population has shrinking options' [webpage]. Council on Foreign Relations. <https://www.cfr.org/refugee-crisis/#!/a-system-under-strain>

Levin, C. and J.L. Self, E. Kedera, M. Wamalwa, J. Hu, F. Grant, A.W. Girard, D.C. Cole, J.W. Low. 2019. 'What is the cost of integration? Evidence from an integrated health and agriculture project to improve nutrition outcomes in western Kenya'. *Health Policy and Planning* 34(9): 646–655. <https://doi.org/10.1093/heapol/czz083>

Lopez, J. and S.T. Sierra, A.M. Rodas Cardona, S. Sara. 2020. 'Implementing the clean clinic approach improves water, sanitation, and hygiene quality in health facilities in the western highlands of Guatemala'. *Global Health: Science and Practice* 8(2): 256–269. <https://doi.org/10.9745/GHSP-D-19-00413>

Lucas, P. and H.B.M. Hilderink, P.H.M. Janssen, S. KC, D.P. van Vuuren, L. Niessen. 2019. 'Future impacts of environmental factors on achieving the SDG target on child mortality-A synergistic assessment'. *Global Environmental Change* 57: 101. <https://www.sciencedirect.com/science/article/pii/S0959378018301262>

Mobula, L., J.H. Nakao, S. Walia, J. Pendarvis, P. Morris, D. Townes. 2018. 'A humanitarian response to the West African Ebola virus disease outbreak'. *Journal of International Humanitarian Action* 3. <https://jhumanitarian-action.springeropen.com/articles/10.1186/s41018-018-0039-2>

Momberg, D.J. and P. Mahlangu, B.C. Ngandu, J. May, S.A. Norris, R. Said-Mohamed. 2020. 'Intersectoral (in)activity: towards an understanding of public sector department links between water, sanitation and hygiene (WASH) and childhood undernutrition in South Africa'. *Health Policy and Planning* 35(7): 829–841. <https://doi.org/10.1093/heapol/czaa028>

OCHA. 2018. 'Collective outcomes: operationalizing the New Way of Working'. April. United Nations Office for the Coordination of Humanitarian Affairs.

<https://agendaforhumanity.org/sites/default/files/resources/2018/Apr/OCHA%20Collective%20Outcomes%20April%202018.pdf>

_____. 2016. 'Global overview of coordination arrangements in 2016'. October. United Nations Office for the Coordination of Humanitarian Affairs. <https://interagencystandingcommittee.org/system/files/global_overview_coord_arrangements_06.10.2016_0.pdf>

Ouedraogo, O. and M.H. Doudou, K.M. Drabo, D. Garnier, N.M. Zagré, D. Sanou, K. Reinhardt, P. Donnen. 2020. 'Policy overview of the multi-sectoral nutrition planning process: the progress, challenges, and lessons learned from Burkina Faso'. *Int J Health Plann Manage* 35(1): 120–139. <https://doi.org/10.1002/hpm.2823>

Ncube-Murakwani, P. and W. Sibanda, S. Dube, N. Weber, Amalima, International Medical Corps | PRO-WASH: Practices Operations and Research in WASH, Save the Children. n.d. 'Does integrating savings, lending, and income generating activities with community health clubs improve the uptake of latrine construction?' [unpublished PowerPoint presentation].

Sommer, M. and M.L. Schmitt, T. Ogello, P. Mathenge, M. Mark, D. Clatworthy, S. Khandakji, R. Ratnayake. 2018. 'Pilot testing and evaluation of a toolkit for menstrual hygiene management in emergencies in three refugee camps in northwest Tanzania'. *Journal of International Humanitarian Action* 3. <https://doi.org/10.1186/s41018-018-0034-7>

Tappis, H. and S. Elaraby, S. Elnakib, N.A.A. AlShawafi, H. BaSaleem, I.A. Saleh Al-Gawfi, F. Othman, F. Shafique, E. Al-Kubati, N. Rafique, P. Spiegel. 2020. 'Reproductive, maternal, newborn and child health service delivery during conflict in Yemen: a case study'. *Conflict and Health* 14(1). <https://doi.org/10.1186/s13031-020-00269-x>

UNICEF and GIZ. 2013. 'Field guide: the three star approach for WASH in schools'. UNICEF Programme Division/WASH. <https://www.unicef.org/kyrgyzstan/reports/field-guide-three-star-approach-wash-schools>

UN. 2015. 'Transforming our world: the 2030 agenda for sustainable development'. United Nations Department of Economic and Social Affairs. <https://sdgs.un.org/2030agenda>

UN Water. 2019. 'Climate change and water. UN-Water policy brief'. UN Water. <https://reliefweb.int/report/world/un-water-policy-brief-climate-change-and-water-september-2019-version#:~:text=In%20the%20new%20policy%20brief,places%20huge%20stress%20on%20ecosystems>

Vidal, J. 2017. 'From heatwaves to hurricanes, floods to famine: seven climate change hotspots'. 23 June. *The Guardian*. <https://www.theguardian.com/environment/2017/jun/23/from-heatwaves-to-hurricanes-floods-to-famine-seven-climate-change-hotspots>

Waite, R.C. and Y. Velleman, G. Woods, A. Chitty, M.C Freeman. 2016. 'Integration of water, sanitation and hygiene for the control of neglected tropical diseases: a review of progress and the way forward'. *Int Health* 8 Suppl 1: i22–27. <https://doi.10.1093/inthealth/ihw003>

WHO. 2022. 'Global analysis of health care waste in the context of COVID-19'. Geneva: World Health Organization. <https://www.who.int/publications/i/item/9789240039612>

_____. 2020. 'Multisectoral preparedness coordination framework'. Geneva: World Health Organization. <https://www.who.int/publications/i/item/9789240006232>

WHO, USAID and UNICEF. 2015. 'Improving nutrition outcomes with better water, sanitation and hygiene: practical solutions for policies and programmes'. Geneva: World Health Organization. <https://apps.who.int/iris/handle/10665/193991>

Wilkinson, A. 2020. 'Local response in health emergencies: key considerations for addressing the COVID-19 pandemic in informal urban settlements'. *Environment and Urbanization* 32(2): 503–522. <https://journals.sagepub.com/doi/full/10.1177/0956247820922843>

CHAPTER 2

A WASH framework to address conflict, COVID-19, and climate change: leveraging the humanitarian–development–peace nexus

Tim Grieve

Introduction

> *We are clear that working 'at the nexus' ... is not an end in itself, but a means to addressing and reducing people's unmet needs, risks and vulnerabilities, increasing their resilience, addressing the root causes of conflict and building peace. (Development Initiatives, 2019)*

The WASH joint operational framework (JOF)

Developing a framework that puts into practice the global humanitarian–development–peace nexus (HDPN) policy in the context of the WASH sector has been a both stimulating and daunting project. For almost 20 years, I worked on this agenda alongside inspiring organizations and professionals across Africa, Asia and the Middle East, forging a deep connection with its critical importance and its people. And most recently, having navigated the twists and turns of a two-year learning journey, the development of the joint operational framework (JOF), commissioned by the German WASH Network with oversight from UNICEF, Sanitation and Water for All (SWA), and the Global WASH Cluster (GWC) is planned for release in 2023. It is based on inputs from more than 40 interviews with key WASH stakeholders across the humanitarian, development, and peace pillars, an ongoing literature review of policy, guidance, and case studies, and more than ten learning workshops and webinars at the global and regional level with inputs from policymakers and practitioners. This chapter outlines the framework and its relevance as a solution to the multiple risks that the WASH sector faces in fragile contexts today.

This chapter marks a point in time in the evolution of the JOF in which it has already undergone a broad, multi-stakeholder, technical review of more than 50 experts. And while the 3Cs of conflict, COVID-19, and climate change are not directly covered in the JOF, they implicitly play a vital part as contemporary challenges in the WASH sector, as will be discussed in this chapter.

The 3 Cs – conflict, COVID-19, and climate change

Shocks and stresses, such as the intersection of climate change, COVID-19, and conflict, have devasted WASH services in vulnerable countries across the world. To highlight the magnitude of the challenge facing these countries, the Central African Republic provides a useful case study. In the Central African Republic, extreme climate events, along with the COVID-19 pandemic, have collided with decades of ongoing conflict. The growing frequency of erratic weather patterns has led to multiple floods and drought, which, combined with poor WASH and water resource management, have destroyed or contaminated entire water supplies, increased the risk of water stress and disease, and exacerbated tensions that have led to conflict and displacement. An increasing scarcity of water resources has led many livestock herders to seek water and pasture for their herds, creating tension between farmers and livestock herders. COVID-19, which started as a disease shock and has contributed to major socio-economic upheavals nationally, has further exacerbated existing inequalities in access to WASH services that had been in existence for decades. Since the start of Sustainable Development Goal (SDG) reporting in 2015, the multiple shocks and stresses faced by the Central African Republic have led to a declining progress toward achieving the water and sanitation SDG goals (WHO & UNICEF, 2021).

The core of the WASH JOF: humanitarian–development–peace nexus.

In contexts where people are highly exposed and vulnerable to recurrent and protracted crises driven by climate change, conflict, and other risks, collaboration between the humanitarian, development, and peace pillars is the key to building resilience, conflict sensitivity, and peacebuilding capacities. When built within WASH systems and communities, these capacities are a prerequisite for:

- addressing and reducing WASH humanitarian needs over the long term;
- achieving the sustainable development of WASH services, and more broadly water resource management, water security, and water-related ecosystems; and
- contributing to both minimizing harm and building peaceful societies.

The desired impact is improved public health, wellbeing, peace, prosperity, and the environment.

A global call to action

To this end, from a global and intersectoral perspective, in 2016 the UN Secretary General released a call to action promoting closer collaboration and coordination between humanitarian, development, and peace pillars (i.e., the nexus approach), supported by the following global agendas:

- The **New Way of Working** (NWOW) as outlined in the Secretary-General's Report of the World Humanitarian Summit (UN, 2016a), and the **Grand Bargain** (IASC, 2016): commonly referred to as the nexus

approach, the NWOW is based on collaboration between diverse stakeholders with complimentary mandates and strengths across the humanitarian, development, and peace pillars.
- The **Agenda 2030** (UN, 2015a): the nexus approach supports the achievement of SDG 6 (ensuring access to water and sanitation for all) through furthering complimentary SDGs relating to resilience and peace, including SDG 1, which is about resilience of the poor and vulnerable; SDG 9 and SDG 11, which focus on resilient and inclusive infrastructure and cities; SDG 13, which covers climate change; and SDG 16, which promotes peaceful and inclusive societies.
- The **Paris Agreement** (UN, 2015b) and **Sendai Framework** (UN, 2015c): these were adopted in 2015 to support the 2030 Agenda through measures to address climate change and reduce disaster risks.
- The **Sustaining Peace Agenda**: the Security Council Twin Resolutions on Sustaining Peace adopted in 2016 recognize the importance of collaboration across the HDPN (UN, 2016b and 2016c)

Purpose of the JOF

The purpose of the JOF is to assist policymakers, directors, coordinators, and practitioners within government, civil society, private sector, UN agencies, banks, donors, and academia at the regional, transboundary, national, and subnational level to integrate (where feasible) resilience, conflict sensitivity, and peacebuilding capacities into existing and new WASH programmes by leveraging the nexus approach.

Leveraging the nexus approach means encouraging collaboration and programming coherence and coordination across humanitarian, development, and peace pillars within the WASH sector, while respecting organizational mandates and acknowledging that solutions are context-specific and locally driven.

The JOF: what it is and what it is not

The JOF sets out the thinking (The JOF and the Nexus), theory of change (Defining a new programme logic), and key steps (Putting the JOF into practice) in applying the triple nexus within the WASH sector, while establishing strong linkages with the integrated water resource management (IWRM) sector. The word 'joint' emphasizes the collaboration required between humanitarian, development, and peace actors. The word 'operational' hints at the suggested practical steps and entry points for policymakers and practitioners.

As such, the JOF is not a new WASH programme or initiative. It is designed primarily for humanitarian–development collaboration. However, where feasible and relevant, the nexus should be extended to include the additional participation of the peace pillar.

The JOF is not a detailed guidance note to be strictly followed but has been designed to be easily adapted by users for their own WASH programming guidance notes and tools.

Tools and resources can be found in Appendix I (links to key guidance and tools published by actors in the WASH sector).

The JOF: where it is relevant

Experience of implementing the nexus approach suggests that it is particularly relevant in contexts prone to protracted (e.g. long-term conflict, water insecurity, etc.) and recurrent (e.g. floods, drought, etc.) crises (IASC, 2020a). In such contexts, the humanitarian, development, and peace pillars collaborate to provide the required stability to implement long-term programmes.

Given the role of climate change as a driver of conflict and protracted/recurrent crises, the JOF is also highly relevant in climate-vulnerable contexts.

The JOF and the nexus

This section gives an insight into the thinking behind the nexus and the JOF. It covers the drivers for action, the linkages between pillars, and the relevant principles.

Drivers for action

Climate change, conflict, and water insecurity are rapidly accelerating the number and magnitude of protracted and recurrent crises globally. Based on current estimates, by 2030, up to two-thirds of the global extreme poor will be living in fragile and conflict-affected contexts (Coral et al, 2020) and more than 100 million will slip into extreme poverty driven by climate change (Jafino et al, 2020). In 2021, 250 million people required humanitarian assistance. This marks a steadily increasing trend in needs of 250 per cent over the last seven years, with the great majority affected living in fragile and conflict-affected contexts (OCHA, 2022). In 2020, 286 million people were international migrants and in 2021, 84 million people were forcibly displaced from their homes – the highest numbers ever recorded in an increasing upward trend – often exacerbating transboundary tension (UNHCR, 2021; IOM, 2022).

Water insecurity and water-related ecosystem degradation, resulting from mismanagement, overuse, pollution, conflict, and climate change, ranked in the top five risks to global economic, social, and political instability (WEF, 2020). Additionally, they are key drivers of displacement and migration due to their impact on health and livelihoods, along with the conflicts they risk triggering (USAID 2023). The situation is predicted to worsen as 40 per cent of the world is expected to live in constant water-stressed environments by 2050 (UNESCO and UN Water, 2020).

Progress towards access to WASH services and safe community WASH behaviour is severely off track. According to WHO and UNICEF (2021), when comparing fragile and non-fragile contexts, the former demand 23 times more effort to achieve the SDG target for safely managed drinking water and 9 times more effort to achieve the target for safely managed sanitation. Infrastructure is often aging, mismanagement is common, WASH outcomes are challenging to sustain over the long term, and markets and supply chains are weak. WASH systems that lack inclusive, trust-building, and accountability measures lead to inequities in access and can expose women and girls to gender-based violence (GBV) when accessing WASH services in schools and communities.

Exposure and vulnerability to shocks and stresses exacerbate water insecurity, the severe lack of WASH services, the mismanagement of water resources, and the loss of water-related ecosystems. Long-term stressors, such as weak institutions, political instability, and climate change, increase vulnerability to shocks, such as floods, conflicts, droughts, earthquakes, and diseases. These crises in turn further weaken and degrade water-related ecosystems and WASH/water resource institutions, systems, and infrastructure, causing disease, loss of life and livelihoods, and dramatic socioeconomic and environmental damage. As the global rate of urbanization continues to increase rapidly, shocks and stresses are devastating urban centres, requiring coordination and engagement with a much larger set of stakeholders and services than in rural areas. In conflict-affected countries such as Yemen, which experienced 122 airstrikes on water infrastructure between March 2015 and January 2021, attacks on drinking water have become a weapon of war (UNICEF 2021).

There is a huge gap in the finance for resilient WASH systems. Over half of the estimated annual capital investment required to meet the SDGs globally (US$60 billion per year) is needed in fragile contexts (UNICEF, 2019). Without resilient WASH systems, humanitarian resourcing needs continue to grow. Global WASH humanitarian appeals remain largely unmet and their funding rate even dropped from 48 per cent to 19 per cent between 2014 and 2021 (GWC, 2021). Challenges continue to prevent the full realization of the Grand Bargain commitment to provide flexible, unearmarked, and multi-year funding (IASC, 2016 and 2022c).

Collaboration between silos is feasible. Significant structural barriers must be overcome to break down the silos between the humanitarian, development, and peace pillars. Different mandates, priorities, planning horizons, funding cycles, and modes of operation have led to norms, culture, and language specific to each pillar, consequently creating disincentives to collaborate (Mason and Mosello, 2016). For example, with respect to funding, humanitarians are often bound by short-term funding cycles, while many development actors lack the capacity to operate in insecure environments over the long term (Tuchel, 2020).

38 ADDRESSING CONFLICT, COVID-19, AND CLIMATE CHANGE

Shared principles

> *In the long term, closer collaboration between humanitarian aid, development and peacebuilding efforts is the only way we will achieve the Sustainable Development Goals and leave no one behind.*
> (UN Secretary General, António Gutteres, OCHA 2022)

There are several principles that humanitarian and development actors share, along with elements of conflict sensitivity and peacebuilding, thus providing common ground and a strong foundation for collaboration, effective coordination, and coherence across all programming phases (see Figure 2.1).

Humanity (one of the core humanitarian principles based on addressing human suffering wherever it is found) is closely related to the development pillar's principle of employing a human rights-based approach (OCHA, 2012).

The six principles 'Leave no one behind', 'Gender equality and women's empowerment', 'Human rights-based approach', 'Sustainable development', 'Resilience', and 'Accountability' are central to realizing the 2030 Agenda and have universal appeal across the pillars (UNSDG, 2019).

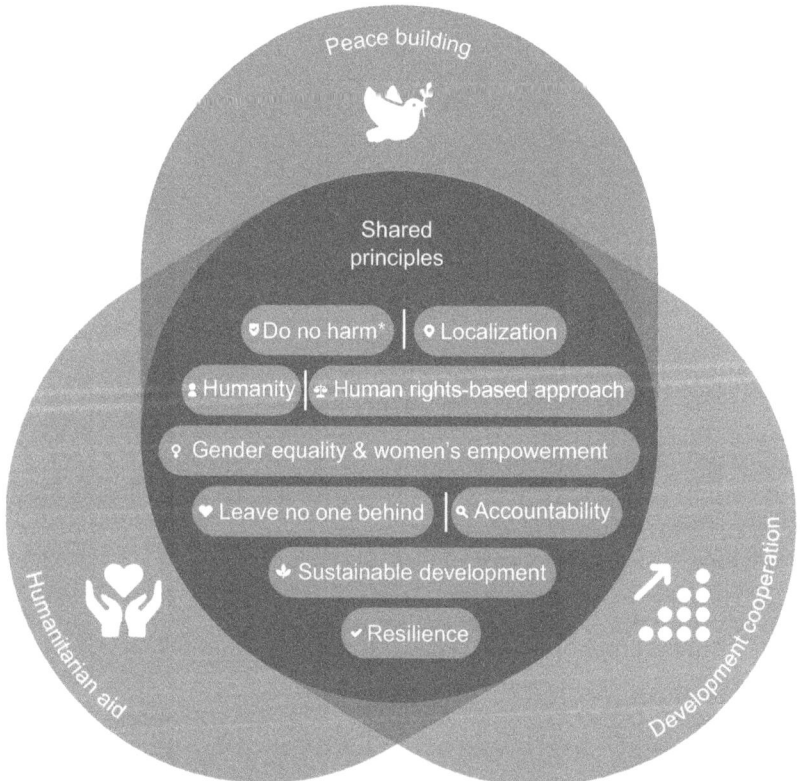

Figure 2.1 Finding common ground in shared principles

The principle of localization, which is recognizing, respecting, and investing in national and local capacity, is also supported across all pillars. Additionally, as conflict over management of water resources intensifies and water security declines across the globe, the principle of 'Do no harm' is a minimum requirement for every water resource management and WASH programme, so that existing conflict is not exacerbated or new conflict created (UNICEF, 2016).

However, in some situations, certain principles do clash. For example, targeting the delivery of aid based on political/security objectives can directly clash with the core humanitarian principles of neutrality and independence across several contexts. The resulting erosion of trust in service providers and authorities, the potential to fuel tensions between communities, and the threat to the safety of frontline workers is well-documented (Perret, 2019). Another example is the over-extraction of groundwater to support vulnerable communities in protracted crises, which negatively impacts long-term water security. These examples are real problems, and they are not easily solved. However, acknowledging and respecting opposing principles while proactively seeking common ground are key to constructively managing effective collaboration across the nexus. This is reflected in the nexus' operational principle of 'respecting diversity, which is explained below.

The nexus' operational principles

The nexus utilizes the linkages between humanitarian, development, and peace actions to achieve collective outcomes. These are 'commonly agreed measurable result(s) or impact(s) enhanced by the combined effort of different actors, within their respective mandates, to address and reduce people's unmet needs, risks and vulnerabilities, increasing their resilience and addressing the root causes of conflict' (OECD, 2022).

Operational nexus principles are key principles required to manage the nexus in challenging environments (see Figure 2.2).

- **'Work together to deliver'** is core to the nexus. Where feasible and relevant, WASH actors should work jointly across all coordination and programming activities, including assessment, analysis, planning, delivery, monitoring, review, and financing. Joint action can be broken down into three elements (OECD, 2022):
  1. Collaboration: working jointly with multiple stakeholders with a strong emphasis on local partnerships.
  2. Complementarity: partnering based on the comparative strength of each pillar and actors' mandate related to the context.
  3. Coherence: ensuring that coordination, programming, and financing is unified across the pillars, including capacity building on key concepts, definitions, and an agreed common terminology.

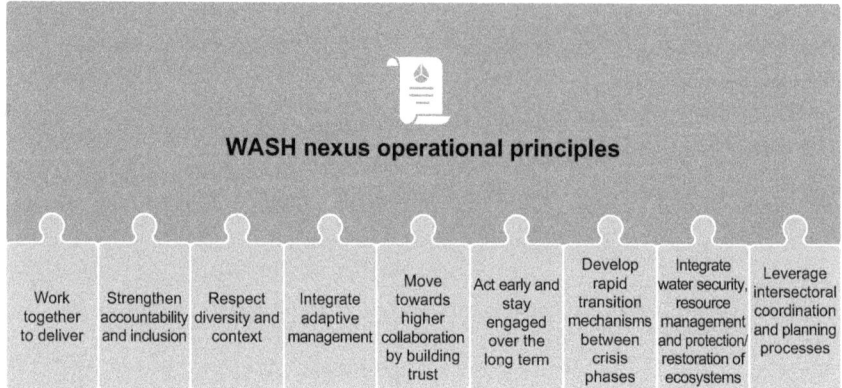

Figure 2.2 The nexus' operational principles

- **Respect diversity** of principles, mandates, roles, and organizational independence, and ensure **context-specific solutions** that are locally led.
- Move **towards higher levels of collaboration** (e.g., shared planning, resources, etc.) from lower levels of collaboration (e.g., information sharing) **based on developing trust**, which can take time.
- **Strengthen systems of accountability**, ensuring that community engagement and feedback mechanisms are developed, and **address inclusion and marginalization** in access to and management of WASH services (Tearfund and UK AID, 2014).
- **Apply adaptive management** within and across organizations collaborating on triple nexus initiatives to adapt to unpredictable operating environments, such as protracted and recurrent crisis settings. The aim is to create an environment of intentional learning and flexible project and activity design. It also requires minimizing the obstacles to modifying programming and creating incentives for adaptive management (USAID, 2018).
- Ensure humanitarian and development partners **act early to prevent and prepare** for shocks and stresses, and **stay engaged and flexible over the long term**.
- Develop **rapid and effective transition mechanisms between crisis phases**, ensuring that water resource and WASH systems enable:
  - humanitarian actors, in consultation with development actors, to focus on sustainability from the start of an emergency response, building on existing water resource/WASH systems and markets;
  - both humanitarian and development actors to develop policies supporting each crisis phase with associated guidance on triggering, standards, data sharing, and associated accountabilities for all stakeholders;

- development actors to support the integration of humanitarian actors' input into long-term assessment, policy, planning, and resourcing processes;
- humanitarian and development actors to collaboratively transform monitoring systems to include relevant real time indicators that incorporate resilience, conflict sensitivity, and peacebuilding capacities (UN, 2020; OECD, 2022; IASC, 2020b; SWA, 2020).

- **Collaborate beyond the WASH sector by linking with the broader water sector** to address water security, resource management, and the protection/restoration of water-related ecosystems. For example, SDG 6.6 calls for action to 'protect and restore water-related ecosystems' and SDG 6.5 ensures that competing interests for domestic use, economic development, and environmental protection are adequately managed (IWRM), providing opportunities for coordination and planning across the nexus, including transboundary cooperation and establishing water rights.
- **Collaborate beyond SDG 6 by linking with existing intersectoral coordination and planning processes** at the country level, which provide multiple benefits to targeted communities across health, education, food security, nutrition, and so on. The success of achieving long-term collective outcomes within these structures is high, as they are often well-established, robust, and well-funded (IASC, 2020a).

Defining a new programme logic

This section outlines the theory of change (TOC) for strengthening WASH systems to enable resilience and sustainability in protracted and recurrent crisis settings, which is underpinned by the WASH triple nexus operational principles described above. The TOC develops the causal links (impact, outcomes, outputs, and approaches) to enable new and existing WASH programmes to integrate (where possible and appropriate) resilience, conflict sensitivity, and peacebuilding capacities into WASH systems.

While the TOC is predominantly WASH-focused, the intersection with IWRM and protecting and restoring water-related ecosystems are priorities. Additionally, in alignment with achieving the overall SDG targets, an intersectoral approach, where possible, is strongly recommended.

The vision: 'by 2030, enhance resilience, conflict sensitivity, and peacebuilding capacities to enable sustainable WASH for all, always and everywhere'.

'All' stresses that the vision is inclusive of all groups, especially the most vulnerable. 'Always' refers to accessibility during and outside of crisis. 'Everywhere' emphasises the relevance for all contexts, including those prone to protracted and recurrent crisis.

Impact, pillar outcomes, and intermediate collective outcomes

Impact: the overall impact of integrating resilience, conflict sensitivity, and peacebuilding into WASH programmes is to 'improve public health, wellbeing, prosperity, peace, and the environment across communities exposed to recurrent and protracted crises'.

Pillar outcomes: the humanitarian, development, and peace pillars each have a WASH outcome, for which they are primarily accountable. The three pillar outcomes are summarized in Figure 2.3, although they are not limited to these.

Intermediate collective outcomes: to address shocks and stresses, a precondition for achieving the WASH Pillar Outcomes is to strengthen WASH systems by integrating and building resilience, conflict sensitivity, and peacebuilding capacities within them. Noting, the term WASH systems can be broadly defined here as an effective network of people (community) and the systems of which they are a part, operating together to deliver WASH services (IRC 2022).

Resilience capacity is the ability of all key WASH stakeholders **to prevent, resist, absorb, adapt, respond, and recover positively, efficiently and effectively** when faced with a wide range of risks, while maintaining an acceptable level of WASH system performance without compromising long-term prospects for sustainable development, peace and security, human rights, and wellbeing for all (UN 2020).

Conflict sensitivity capacity is the ability of a WASH organization '**to understand** its operating context, the interaction between its interventions and the context, **and act** upon this understanding **to avoid negative impacts** ("do no harm") and **maximise positive impacts** on conflict factors'(UNICEF 2020, UN-IASC 2020b).

Peacebuilding capacity is the ability of key WASH stakeholders **to address the root causes of violence** that impact on the performance of a WASH system (noting that the WASH system itself may be one of the root causes) and **to contribute to the peace and development** of the community (UNICEF 2020, UN-IASC 2020b). By building conflict-sensitive and peacebuilding capacities into the management of water resources, water-related ecosystems, and the delivery of WASH services, the broader water sector can play a significant role in contributing to peaceful societies.

Within the TOC, the resilience, conflict sensitivity, and peacebuilding capacities are labelled **WASH intermediate Collective Outcomes**. They are:

- Considered intermediate outcomes, as they are a step towards achieving the WASH Pillar Outcomes;
- Considered collective outcomes as they require a nexus approach to enable them (outlined in Operational Principles below);
- Bundled together as they are mutually reinforcing. Conflict sensitivity and peacebuilding capacities strengthen social cohesion within and

FRAMEWORK TO ADDRESS CONFLICT, COVID-19, AND CLIMATE CHANGE   43

Protracted and recurrent crisis	Approaches	Outputs	Intermediate collective outcomes	Pillar outcomes	Impact
Stresses e.g. climate change, weak institutions, political instability	Risk informed	Resilient WASH service providers, infrastructure and water resources	Anticipative and absorptive capacities	**WASH humanitarian assistance** WASH humanitarian needs are addressed and reduced (NWOW)	Improve public health, well-being, prosperity, peace, and the environment across communities exposed to recurrent and protracted crisis
		Resilient community WASH behaviour			
	Conflict sensitivity & Peacebuilding	WASH Governance enhanced	Resilience, conflict sensitivity and peacebuilding capacities	**WASH development cooperation** WASH services and behaviours are sustainable and resilient to shocks and stressors (SDG 1, 6, 9, 13, NWOW)	
Shocks e.g. floods, conflict, droughts, earthquakes, disease	Strengthening System	Coordination, planning, information management linked	Preventative and adaptive capacities	**WASH peacebuilding** WASH contributes to building esilient, inclusive, and peaceful societies (SDG 1, 11, 16, NWOW)	
		Flexible and sustainable financing			

Figure 2.3 Theory of change

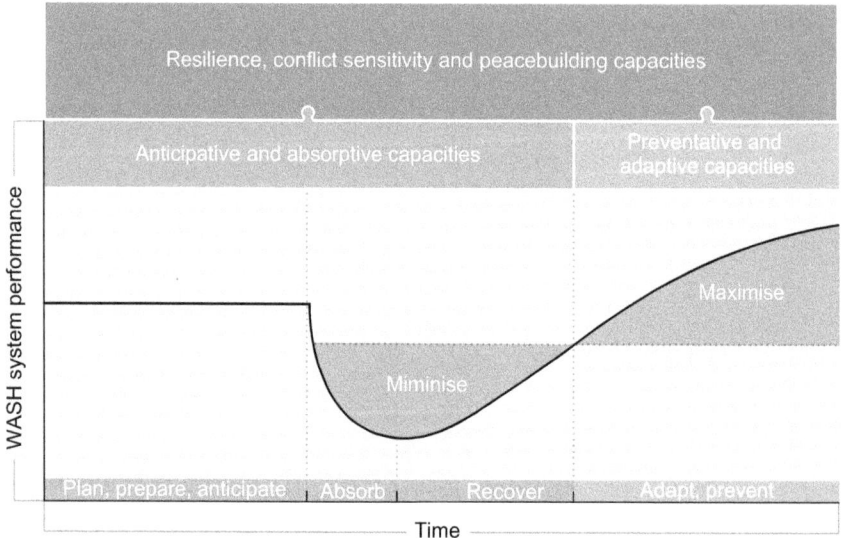

Figure 2.4 WASH Intermediate Collective Outcomes

across communities, and between communities and service providers/authorities. Social cohesion is foundational for building WASH systems' resilience. In turn, resilience capacity provides the stability for establishing conflict-sensitive and peacebuilding capacities within WASH systems;
- Placed into sub-categories ('anticipative and absorptive capacities' and 'preventative and adaptive capacities') based on the resilience capacities outlined in the UN Common Guidance on Helping Build Resilient Societies (UN 2020).

The diagram below (Figure 2.4.) demonstrates the relationship between these capacities and WASH Systems and how this evolves over time when faced with shocks (adapted from OECD 2014). As these sub-categories of resilience, conflict sensitivity and peacebuilding capacities are built and further shocks and stresses are experienced, WASH system performance will incrementally improve.

Anticipative and absorptive capacities - minimise WASH system underperformance (red)

Resilience, conflict sensitivity, and peacebuilding capacities can first be grouped into those that ensure a WASH system can anticipate, prepare for, respond to (absorb) and recover from shocks (such as floods, conflict, or disease outbreaks) based on achieving a minimum humanitarian standard. Strengthening anticipative and absorptive capacities will minimise WASH system underperformance, as represented by the critical red area in Figure 2.4.

- Resilience example – building anticipative capacity: developing or linking the WASH system to an existing disaster early warning system,

protocols and a forecast-based financing mechanism, which automatically allocates funding for pre-defined early actions once a forecast trigger has been reached.
- Resilience example – building absorptive capacity: strengthening the long-term preparedness and emergency response capacity of a WASH service provider to ensure business continuity (i.e., uninterrupted delivery of WASH services) in times of crisis.
- Conflict sensitivity example – anticipative capacity: by using a combination of conflict analysis (ranging from a basic conflict sensitivity checklist to more formal reports) and linking with 'real-time' information networks (e.g., informal community, formal security sources etc.), WASH organisations can increase their capacity to anticipate conflicts in an ongoing manner, and prepare and adjust programming accordingly to minimise negative effects.
- Conflict sensitivity and peacebuilding example – building absorptive capacity: establishing a transparent and inclusive public forum where groups such as refugees and the host community can both avoid conflict and create a mutually beneficial outcome (i.e., access to equitable safe water and sanitation services).

Preventative and adaptive capacities - maximise WASH system performance (green)

Secondly, resilience, conflict sensitivity, and peacebuilding capacities can be further grouped into capacities that ensure a WASH system can both prevent (or in most cases reduce) exposure to shocks and long-term stresses such as climate change, and most importantly can incrementally and fundamentally adapt to them. Strengthening preventative and adaptive capacities will maximise WASH system performance, as represented by the critical green area in Figure 2.4. Organisations are encouraged to integrate 'adaptive management' processes (as described in section 2) which require an investment in capacity of systems and personnel, as well as a shift in culture. For example, the integration of 'real-time' data into programme and management systems will enable a shift to a more rapid and informed decision making, which is necessary for addressing ongoing and future risks.

- Resilience example – building preventative capacity: flood/climate-proofing critical WASH infrastructure and services and minimizing damage to water-related ecosystems.
- Resilience example – building adaptive capacity: diversifying water resources and delivery mechanisms (i.e., developing alternative power and water sources) to ensure business continuity should the primary sources fail during a crisis. Diversifying power and water is an example of deliberately building redundancy (or 'back-ups') into WASH systems, which is a key component of resilience (World Bank et al. 2021, UNDRR 2022).

Building preventative and adaptive capacity from a conflict sensitivity and peacebuilding perspective is about ensuring processes and mechanism are integrated within the WASH system that promote collaboration, inclusion, and accountability (Tearfund 2014).

- Peacebuilding example – building preventative and adaptive capacity: the meaningful inclusion of a representative group of stakeholders in WASH decision-making bodies that allocate and manage water resources, along with building or using existing community mechanisms to resolve water-related disputes, can provide the opportunity to address the root cause of conflict between opposing communities and enhance trust in the service provider and authorities.
- Conflict sensitivity example – building preventative and adaptive capacity: undertaking a conflict analysis, even a basic one such as a checklist, can help WASH organizations understand conflict dynamics within the community, especially regarding allocation of water and energy resources. WASH programme managers/coordinators can use this information to both prevent WASH programmes from exacerbating existing community tensions and develop capacity for ongoing programme adaptations by seeking opportunities to create a positive effect on the conflict, depending on expertise and experience.

Outputs

To achieve the intermediate collective outcomes described above, it is recommended to integrate resilience, conflict sensitivity, and peacebuilding capacities across five key WASH outputs outlined in Table 2.1. The outputs capture key elements of the WASH sector building blocks set out by both SWA and the Agenda for Change (SWA, 2020; Huston and Moriarty, 2018).

Approaches

In order to achieve the JOF outputs, the triple nexus operational principles outlined in Figure 2.3 are foundational to the key approaches described below. Links to useful guidance tools can be found in Appendix I.

A **risk-informed** and context-specific way of working is a minimum requirement. It begins with an analysis of the local context to understand the multiple and interconnected dimensions of risk, including conflict (UNICEF 2018). This analysis then provides the evidence and direction for building risk-informed capacities such as resilience.

Conflict sensitivity is foundational, while **peacebuilding capacity** is applicable where feasible and relevant. Conflict sensitivity and peacebuilding capacities can be applied across three levels:

- Connecting WASH institutions and communities (e.g., via a service provider-community feedback mechanism)
- Enhancing relationships at the community level (e.g., through the allocation and management of water resources)
- Enhancing individual capacities (e.g., by empowering women and indigenous WASH representatives (UNICEF, 2016))

Table 2.1 JOF outputs

1. Resilient WASH service providers, infrastructure, and water resources	2. Resilient community WASH behaviour	3. WASH policies, laws, guidance, and standards linked	4. Coordination, planning, information management linked	5. Flexible and sustainable financing
Enhanced resilience, conflict sensitivity, and peacebuilding capacities of WASH service providers (including markets), infrastructure, and water resource management	Enhanced resilience, conflict sensitivity, and peacebuilding capacities within communities practising WASH behaviours	Resilience, conflict sensitivity, and peacebuilding integrated into WASH policies, laws, guidance, and standards at the national, subnational, and local level	Coordination, planning, review, and information systems linked across the WASH sector	Flexible and sustainable financing strategies enabled to ensure that both financing and funding is adaptive to unpredictable environments, especially those that experience protracted and recurrent crises
1.1 Allocation, upgrade, and management of WASH and water resource infrastructure enhanced by integration of resilience, conflict sensitivity, and peacebuilding capacities	2.1 Community WASH knowledge and behaviour enhanced to address shocks and stresses	Enhanced resilience, conflict sensitivity, and peacebuilding capacities of policymakers and service authorities	Resilience, conflict sensitivity, and peacebuilding (where relevant), integrated into relevant platforms and processes	5.1 Landscape analysis of WASH, resilience, and peacebuilding financing and funding opportunities, including leveraging existing mechanisms
	2.2 Community monitoring systems and anticipatory action enhanced and linked to early warning systems and forecast-based financing systems	3.1 Knowledge of disaster and climate risks generated and shared	Existing government-led systems prioritized	
1.2 WASH service delivery models enhanced to absorb (i.e. business continuity) and adapt to shocks and stresses			4.1 WASH stakeholders mapped to facilitate collaboration	5.2 WASH resilience and peacebuilding (where feasible) integrated into country-level financing strategies
		3.2 Resilience, conflict sensitivity, and peacebuilding, where feasible, feature prominently in national WASH policies, plans, and programmes	4.2 Joint assessment, planning, monitoring processes, and coordination platforms identified to facilitate participation of humanitarian and development actors	

(Continued)

Table 2.1 Continued

1.3 Water resources diversified and redundancy built into WASH systems to prevent failure and collapse	2.3 Opportunities leveraged to build social cohesion through WASH programmes	3.3 WASH resilience, conflict sensitivity, and peacebuilding integrated into standards and programming guidance	4.3 Resilience and peacebuilding integrated into WASH Joint Sector Reviews and WASH Bottleneck Analysis (WASHBAT)	5.3 Pre-crisis risk assessment of WASH institutions undertaken, flexible and forecast-based financing mechanisms built
1.4 Smart technologies for integrating resilience into WASH systems investigated and implemented	2.4 Local markets and supply chains strengthened to increase availability of resilient WASH products and services, and demand strengthening	3.4 Enhanced systems of accountability between policymakers, service providers, civil society organizations, and communities, ensuring that roles and responsibilities are clearly defined among WASH humanitarian and development actors	4.4 Joint context and risk (including conflict) analysis completed as a foundational element of WASH programming	5.4 Development banks/international financing institution (IFI)-commissioned financial research/evaluations into areas affected by crisis
1.5 Nature-based solutions prioritized to protect and restore water-related ecosystems	2.5 Community engagement dialogue mechanism set up for responsive communication and to resolve conflicts	3.5 Enhanced WASH sector regulation of services to adequately cover all stages of a crisis	4.5 Humanitarian and development information management systems linked, covering WASH gaps, risks, and vulnerabilities	5.5 Enhanced WASH service creditworthiness by improving their long-term performance
		3.6 Local and national civil society organizations included in national and local decision making around planning, policy enactment, and delivery	4.6 Contingency plans periodically updated to address shocks and stresses	5.6 Financial management capacity of local private sector, government, and NGOs in the WASH Sector built
			4.7 Plans for the transition to government-led national coordination platforms prepared and implemented, and the WASH cluster deactivated (if applicable)	5.7 Advocacy for predictable, unearmarked and flexible multi-year funding and the development of innovative financing models conducted

The aim of the **system strengthening** approach, along with a risk-informed approach, is to first identify the linkages between shocks and stresses and the vulnerability and exposure of WASH services in a given geographic area, and to then address them (UN, 2020, Tillet et al. 2020).

In addressing them, the approach aims to understand where resilience, conflict sensitivity, and peacebuilding capacities are best placed within and across the delivery of WASH services, and to build them in a way that leverages the interconnectedness of these WASH systems.

Intervention levels

The framework covers three levels of interventions for strengthening resilience, conflict sensitivity, and peacebuilding in the WASH sector:

- **Regional/transboundary**: strengthen the coordination, knowledge management, and technical assistance across country borders and within regions. Transboundary is equally relevant, as water-related ecosystems, disease transmission, and migrant and refugee flows are often a transboundary challenge.
- **National/subnational level**: strengthen enabling environment, management, and monitoring of water resources, WASH services, infrastructure, and community behaviours.
- **Local level**: improve access to WASH services and enhance community WASH behaviour.

Key steps: putting the JOF into practice

This section outlines key steps to operationalizing the WASH nexus approach. Connections are made to the outputs from the previous section and key entry points are provided that link policymakers and practitioners with in-country processes and coordination structures commonly operating in protracted and recurrent crisis contexts. While not the sole focus of the framework, the 3Cs are a combination of contemporary risks that affect the delivery of WASH services and can be addressed using the steps outlined in this section.

In adopting the steps, please note the following assumptions:

- The steps do not necessarily need to be undertaken in a linear fashion. For example, where there are existing platforms and processes for humanitarian and development actor cooperation in the WASH sector, it is recommended to begin with Step 7 (assessing the WASH context, risks, and needs) and then go back to either Step 4 or 5 to select partners capable of addressing the assessment recommendations.
- These steps can be completed outside of the acute phases of an emergency response. However, should the preparation not be in place, these steps can be rapidly followed while adhering to local coordination and planning processes.

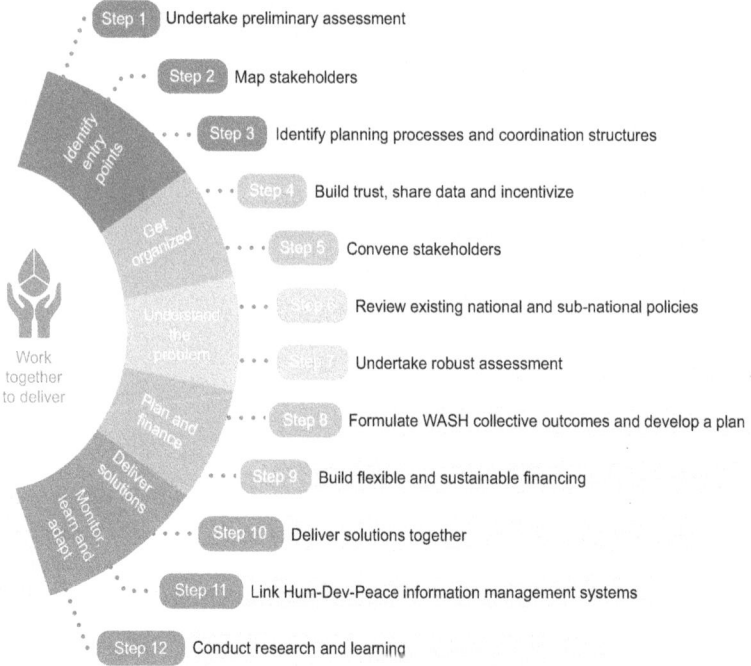

Figure 2.5 Key steps in operationalizing the nexus

- There is no additional step for programme delivery provided for after Step 6, as each programme's delivery will be unique to the context, the scope, and the nature of the planning process.
- Most importantly, policymakers and practitioners are encouraged to seek out local planning processes and coordination structures that are unique and local to the setting and may not be part of UN or national government bodies.

Identify entry points

Step 1: conduct a preliminary assessment to identify WASH needs, risks, and vulnerabilities

Prior to initiating a triple nexus collaboration, a preliminary assessment should be undertaken to determine the key needs, vulnerabilities, and risks faced by the targeted population. This assessment should be designed to provide sufficient information for an overall assessment and encourage other actors to want to collaborate.

Step 2: conduct stakeholder mapping to determine suitable partners for collaboration (output 4.1 in Table 2.1)

To build a collaboration, the actor or group of actors who undertook the rapid assessment need a practical understanding of potential partners in the

Table 2.2 Stakeholder mapping actions and responsible coordination platforms

Level	Action	Responsible coordination platform
Regional/ transboundary	Develop a regional/ transboundary WASH stakeholder map	River-/basin-level authorities, neighbouring countries' health and WASH, water resource authorities
National/ subnational	Develop a national/ subnational WASH stakeholder map	National/subnational humanitarian–development platform identified in Step 1 with assistance from WASH cluster coordinators (and other relevant WASH leads if the cluster is not operational) and national development WASH platform leads
Local	Using national mapping as a starting point, develop a local WASH stakeholder map	Local humanitarian and development platforms identified in Step 1

sector. A formal or informal stakeholder mapping exercise will identify which actors operate within a given geographic area and with which mandate(s) (USAID 2021). If the stakeholders are already well-known through existing networks, then this step can be skipped. Table 2.2 proposes required actions and responsible parties. As the water sector is fragmented, the stakeholder analysis can draw on IWRM coordination bodies and stakeholders to complement mapping of the WASH stakeholders.

Step 3: identify most suitable planning process and coordination structures to launch collaboration (output 4.2 in Table 2.1)

A joint humanitarian and development coordination platform that supports a planning process based on achieving collective outcomes should be identified. Ideally, this will be an existing structure with a trusted leadership either within the WASH sector or within or across multiple sectors inclusive of the WASH sector. Local planning processes and coordination systems should be prioritized and supported in alignment with the principles of localization and sustainability.

An additional benefit of selecting an existing platform is that, in many cases, the government, the UN, and other bodies have established long-term, well-resourced coordination and planning processes in protracted and recurrent crisis settings (UN, 2020a). Table 2.3 provides entry points for such in-country intersectoral planning processes that draw on existing coordination platforms and coordinating actors.

Get organised

Step 4: build trust, share data, and incentivize

Collaboration is based on trust. The next step is therefore to ensure that sufficient incentives for collaboration are provided and are based on building trust. A WASH cluster analysis of collaboration between WASH humanitarian

Table 2.3 Identifying the most suitable coordination platform and planning process

Level	Entry points for planning	Responsible coordination platform or actor
Regional/ transboundary	Investigate existing platforms, especially those used by IWRM sector, IOM regional response plans, and so on	Regional platforms, river-/basin-level authorities, neighbouring countries' health and WASH, water resource authorities, UN agencies, INGOs
National/ subnational	Government planning and budgeting processes within the WASH sector Humanitarian and development actors can engage in the periodic (typically annual) WASH Joint Sector Reviews and WASH-BAT (see output 4.2, Table 2.1)	WASH sector coordination platforms (led by the line ministry and sometimes co-led by a donor, bank, or UN agency), UNICEF (WASHBAT)
National/ subnational	Utility planning processes (including public private partnerships) Humanitarian and development actors are encouraged to engage in these processes, where possible	Utility CEOs, line ministry
National/ subnational	UN Sustainable Development Cooperation Framework (UNSDCF) The UN promotes 'collective outcomes' in protracted crisis settings. Humanitarian WASH actors can engage in the annual review of both the Joint Work Plans and the Country Common Assessment (CCA) (UNSDG, 2019)	Co-leads of the relevant results groups and sub-groups For establishing contact, lead actors can be found in the UNSDCF country document. Dual-mandate UN agencies, such as UNICEF and UNDP, are well-placed to provide support, along with UN Office for the Coordination of Humanitarian Affairs (OCHA) Resident/Humanitarian Coordinator (RC/HC) and Humanitarian Country Team (HCT)/UN Country Team (UNCT)
National/ subnational	Humanitarian Needs Overview (HNO) and Humanitarian Response Plan (HRP) Development WASH actors can engage in the technical working groups (TWGs) and participate in the HNO and HRP annual processes within the WASH cluster (OCHA, 2021)	National or subnational WASH cluster coordination platform led by the WASH cluster coordinator (typically government and UNICEF) Coordination platforms identified under the UNSDCF can also facilitate

(Continued)

Table 2.3 Continued

Level	Entry points for planning	Responsible coordination platform or actor
National/ subnational	Recovery and Peacebuilding Assessment (RPBA)	Government, UN, World Bank, and the EU
	Humanitarian actors can engage throughout the process (UN et al, 2017)	Leadership at the national level is context-specific. WASH sector contacts are UNICEF, UNDP, INTPA, ECHO and World Bank
National/ subnational	Refugee Response Plans (RRPs)	National or subnational WASH sector coordination platform led by the WASH sector coordinator (typically UNHCR and/ or government)
	Development WASH actors can engage in the TWGs and participate in the RRP annual planning processes (UNHCR, 2022)	
National/ subnational	IASC Framework on durable solutions for internally displaced persons. Entry points for humanitarian and development actors transition towards long term solutions (IASC, 2010)	Government- and UN-led
Local	Locally led planning and budgeting processes	Local government-supported platforms, especially supported by disaster management authorities
	Humanitarian and development actors can engage in the annual review of plans, which is often led by government	

and development partners in Burkina Faso demonstrated that levels of collaboration vary significantly (WASH Cluster Burkina Faso, 2022). Where there are low levels of trust between partners, networking and information sharing is a good place to start. According to the continuum of collaboration (see Figure 2.6) trust is built over time, with higher levels of collaboration achieved when resources, planning processes and capacity building are well coordinated or shared.

Step 5: convene stakeholders and determine their comparative advantages for specific roles in the HDPN process in a transparent and inclusive way.

In order to determine the best fit for collaboration, a transparent process for evaluating the comparative advantage of each potential partner is recommended for development. This is a sensitive process that will require the trust of partners (as described in Step 4). Additionally, the coordination platform needs to adopt a common terminology that is context-specific and based on knowledge and understanding of local preferences and sensitivities (IASC, 2020a).

54   ADDRESSING CONFLICT, COVID-19, AND CLIMATE CHANGE

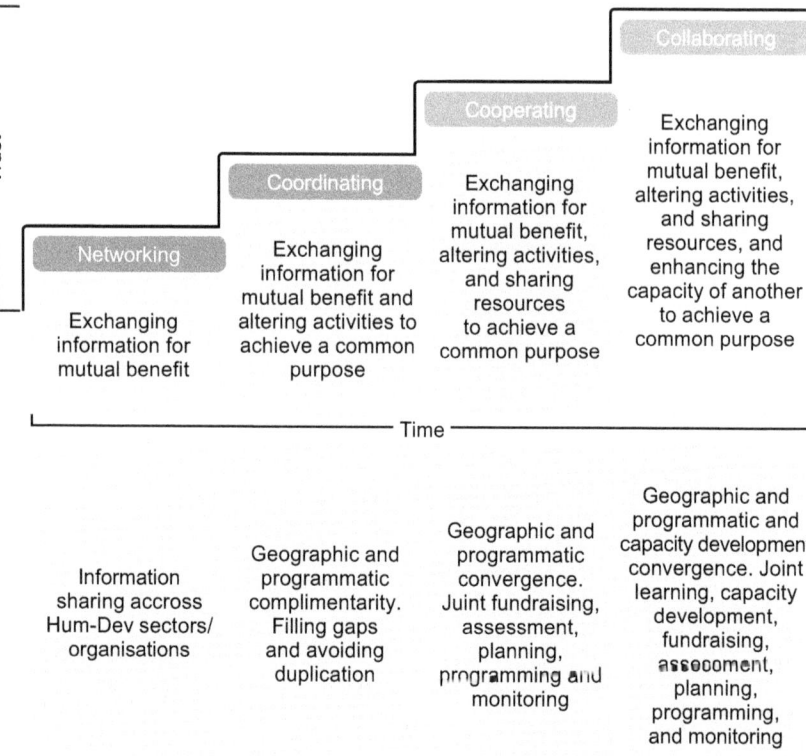

Figure 2.6 Collaboration continuum

Table 2.4 Coordination platforms to convene stakeholders and determine comparative advantage of actors

Level	Action	Responsible coordination platform
Regional/ transboundary	1. Convene stakeholders 2. Evaluate mandates, experiences, and capacities of each potential actor 3. Select actors and formalize collaboration with defined roles and responsibilities	Regional platforms, river-/basin-level authorities, neighbouring countries' health and WASH, water resource authorities, UN agencies, INGOs
National/ subnational		WASH sector coordination structures (led by the line ministry and sometimes co-led by a donor, bank, or UN agency), including relevant platforms identified in Step 2
Local		Local government supported platforms, especially those supported by disaster management authorities

Table 2.5 Entry points for reviewing existing and subnational priorities

Action	Purpose	Entry points for alignment with relevant processes identified in step 2
Review development and humanitarian policies and plans	To determine the extent to which WASH resilience and peacebuilding are embedded	Key entry points in government (and utilities) planning and budgeting processes, including joint WASH sector reviews
Review WASH policies and plans	To determine the extent to which resilience and peacebuilding are embedded based on SDGs 1 (goal 1.5: resilience), 13 (climate) and 16 (peacebuilding)	Annual CCA reviews as part of the 'Cooperation Framework' HNO step 2: secondary data review
Review resilience and peacebuilding policies and plans	To determine the extent to which WASH outcomes are embedded based on SDG 6 (WASH and water resource management)	RPBA step 1: pre-assessment

Understand the problem

Step 6: review existing national and subnational priorities (outputs 3.2 and 3.3 in Table 2.1)

An assessment of the links between WASH priorities, resilience, and peacebuilding is useful in identifying synergies, finding opportunities for strengthening them, and proposing entry points for collective outcomes to be enhanced by collaboration with other sectors, such as health, food security, and energy. These sectors have strong synergies with WASH and water resource management and share priorities on resilience and peacebuilding. Table 2.5 outlines proposed action points, their purpose, and entry points into existing in-country processes.

Step 7: conduct a robust joint assessment of WASH context, risks, and needs (output 4.3 in Table 2.1)

Conducting a joined-up assessment and analysis of WASH context, risks (including conflict), and needs provides the evidence and direction for building risk-informed capacities, such as resilience and conflict sensitivity, as outlined in output 4.3 and Step 2 of the nexus approach. Table 2.6 outlines relevant entry points.

Table 2.6 Entry points for conducting a joint assessment of WASH context, risks, and needs

Level	Entry points for alignment with relevant processes identified in Step 2
National/ subnational	Engage in government and utility risk assessment and planning processes
National/ subnational	UNSDCF: annual reviews of the CCA

(Continued)

Table 2.6 Continued

Level	Entry points for alignment with relevant processes identified in Step 2
National/ subnational	HNO, step 3: collect primary data
	HNO, step 4: conduct joint intersectoral needs analysis
	Since 2020, countries preparing humanitarian responses within the Humanitarian Programme Cycle have been using the Joint Intersectoral Assessment Framework (JIAF) to inform their country Humanitarian Needs Overview (HNO), which outlines opportunities for development actors to engage related to collective outcomes
National/ subnational	RPBA, step 4: assessment of recovery and peacebuilding needs, with opportunities for humanitarian actors to engage

TOOLS: see Annex I for useful tools.

While a joint assessment of primary data is ideal, if this presents a major obstacle to implementation, then a secondary data assessment or joint analysis of existing data sets (UNICEF and WHO's Joint Monitoring Programme, etc.) and assessments is worth considering as the basis for planning.

Plan and finance

Step 8: formulate WASH collective outcomes and develop a joint plan (outputs 1–5 in Table 1)

A joint definition of the WASH problem statement, including clear definitions for WASH resilience, conflict sensitivity, and peacebuilding capacities will provide clarity to all stakeholders on the problem itself and the type of capacities that need building (World Bank, 2017). It is recommended that these definitions include:

- to what the project/programme is building resilience, conflict sensitivity, and peacebuilding capacities (e.g. floods, conflict, climate change, drought, etc.);
- to whom the project/programme is providing resilience, conflict sensitivity, and peacebuilding capacities (e.g. households, communities, WASH service providers, local government, a sector, a country, etc.).

The formulation of WASH collective outcomes is based on the definitions above and is recommended to include:

- an aim at the intermediate collective outcome level (see section 'Defining a new programme logic');
- a span of a minimum three to five years, with longer timeframes encouraged (IASC, 2020a);
- a target level of engagement (i.e. national level and transboundary, subnational level or local level); and

- the use of the SMART framework (i.e. specific, measurable, achievable, relevant, and time-bound).

Lastly, the development of a joint plan or results framework should be based on the:

- development of a context-specific TOC, outlining the links between approaches, outputs, and intermediate collective outcomes, based on the TOC proposed in the section titled 'Defining a new programme logic.' Assumptions and risks should be made explicit, tested, and managed where possible;
- assignment of agencies' responsibilities for each output and outcome. Specific contributions may include those delivered in existing funded programmes, those in the pipeline, or unfunded programmes that target gaps identified in the joint analysis.

Note: this outline may be aspirational only for certain collaborations that have yet to reach this level. This should not discourage collective outcomes. As per Step 4, collective outcomes can be based on separate planning and funding exercises where collaboration is at the coordination level (e.g., targeted geographic convergence).

Table 2.7 outlines the relevant entry points at the national, subnational, and local levels.

Table 2.7 Entry points for developing collective outcomes

Level	Entry points for alignment with relevant processes identified in Step 2
National/ subnational and local	Government budget and planning processes: the annual WASH Joint Sector Reviews
National/ subnational and local	Water utility planning processes: entry points will vary based on context
National/ subnational	UNSDCF: annual work plan reviews
	HRP, step 5: define the scope of the HRP and formulate initial objectives
	HRP, step 6: conduct response analysis
	HRP, step 7: finalize strategic and specific objectives and associated indicators
	If collective outcomes have been agreed upon in a country, the HRP strategic objectives should connect or align. If they have not yet been agreed, the HRP strategic objectives should inform the formulation of collective outcomes (OCHA, 2022), along with those of development plans such as the UNSDCF
	HRP, step 8: formulate projects/activities and estimate costs of the response plan
	RPBA: prioritization and presentation of priorities in a strategic, implementable recovery, and peacebuilding plan and results matrix
	RRP, steps 2–5

Step 9: build flexible and sustainable WASH financing (output 5)
As outlined in output 5, financing covers the need for:

- a financing landscape analysis and the integration of WASH resilience into country-level financing strategies (Poole & Scott 2018);
- building multi-year, flexible financing mechanisms (IASC 2016, BMZ 2021);
- leveraging IFIs, commercial banks, and microfinance institutions to commit long term in fragile contexts (German WASH Network et al. 2021);
- de-risking WASH service providers (from the perspective of finance institutions) by improving their creditworthiness and building financial management capacity of local institutions (German WASH Network et al. 2021);
- ensuring that emergency preparedness plans (business continuity) for acute crises are regarded as 'no-regrets' investments and developing forecast-based funding mechanisms that anticipate the funding requirements for a crisis (World Bank 2020).

Table 2.8 outlines the financing entry points:

Table 2.8 Entry points and coordination platforms for building flexible and sustainable financing

Entry points for alignment with relevant processes identified in Step 2	Responsible coordination platform
Government planning and budgeting processes: identify opportunities to influence grants and loans	WASH Joint Sector reviews led by line ministries, intersectoral government platforms, platforms hosted by finance ministries, donors and commercial banks, IFIs, or MFIs
Water utilities: identify opportunities for improving investment, de-risking, and business continuity	Government line and finance ministries, water utilities, IFIs etc
UNSDCF: review the funding framework and all work plans on an annual basis	Co-leads of the relevant results groups and sub-groups
HRPs: launch annually for funding at the national level	National or subnational WASH cluster coordination platform led by the WASH cluster coordinator
RPBA: validation and finalizing phase	Government, UN, World Bank, and the EU

Deliver solutions

Step 10: deliver solutions together (outputs 1–5 in Table 1)
Establish mechanisms to execute the plans in Step 8, ensure frequent coordination and set up monitoring, learning, and adaptation processes as per Step 9. Ensuring that each partner delivers and shares information and lessons learned will be critical in terms of building trust and incentivizing continued and further collaboration as per Step 4.

Note that each WASH programme will have its own unique delivery mechanism based on the structure of the collaboration and the context.

Monitor, learn, and adapt

Step 11: develop a data-sharing platform between humanitarian, development, and peace pillars (output 3.4 in Table 2.1)

By developing a data-sharing platform that links humanitarian, development, and peace pillars, the aim is to improve coordination and programming coherence, and gradually move towards fully linking WASH humanitarian, development, and peace information management systems. This includes accountability mechanisms that are relevant, context-specific and linked with existing national data systems, thus enabling:

- monitoring dynamic outcomes, such as resilience, conflict sensitivity, and peacebuilding capacities;
- humanitarian actors to focus on sustainable WASH services from the start of an emergency response based on leveraging development infrastructure and service delivery models; and
- development actors to transition more effectively from recovery into development by leveraging the systems developed by humanitarian actors.

Ideally, the monitoring systems will be 'real time' so that WASH actors and systems can learn, adapt, and make better decisions both during a crisis and beyond (see 'Adaptive management' as nexus operational principle outlined in the section 'the JOF and the nexus'). Table 2.9 provides possible entry points with relevant in-country processes.

Table 2.9 Entry points for developing a shared data, monitoring, and learning platform

Outputs	Entry points for alignment with relevant processes identified in Step 2	Responsibility
Aligned with 'Output 4: Coordination, planning and information management linked' within Section 'Defining a new programme logic'	Review of government and utility data management processes	Government statistical office, line ministries, and utilities data focal points
	HRP, step 9: conduct After Action Review	National or subnational WASH cluster coordination platform led by the WASH cluster coordinator (typically government and UNICEF)
	RPBA: validation and finalizing phase	Government, UN, World Bank, and the EU

Step 12: conduct research and learning from the programme (outputs 1.5 and 3.1 in Table 2.1)

Research and learning provide the evidence to improve nexus coordination, programming, and financing in the WASH sector, as well as underpinning advocacy to drive the agenda forward. Building resilience and peacebuilding capacities in the WASH sector is a relatively new field, presenting significant opportunities and challenges for evaluation.

When developing evaluation methods, the following points should be considered:

1. Given resilience is unobservable, the development of multiple proxy and process indicators will be better suited than one universal indicator (Sturgess and DFID, 2014; World Bank, 2017). Examples of proxy indicators include:
   - peacebuilding: percentage of target beneficiaries who express that they experienced increased trust in members of another community/ or public institutions (UNICEF, 2016);
   - resilience: percentage of days water service provider deliver minimum quantity of water to community (households and institutions) during shocks and stresses.
2. The effect of resilience building can only be proven in the face of shocks and stresses, making it challenging to ensure evaluations are flexible enough with their timeframes to capture these events.
3. Building resilience capacity may take time, creating the additional challenge of ensuring sufficient timeframe to capture results.
4. Given these challenges, qualitative analysis (combined with quantitative analysis where possible) is the preferred method of evaluation, including any one of the following (World Bank, 2017):
   - a theory-based analysis, using the WASH programme's TOC, to identify and confirm causal processes, and articulate supporting factors and mechanisms at work in the context;
   - a descriptive study, making comparisons across and within cases (e.g., across and within households) to determine causal links and overall implications of the WASH programme design;
   - a participatory annual study; for instance, following key stakeholders within a utility throughout each step of the WASH programme can provide validation of the causal links underpinning the capacity building intervention, from the perspective of the stakeholders.

What's next?

To operationalize the WASH nexus at the country level, the following actions are recommended:

- Mainstream the nexus approach in WASH programmes at the national and subnational level, especially in protracted and recurrent crisis contexts.
- Create an enabling environment in key countries for implementing the WASH nexus approach, leveraging existing planning architecture and coordination structures where possible.
- Adopt flexible and sustainable financing strategies into protracted and recurrent crisis contexts, and leverage financing to achieve the SDGs.

- Advocate for predictable, un-earmarked and flexible multi-year funding, and the development of innovative financing and forecasting models.
- Continue to build key evidence, learning and capacity.

As stated in the introduction, the WASH JOF is an evolutionary document that will be published in 2023. We hope that you can apply the framework to your own context and that you may provide useful feedback to the German WASH network (https://www.washnet.de/en/) on how it can be improved for future editions.

Appendix I WASH resilience, conflict sensitivity, and peacebuilding tools

Useful tools for the humanitarian-development-peace (triple) nexus approach

A risk-informed and context-specific way of working:

UNICEF's guidance on risk informed programming: <https://www.unicef.org/documents/guidance-risk-informed-programming>
UNDP's environmental and social screening procedure: <https://www.undp.org/publications/undps-social-and-environmental-screening-procedure-sesp>

Conflict sensitivity and peacebuilding:

UNICEF's guide to conflict analysis: <https://www.unicef.org/documents/unicef-guide-conflict-analysis>
USAID's water and conflict toolkit: <https://www.globalwaters.org/resources/assets/water-and-conflict-toolkit-programming-0>

WASH system strengthening tools:

IRC's WASH system strengthening course covering the basics: <https://www.ircwash.org/news/wash-system-strengthening-basics>
IRC's WASH system strengthening approach – tools for practitioners: <https://www.washagendaforchange.org/wp-content/uploads/2020/04/ssi_toolbox_08apr20.pdf>
Agenda for Change's WASH discussion paper with useful case studies: <https://washagendaforchange.org/blog/applying-wash-systems-approaches-in-fragile-contexts/>

Adaptive management tools:

USAID's adaptive management toolkit: <https://usaidlearninglab.org/qrg/adaptive-management>
Mercy Corps adaptive management tools: <https://www.mercycorps.org/research-resources/adaptive-management-tools-system>

Useful tools for the key steps - putting the JOF into practice

Step 2: Identify best planning process and coordination structures to launch collaboration

UNICEF WASH bottleneck analysis tool (BAT): <https://www.washbat.org/>
UN's sustainable development cooperation framework (UNSDCF): <https://unsdg.un.org/sites/default/files/2019-10/UN-Cooperation-Framework-Internal-Guidance-Final-June-2019_1.pdf>

UN, WBG and EU's joint recovery and peacebuilding assessments (RPBAs) 'A Practical Note to Assessment and Planning': <https://www.recoveryandpeacebuilding.org/content/rpba/en/home/partnership-documents.html>

UNHCR's refugee response plans (RRPs): <https://emergency.unhcr.org/entry/55127/interagency-unhcrled-refugee-response-plans>

UN OCHA's humanitarian needs overview (HNO) and humanitarian response plan (HRP): <https://assessments.hpc.tools/km/hno-hrp-step-step-guidance-2021>

Step 6: WASH context, risk, and needs assessment

In conjunction with tools outlined above under 'A risk-informed and context-specific way of working', and 'Conflict sensitivity and peacebuilding'

Useful tool to assess WASH context, risks, and needs at the local level

UN OCHA's joint intersectoral assessment framework (JIAF): <https://www.jiaf.info>

UNDP's environmental and social screening procedure: <https://www.undp.org/publications/undps-social-and-environmental-screening-procedure-sesp>

Mercy Corps risk and resilience assessment tool: <https://resiliencelinks.org/system/files/documents/2019-08/gn01_riskandresilienceassessments_final508_1.pdf>

CALP network basic needs assessment toolbox: <https://reliefweb.int/report/world/basic-needs-assessment-guidance-and-toolbox>

References

BMZ. 2021. 'The humanitarian–development–peace nexus: a literature review'. <https://www.bmz.de/en/news/publications/publikationen-reihen/materialie530-humanitarian–development–peace-nexus-79796>

Coral, P. and A. Irwin, N. Krishnan, D. Mahler, T. Vishwanath. 2020. 'Fragility and conflict: on the front lines of the fight against poverty'. World Bank Group. <https://openknowledge.worldbank.org/bitstream/handle/10986/33324/9781464815409.pdf>

Development Initiatives. 2019a. 'Key questions and considerations for donors at the triple nexus: lessons from UK and Sweden'. <https://devinit.org/documents/677/key_questions_and_considerations_for_donors_at_the_triple_nexus_lessons_from_U_lyhl5ro.pdf>

German WASH Network, SWA, GWC and UNICEF. 2021. 'Triple nexus in WASH: global event report'. <https://www.washnet.de/en/triple-nexus-wash/#postTabs_ul_9126>

GWC. 2021. 'Annual report'. <https://www.washcluster.net/sites/gwc.com/files/2022-10/AR2021FINAL.01%20%281%29.pdf>

Huston, A. and P. Moriarty. 2018. 'Building strong WASH systems for the SDGs: understanding the WASH system and its building blocks'. IRC working paper. <https://www.ircwash.org/news/building-blocks-strong-and-healthy-wash-systems>

IASC. 2010. IASC Framework on Durable Solutions for Internally Displaced Person, <https://interagencystandingcommittee.org/other/iasc-framework-durable-solutions-internally-displaced-persons>

IASC. 2016. 'The grand bargain: a shared commitment to better serve people in need'. <https://interagencystandingcommittee.org/grand-bargain/grandbargain-shared-commitment-better-serve-people-need-2016>

———. 2020a. 'Light guidance on collective outcomes'. <https://interagencystandingcommittee.org/inter-agency-standing-committee/un-iasc-light-guidance-collective-outcomes-0>

———. 2020b. 'Issue paper – Exploring peace within the humanitarian–development–peace nexus'. <https://interagencystandingcommittee.org/humanitarian-development-collaboration/issue-paper-exploring-peace-within-humanitarian-development-peace-nexus-hdpn>

———. 2020c. 'Humanitarian Financing' <https://interagencystandingcommittee.org/results-group-5-humanitarian-financing>

IRC. 2022. 'WASH Systems'. <https://www.ircwash.org/washsystems>

IOM. 2022. 'World migration report'. <https://publications.iom.int/books/world-migration-report-2022>

Jafino, B. and B. Walsh, J. Rozenberg, S. Hallegatte. 2020. 'Estimates of the impact of climate change on extreme poverty by 2030'. World Bank Group. Policy research paper 9417. <https://openknowledge.worldbank.org/handle/10986/34555>

Mason, N. and B. Mosello. 2016. 'Making humanitarian and development WASH work better together'. ODI. <https://odi.org/en/publications/making-humanitarian-and-development-wash-work-better-together>

OCHA. 2022. Video message of UN Secretary-General, Antonio Gutteres, on the launch of the Global Humanitarian Overview 2022. <https://www.unocha.org/2022gho>

———. 2021. 'HNO–HRP step by step guidance 2021'. <https://assessments.hpc.tools/km/hno-hrp-step-step-guidance-2021>

OCHA 2012. 'OCHA on message: humanitarian principles'. <https://www.unocha.org/sites/unocha/files/OOM_Humanitarian%20Principles_Eng.pdf>

OECD. 2022. 'DAC recommendation on the humanitarian–development–peace nexus'. OECD Legal Instruments. <https://legalinstruments.oecd.org/public/doc/643/643.en.pdf>

———. 2020. 'States of fragility 2020'. Paris: OECD Publishing. <https://www.oecd.org/dac/states-of-fragility-fa5a6770-en.htm>

OECD. 2018. 'Operationalising the "nexus": principles and approaches for strengthening and accelerating humanitarian, development and peace coherence'. Development Assistance Committee (DAC)'. <https://www.oecd.org/development/conflict-fragility-resilience/docs/Final%20summary_DAC_Roundtable%20Nexus_19Nov.pdf>

———. 2014. 'Guidelines for resilience systems analysis: how to analyse risk and build a roadmap to resilience'. Paris: OECD Publishing. <https://doi.org/10.1787/3b1d3efe-en>

Perret, L. 2019. 'Operationalizing the humanitarian-development-peace nexus: Lessons learned from Colombia, Mali, Nigeria, Somalia and Turkey', IOM Geneva, <https://publications.iom.int/system/files/pdf/operationalizing_hdpn.pdf>

Poole, L. and R. Scott. 2018. 'Financing for stability: Guidance for Practitioners', OECD Development Policy Papers, No. 11, OECD Publishing, Paris, <https://doi.org/10.1787/5f3c7f33-en.>

Sturgess, P. and DFID. 2016. 'Measuring resilience. Evidence on demand'. <http://dx.doi.org/10.12774/eod_tg.may2016.sturgess2>

SWA. 2020. 'Strategic framework 2020–2030: all, always and everywhere'. <https://www.sanitationandwaterforall.org/sites/default/files/2020-04/SWA%20Strategy%202020-2030%20EN%20Web.pdf>

Tearfund and UK Aid. 2014. 'How WASH can contribute to peace- and state-building'. <https://assets.publishing.service.gov.uk/media/57a08a51ed915d622c000695/60989-WASH-PBSB-summarynote.pdf>

Tillett, W. and J. Trevor, J. Schillinger, D. DeArmey. 2020. 'Applying WASH systems approaches in fragile contexts: a discussion paper'. <https://washagendaforchange.org/wp-content/uploads/2020/10/WASH-Syst.-Str_Fragile-Contexts_Final.pdf>

Tuchel, L. 2020. 'Multi-year humanitarian funding: global baselines and trends'. Development initiatives. <https://devinit.org/documents/706/Multi-year_humanitarian_funding_Global_baselines_and_trends.pdf>

UN, World Bank, and European Union. 2017. 'Joint recovery and peacebuilding assessments (RPBAs): a practical note to assessment and planning'. <https://www.recoveryandpeacebuilding.org/content/rpba/en/home/partnership-documents.html>

UNDRR. 2022. 'Resilience'. [web page] <https://www.preventionweb.net/understanding-disaster-risk/key-concepts/resilience>

UN. 2020. 'United Nations common guidance on helping build resilient societies'. <https://unsdg.un.org/sites/default/files/2021-09/UN-Resilience Guidance-Final-Sept pdf>

———. 2016a. 'Resolution A/71/353 – Outcome of the world humanitarian summit'. <https://agendaforhumanity.org/sites/default/files/A-71-353%20-%20SG%20Report%20on%20the%20Outcome%20of%20the%20WHS.pdf>

———. 2016b. '70/262. Review of the United Nations peacebuilding architecture'. <https://undocs.org/A/RES/70/262>

———. 2016c. 'Resolution 2282'. <https://undocs.org/S/RES/2282(2016)>

UN. 2015a. 'Resolution A/RES/70/1 – Transforming our world: the 2030 agenda for sustainable development'. <https://sdgs.un.org/2030agenda>

———. 2015b. 'Paris Agreement'. <https://unfccc.int/process-and-meetings/the-paris-agreement/the-paris-agreement>

———. 2015c. 'Sendai Framework for Disaster Risk Reduction 2015–2030'. <https://www.undrr.org/publication/sendai-framework-disaster-risk-reduction-2015-2030>

UNESCO, UN-Water, 2020: United Nations world water development report 2020: Water and climate change, Paris, UNESCO, <https://www.unesco.org/en/wwap/wwdr/2020>

UNHCR. 2022. 'Inter-agency UNHCR-led refugee response plans'. *Emergency Handbook*. <https://emergency.unhcr.org/entry/55127/interagency-unhcrled-refugee-response-plans>

———. 2021. 'Mid-year trends 2021'. [web page] <https://www.unhcr.org/mid-year-trends.html>

UNICEF (2021), 'Water under fire volume 3: attacks on water and sanitation services in armed conflict and the impacts on children, retrieved 21 March 2023'. <https://www.unicef.org/reports/water-under-fire-volume-3>

UNICEF. 2020. 'The core commitments for children in humanitarian action'. <https://www.unicef.org/emergencies/core-commitments-children>

———. 2019. 'Water under fire, volume 1: emergencies, development and peace in fragile and conflict affected contexts'. <https://www.unicef.org/reports/emergencies-development–peace-in-fragile-and-conflict-affected-contexts-2019>

———. 2018. 'Guidance on risk informed programming'. <https://www.unicef.org/documents/guidance-risk-informed-programming>

UNICEF. 2016. 'Conflict sensitivity and peacebuilding programme advice'. <https://www.unicef.org/media/96576/file/Programming-Guide-Conflict-Sensitivity-and-Peacebuilding.pdf>

UNSDG. 2019. 'United Nations sustainable development framework: internal guidance'. <https://unsdg.un.org/sites/default/files/2019-10/UN-Cooperation-Framework-Internal-Guidance-Final-June-2019_1.pdf>

USAID. 2023. 'Water and peace: a toolkit for programming'. <https://www.globalwaters.org/resources/assets/water-and-conflict-toolkit-programming-0>

———. 2021. 'USAID water and development technical series: humanitarian–development coherence in WASH or WRM programs'. Technical brief No. 8. <https://www.globalwaters.org/resources/assets/usaid-water-and-development-technical-series-humanitarian–development-coherence>

———. 2018. 'What is adaptive management?' *Learning Lab*. 8 February. <https://usaidlearninglab.org/lab-notes/what-adaptive-management-0>

WEF. 2020. 'The global risks report 2020'. <https://www.weforum.org/reports/the-global-risks-report-2020>

WHO & UNICEF. 2021. 'Progress on household drinking water, sanitation and hygiene 2000-2020: five years into the SDGs'. <https://www.who.int/publications/i/item/9789240030848>

World Bank. 2017. 'Evaluation of resilience-building operations: operational guidance paper for project task teams'. <https://documents1.worldbank.org/curated/en/669941506093754016/pdf/119937-WP-PUBLIC-P155632-68P-ReMEEvaluationGuidanceFinal.pdf>

World Bank. 2020. 'Crisis and disaster risk finance: Short notes on COVID-19'. <https://interagencystandingcommittee.org/other/iasc-framework-durable-solutions-internally-displaced-persons>

World Bank, ICRC, UNICEF. 2021. 'Joining forces to combat protracted crises: humanitarian and development support for water and sanitation providers in the Middle East and North Africa'. <https://openknowledge.worldbank.org/handle/10986/35122>

CHAPTER 3

Integrating WASH with health in humanitarian settings

Nikolas Sorensen and Mariëlle Snel[1]

Introduction

Safe and clean water, adequate sanitation, good hygiene practices, and a healthy living environment are essential for individuals, families, and communities to survive and develop. This is particularly true for children under five, where water and sanitation-related diseases are one of the leading causes of death. Mara et al (2010) stated that '[a]dequate sanitation, together with good hygiene and safe water, are fundamental to good health and to social and economic development'. However, how we build the connections between WASH and health programming has a critical impact on the success of health services, particularly in humanitarian settings. According to the CDC (2022), '[u]niversal access to safe drinking water, adequate sanitation, and hygiene has the potential to reduce the global disease burden by 10%'. This is particularly true of diseases that cause diarrheal deaths, typically obtained through unsafe drinking water and sanitation practices. The WHO reported in 2022 that 'microbiologically contaminated drinking water can transmit diseases such as diarrhoea, cholera, dysentery, typhoid and polio and estimated to cause 485,000 diarrhoeal deaths each year' (WHO, 2022a).

To date, WASH interventions have been shifting toward more durable solutions, focusing on restoring water supply resources and improving sanitation infrastructure that supports behaviour change activities designed to reduce water-borne/diarrheal diseases and enhance the quality of health service provision for those affected families and their children in camps, returnee sites, host communities and/or households. Through multisectoral integration approaches, it is possible to provide quality health and WASH services in household and non-household settings, including in schools, temporary learning centres, health care facilities, and refugee and IDP contexts. Here we define integration as the coordinated blending of WASH programming with health services to improve the overall health and safety of individuals, families, and communities. Integration requires a joint, multisectoral approach to assessment, data sharing, programme design, and implementation, and the sharing of results and impact, which culminates in a united understanding of humanitarian contexts and deeper partnerships leading to more robust outcomes (Parikh et al, 2020).

Conflict, COVID-19, and climate change (3Cs) are three of the most significant compounding factors impacting WASH and health services worldwide. In the recent Lancet Countdown Report, Romanello et al (2021) argued that climate change and COVID represent a converging crisis. They pointed out that we do not have the luxury of focusing on just one of them. There will be a continual need to invest in community resilience and disaster risk reduction while also grappling with the health-related measures around conflict, COVID and pandemics, and climate change. A key publication by the International Federation of Red Cross and the Climate Centre from 2020 revealed that 'at least 51.6 million people globally affected by an overlap of floods, droughts or storms and the COVID-19 pandemic' (Walton and van Aalst, 2020). The COVID-19 pandemic is compounding the needs of individuals, families, and communities already affected by other climate change-related emergencies.

There is a significant lack of water, hygiene, and sanitation services worldwide. The latest data from the WHO/UNICEF Joint Monitoring Program on Water Supply, Sanitation and Hygiene indicate that about 1.6 billion people worldwide lack access to clean drinking water in the home, 1.9 billion lack adequate handwashing facilities, and 2.8 billion lack safe sanitation services (WHO and UNICEF, 2021). Safe and affordable access to water is a human right and is a crucial part of sustainable development goals (SDGs) 6.1 and 6.2. Furthermore, safe and affordable access to WASH services is critical to improving individuals' and families' health, quality of life, education, and economic outcomes (UNICEF and WHO, 2021). As far back as 2014, the WHO and the UN were estimating that, for every $1 investment into WASH programming, there was a $4.3 return on investment through the 'reduced healthcare costs, reduced pollution of water and land resources, and gains in quality of life (such as improved school attendance, fewer sick days, greater privacy, safety, and sense of dignity)' (IISD, 2014). WASH services are the vital foundation for improving people's health, economic, educational, and social quality of life, particularly in martialized and disenfranchised groups living in humanitarian contexts.

Most of the discussion in this chapter will focus on the unique health concerns faced by individuals, families, and communities living in refugee and IDP camps, schools, health care facilities, and other humanitarian contexts, and the compounding impact the COVID-19 pandemic has had on health care services in these contexts.

Conflict and climate change

The impacts of the 3Cs have tremendously affected people's health globally. This impact is devastatingly true for marginalized groups living in humanitarian contexts. Robust health systems rely on safe and consistent access to

WASH services. Conflict has a notable impact on the health of individuals, families, and communities, as it destroys vital infrastructure, breaks supply chains, and restricts access to critical water, hygiene, and sanitation services. While conflict destroys health systems and infrastructure, COVID-19 and climate change impact health care outcomes by straining systems, which is a critical concern when those systems are already fragile or non-existent, like those within conflict zones. Conflicts grow as people face increasing scarcity in vital resources, particularly water, which will be one of the most critically vital resources in the coming century. As the impacts of climate change increase and water resources dry up, move, and become more unpredictable, conflict over water resources will increase. The overlapping impact of climate change and conflict will have significant health-related implications on the lives of individuals, families, and communities, especially marginalized groups.

Climate change is also going to have a significant impact on global health and economic systems, institutions, and infrastructure. Climate-related forced migration is on the rise and is anticipated to be one of the most significant humanitarian issues of the coming century. In a recent study, Jones et al (2020) noted that '[c]limate change will significantly impact water security and access, which will, in turn, have a significant impact on the health of communities. Cholera and other health risks increase in areas of poor WASH infrastructure and behavior'. With climate-related forced migration on the rise, the risks of conflict and health-related concerns increase, as health systems are strained, and safe and consistent access to WASH services is jeopardized (Howard et al, 2016). Integration and coordination between health care systems, environmental management, and WASH implementors are required to meet people's needs effectively in ever-changing contexts. Deola et al (2021) noted that understanding the relationship between climate change and environmental degradation is essential to preventing and responding to infectious diseases. They go on to state that this understanding requires

> *'an indepth understanding of the relationship between public health and the environment – including aspects such as water resource management and water safety, air and soil pollution control, vector control, treatment and disposal of chemical weapons, hazardous waste management, and human waste treatment and management'.*

Many of these linkages already exist in many parts of the world but require proactive re-evaluation as institutions and systems prepare for migration and population shifts. And in areas where institutions, systems, and infrastructure are lacking due to low investment, conflict, or instability, increased advocacy and planning by external actors are needed to anticipate and plan for increased needs.

Health impacts of WASH in non-household settings

Non-household settings, as we have argued in the past (Kendall and Snel, 2016; Sorensen and Snel, 2020; Snel and Sorensen, 2021), play a critical and unique role in connecting WASH programming with the long-term health, education, and economic potential of individuals, families, and communities. Inadequate WASH services and practices lead to an increase in water-borne illness and diarrhoea, which prevents individuals from going to work and children from attending school classes. Each day of missed work or school has a compounding impact on the future livelihood potential of that child, individual, and family.

In humanitarian contexts, there is a further deepening in the economic and educational opportunities facing marginalized groups as increased barriers, such as changes in access, geography, health, and safety, prevent consistent, long-term access to health and educational opportunities. Often due to social, cultural, and biological differences, the health-related barriers of unsafe WASH facilities particularly impact women and girls. Schmitt et al (2021) argued that '[g]lobal evidence suggests that during humanitarian emergencies, girls and women experience increased challenges in relation to managing their WASH-related needs given the frequent lack of reliable access to safe, private and comfortable toilets and bathing facilities'. Focusing on integrating WASH in communities and non-household settings, such as temporary learning centres and emergency health care centres in humanitarian settings, is vital to the long-term health of individuals, families, and communities, as well as the long-term economic, educational, and social success of those living through emergencies. There is growing evidence that new participatory responses to menstrual hygiene management are particularly impactful in not only protecting the health of women and girls but increasing women's and girls' safe access to, and participation in, educational and economic activities (Schmitt et al, 2021).

It is also critical to note that WASH and health consideration for those living with disabilities is essential, especially in non-household settings like schools and health care facilities (particularly temporary learning and health centres). These individuals have increased health needs and an increased risk of coming in contact with infectious diseases when disability access is inadequate. Improving the long-term health, education, and economic potential of individuals with disabilities requires early planning and implementation of adequate disability mainstreaming, particularly in non-household settings.

Schools in emergency settings

In a recent study on the importance of WASH in schools for improving psychosocial health and recovery after humanitarian conflict, Pacheco et al (2021) noted that '[t]he literature identifies schools as vital centres of support for children and their communities following a hazard event'. This is partly due to schools' role as vital places for teaching resilience and building future economic capabilities for children. However, Pacheco et al also highlight that the success of resilience building and psychosocial support that schools have for vulnerable children requires safe and reliable WASH services to be in place to maintain their health and, therefore, protect long-term access to schools for marginalized children. This is accomplished, as Mooijman et al (2010) pointed out, because WASH services in schools

> 'improve health, and enhance the learning environment, while special protection measures address concerns for safety and security, including gender-based violence. Safe, inclusive, "child-friendly" school environments contribute to quality learning experiences that integrate relevant life skills (e.g. health and hygiene; HIV/ AIDS prevention) into education'.

Protecting the future potential of individuals, families, and communities, particularly that of women and girls and those living with disabilities, requires the effective and safe integration of WASH programming into schools and temporary learning centres early in a crisis. This allows for consistency in health teaching, access, and practice at all locations children have access to during an emergency.

Temporary health centres

In humanitarian emergencies, health care facilities, including temporary and mobile health care clinics, are not only vital to maintaining safe and consistent health care but require safe and consistent access to WASH services to be successful. Recent reports by the WHO found significant gaps in the quality of WASH services in health care facilities globally, reporting that one in four health care facilities lack basic access to safe water services, resulting in some 857 million people worldwide who risk illness from contaminated water when accessing health services (WHO, 2020; WHO and UNICEF, 2022). Furthermore, the most recent indicators show that nearly 50 per cent of health care facilities globally lack hand hygiene services (WHO and UNICEF 2022). These deficiencies are particularly true globally in the least developed countries. Implicitly, health care facilities with safe and effective WASH services have higher quality care, more consistent health outcomes, and better community participation and trust because there is a lower risk of visit-related infections (Kendall and Snel, 2016).

In humanitarian contexts, temporary health centres and mobile clinics represent an excellent opportunity to connect WASH information and services with health treatment, improving the long-term health of marginalized people. In humanitarian settings, integrating mobile clinic health teams with WASH technicians and staff can significantly increase the reach and impact of health services in remote or hard-to-reach communities. McGowan et al stated that

> '[m]obile clinics have the potential to provide a useful platform for delivering WASH-related hygiene information, education, and communication (IEC) materials, household WASH supplies (e.g. chlorination kits), and routine maintenance of local WASH infrastructure (e.g. water pumps, latrines) if mobile clinic staff are joined by WASH technicians'.

This integration takes coordination and planning but has excellent potential for improving health outcomes and strengthening resilience.

Integrating WASH with health in humanitarian settings

Whether it is due to conflict, climate change, or some other artificial or natural disaster, humanitarian contexts amplify the health risks of those impacted. McGowan et al (2020) noted the complex health considerations emergencies create, stating that humanitarian contexts have high infection and death rates due to increased 'risk factors including: population displacement, widespread damage to societies and economies, and the need for large-scale humanitarian assistance'. These risks are compounded by the destruction of WASH and health infrastructure and resources for care. Successful health systems are depended on consistency and the ability to anticipate future needs. Humanitarian contexts, especially sudden-onset disasters, hamper the ability of health services to address changes in individual needs and can lead to long-term health consequences.

Many of the linkages between WASH and health services are undisputable. There is a significant increase in the risk of infectious diseases in health care facilities that lack adequate WASH services (Kanyangarara et al, 2021). However, how common-sense connections translate into coordinated programme design and implementation is often missing. This disparity is compounded in humanitarian contexts by funding gaps, differences in short-term and long-term priorities, and complex differences in capabilities that stand in the way of coordination and cooperation between WASH and health sector responders. Although there is substantial agreement on the connections between WASH and health services, and between WASH and education, psychosocial services, and economic capability, expensive infrastructure requirements for sustainable WASH services often stand in the way of WASH funding and implementation in humanitarian settings. However, setting up long-term WASH priorities is essential to early crisis response. Pacheco et al (2021) argued the importance of WASH considerations across the emergency, transitional, and post-emergency phases, and stated that 'prioritising WASH in early and longer-term stages of response is essential to building resilient communities, which are well-equipped for future hazards given their recurring nature'.

WASH is an essential link between people and health. As soon as safe water services are disrupted for any reason, be it infrastructure damage due to conflict, the strain on systems due to forced migration, or moving water systems due to climate change, health systems suffer (WHO, 2022b). Trucking water and providing hygiene kits immediately after an emergency are essential and, depending on the geopolitical context, may be relatively easier compared to the difficulty that comes with repairing and building infrastructure from scratch, which in a humanitarian context requires long-term planning on a short-term timeline.

The earlier critical decisions about WASH infrastructure can be made in a crisis, the greater the impact WASH services can have on the health of individuals, families, and communities. Emmett Kearney, a senior WASH officer for UNHCR, stated that WASH responders in humanitarian contexts

> 'need to think longer term, work out what all the needs are, who has funding for what, and who can fill the gaps. [They] also have to prioritize within each sector and draw up a plan in consultation with the local authorities, refugees and other stakeholders. And that all has to happen early on because the decisions made in the first weeks and months of an emergency have an impact on the type of services available in five or ten years' (WHO, 2022b).

Effective WASH services of the quality needed to improve health outcomes, save lives, and increase quality of life in humanitarian settings require an integrated mindset. Long-term development priorities must be considered early and quickly during the onset of a humanitarian context and pivoted as priorities and contexts change.

In the case study of the Molai health stabilization centre mentioned in box 3.1, we highlight the role Save the Children played in increasing access to WASH services across vulnerable communities in Borno state, Nigeria, as well as in a health treatment centre. As we mentioned above, the WHO and UNICEF recently reported that about half of health care facilities globally lack adequate access to handwashing stations, and 25 per cent lack access to adequate access to clean and safe water (WHO and UNICEF, 2022). In addressing the health needs of IDPs and refugees in this area of Nigeria, and their impact on the local community, integrating WASH services with the Molai health stabilization centre was vital to addressing the health needs of children under the age of five.

Box 3.1 Case study: Molai health stabilization centre in Borno, Nigeria

Save the Children

Acknowledgment: Mariëlle Snel

Save the Children's WASH programmes are integrated into all sectors in order to provide essential WASH services while aiming to build local capacity, ensure gradual integration into government-provided services, assist IDPs, build capacities to attain self-reliance, and further develop sustainable solutions to the services in both camps and host communities across the state.

(Continued)

Box 3.1 Continued

Save the Children's programming focuses on the prevention of malnutrition and stunting through hygiene promotion and improved water and sanitation infrastructure. Lack of access to water and sanitation and poor hygiene practices directly contribute to malnutrition through diarrhoea and other water-borne diseases. Activities to prevent the spread of water-borne diseases, such as cholera, hepatitis E and malaria, which pose a great risk to the lives of children and their families, are a top priority for improving the lives of those served. To date, Save the Children has constructed/rehabilitated more than 45 solar-motorized boreholes and 110 hand pumps within Maiduguri Metropolitan City in and around the local government areas of Jere, Magumeri, Mafa, Kaga, Damboa, and Biu for users in IDP settlements, host communities, health facilities, and schools. Save the Children has actively responded to a cholera outbreak in Borno state, reaching 25,350 individuals, disinfected more than 100 latrines and 2,500 infected household environments, chlorinated more than 100 water points, and collected and tested 90 water samples from 10 different locations across Jere, Magumeri and Mafa and Borno state. Since 2018, with the cholera outbreak in Borno state, Save the Children International committees have managed to strengthen community stakeholder collaboration. At the time of this publication, such services were ongoing. Community structures in some local government areas have taken up the responsibilities of operations and maintenance of WASH facilities in their respective communities. At the time this case study was written, there was a continued need to respond to cholera outbreaks with more pre-positioning of non-food-item to newly emerging and reoccurring outbreaks as well as to other emergencies, such as new displacements. This required the provision of portable and safe drinking water and sanitation services in communities and the necessary manpower to distribute and monitor them.

Water user committees were established across six locations with ten committee members each (five women and five men), and trained on operations and maintenance of water points. Chlorination of water points is ongoing, especially at the Molai stabilization centre and in host communities with online chlorine dosing pumps. For communities affected by cholera that did not have online chlorination systems for water points, Save the Children conducted bucket chlorination and distributed water purification tablets for water treatment, with a particular focus on mothers of children ages five and under admitted at outpatient therapeutic programme sites in November to December 2021.

Molai health stabilization centre

The Molai health stabilization centre is a unique example of where children under the age of five come with cases of acute malnutrition and often with medical complications. It has an average of 60 patients a month (depending on the season) arriving at the centre. The children are brought here through a Save the Children referral system in the communities. Once a child is brought into the centre, they are assessed for malnutrition symptoms and medical complications, such as diarrhoea and vomiting. Save the Children has a robust nutrition department that is committed to providing life-saving nutrition interventions to the children of Borno. Nutrition programme activities include the provision of care for prevention, treatment, and management of moderate acute malnutrition through outpatient therapeutic programmes, treatment of children with severe acute malnutrition without complications, and management of moderate acute malnutrition through targeted supplementary feeding programmes. This is a key component within fundamental community management of acute malnutrition programmes in nutrition and WASH intervention. Save the Children has been at the forefront in promoting, protecting, and supporting appropriate infant and young child feeding at the community and health facility levels. Save the Children aims to strengthen community capacity and linkages to enhance early detection of malnutrition and referral to facilities through community volunteers and caregivers. This also contributes to localization efforts.

(Continued)

> **Box 3.1** Continued
>
> In terms of WASH facilities at the Molai health stabilization centre, Save the Children provided one solar-powered twin water tank with a capacity of 5,000 litres of water each.[2] Additionally, it provided an underground reservoir, which stores around 1,600 litres of water. Approximately 500 litres of water are used every day. This is seasonally dependent. In terms of sanitation facilities, there are two pour-flush latrines for staff (one for men and one for women) in addition to five semi-flush latrines for patients. There are hygiene promotion sessions for the mothers of the children that have been submitted to the centre, as well as for the staff. Hygiene kits, which contain various hygiene products, are also provided to mothers.[3]

The postponement of the long-term infrastructure needs of WASH services can have significant health risks for people living in acute emergency settings. Some of the most significant shortcomings in integrating WASH and health services result from the lack of coordination between the two sectors. This is particularly true in forced displacement, where health and WASH infrastructure is non-existent or overwhelmed. In a discussion contextualizing the impact forced migration can have on displaced populations' health, Deola et al (2021) stated that health risks increase when people 'leave behind their social networks, livelihoods, service providers, and infrastructures. Displaced people often see their health weakened during their displacement journey because they lack food and adequate nutrition, safe water and sanitation services, and often do not have the resources to maintain basic hygiene'. In such contexts, humanitarian health service providers are often overwhelmed by unknowns, like patient health backgrounds, which can lead to inefficiencies and ineffective coordination.

As the complexity, number, and length of humanitarian crises continue to increase, the gaps in WASH and health services are growing, significantly impacting the health and dignity of those living in humanitarian conditions. Deola et al (2021) noted that these compounding circumstances result in 'considerable gaps in the coordination between sectors of assistance; inadequate funding for public health response; and a plethora of humanitarian agencies responding to crises, resulting in competition for funding.' These problems significantly impact the ability of humanitarian responders and organizations to meet not only the very real needs but also the aspirations of individuals, families, and communities living in humanitarian and displacement contexts. There is a strong need for more robust frameworks that incentivize collaboration and integration to meet needs better and prevent service overlap and gaps in capabilities. We do not suggest we have the answer, but we want to highlight below some recent integration efforts connecting WASH services, health care facilities, and COVID responses in humanitarian contexts that show promise and suggest integrative paths forward to improve health outcomes.

Addressing COVID-19 in refugee and IDP camp settings

The impact of the COVID-19 pandemic on the health and wellbeing of individuals, families, and communities has been substantial. This is especially true with marginalized groups, such as those living in humanitarian contexts.

COVID-19 is spread from person to person through respiratory droplets caused by coughing, sneezing, or inadequate handwashing and sanitation practices. This mode of transmission is uniquely dangerous in densely populated areas like those found in refugee and IDP camps or other informal settings (Alawa et al, 2020; Ali et al, 2022; Shammi et al, 2020). One of the best means of addressing the spread of the COVID-19 virus requires social distancing for several days, which in humanitarian camp settings is increasingly difficult, mainly due to high population densities, cramped housing, and shared community spaces.

Most countries hosting large numbers of refugees and IDPs fall on the list of low- or middle-income countries that struggle to fund and manage health and WASH services adequately. These countries are acutely vulnerable to the spread of viruses like COVID-19 due to limits in their ability to respond effectively. Alawa et al (2020) indicated that 'despite this reality, aid agencies, international actors, and donor governments have been slow to coordinate a multifaceted response, and few policies have been put forth to develop sufficient test–treat–isolate capacity and to equip medical facilities and health personnel with the resources necessary to care for patients with COVID-19'. Furthering this argument, the authors noted that in humanitarian contexts, where health capabilities are already limited, vital resources would be shifted toward treating COVID-19 patients, and patients with other, more severe ailments and diseases will suffer.

In humanitarian settings, WASH practitioners must provide a variety of interventions, including delivery or access to safe drinking water, management and treatment of wastewater and excrement, as well as the delivery of hygiene kits and presentation of various water, hygiene, sanitation information, and behaviour change programming. However, all of this must be implemented in unstable emergency conditions often marred by additional outbreaks of conflict, disease, and other forms of instability. Many interventions, typically used in more stable development conditions, are unusable in these conditions, significantly reducing the options WASH practitioners have at their disposal (Ramesh et al, 2015). It is precisely under these conditions that integrative responses are most useful, particularly when combining WASH with health. In a 2021 report, Jeffries et al highlighted the success of a 'joint assessment team' developed in 2019 by the WHO in the Coxs Bazar Rohingya refugee camps in Bangladesh. This assessment team brought together humanitarian WASH and health practitioners to investigate and respond to cases of acute watery diarrhoea in the camps. Emphasizing what made this joint collaboration successful, Jeffries et al explained that for each case,

> '[c]ase investigation and active case search[es] including stool specimen collection by the health actors as well as water quality testing and hygiene promotion activities by the wash actors. Importantly, [joint assessment teams] reported to the camp authorities as a joint WASH and health team which improved inter-sectoral coordination at the field level. This collaborative approach also helped address resource

limitations, ensuring sufficient availability of staff to investigate all alerts and avoiding over-reliance on single health partner agencies'.

Successful integration between the WASH and health sectors requires a deeper commitment to service outcomes over single actor impact. As the case in Bangladesh highlighted, bringing various actors together increased human resources to the point that every situation could be investigated and responded to individually, amplifying their impact on the lives of Rohingya individuals, families, and the Rohingya community.

Disease outbreaks are not new to humanitarian WASH and health responders, and COVID was no exception (Abdelaziz et al, 2021). However, the global nature of the COVID-19 pandemic made it a unique system stressor and a learning opportunity for the field. As with many outbreaks in humanitarian settings, priority interventions were focused on increasing handwashing stations and on the safe distribution of proper hygiene and sanitation practices. This was critically needed early in the pandemic for high-risk portions of the population, like the elderly and disabled (Cortez and van Blerk, 2021). Even in areas with seasoned humanitarian WASH and health responders, COVID-19 presented a unique learning curve as already weak systems and resources were stressed, highlighting vital areas for future improvement. Looking at displacement settings in Ethiopia, Somalia, and South Sudan, Abdelaziz et al (2021) noted that even in places where humanitarian WASH and health responders had been working for quite some time, the response was not always perfect, as many locations, due to funding gaps or weaknesses in local and national governments responses, did not have proper facilities to implement appropriate countermeasures to address the spread of COVID-19. These gaps often led to poorly maintained WASH infrastructure and services, which compounded the risk of COVID-19 spread in marginalized and at-risk communities.

The case of Ethiopia, Somalia, and South Sudan highlights the unique burden COVID-19 brought to the health of those living in hard-to-reach and unstable parts of the world. As Abdelaziz et al (2021) stated further, 'fear around COVID-19 can lead to the spread of misinformation and increased xenophobia and stigma'. Places that are hard to reach, struggle with overcrowding due to conflict and forced migration, and lack adequate WASH and health services significantly are at increased risk of disease spread, further conflict, and marginalization.

In humanitarian contexts, the actual impact of COVID-19 is still unknown. There has been much talk about the potential of widespread COVID-19 cases in refugee and IDP camps. Still, many of these locations globally have limited testing available, significantly reducing WASH and health practitioners' ability to assess and respond to the pandemic. As Alawa et al (2020) argued, 'due to overcrowding, poor WASH tools, and limited availability of advanced health services, it is expected that rates of transmission and mortality will be higher in humanitarian settings'.

However, there is some evidence that, with adequate early response, this does not have to be the case. A 2022 report by Ali et al looked at how integrated programming can be used to address the spread of COVID-19 in humanitarian settings, highlighting some success in the state of South Kordofan within Sudan. In South Kordofan, refugees and IDPs make up most of the population and are therefore considered at high risk for the spread of the COVID-19 virus. Under the leadership of the WHO, a rapid response team was formed to improve the surveillance and tracking of the virus and to prioritize education and dissemination of vital health risks and prevention measures, including WASH-related training and water quality management. Reporting on the impact of this integration between WASH and health responders, Ali et al noted that:

> [t]his early preparedness, including proper training, coordination and follow-up, has significantly contributed to limiting the spread of COVID-19 in this humanitarian region of the country, with the detection of only 50 cases and 4 deaths reported up to 28 April 2021 out of the total state population of 1 862 998. These cases and related deaths are significantly low compared with other states of Sudan, such as Khartoum and Gaziera. However, these states are not impaired by the additional risk of a humanitarian situation like South Kordofan. More importantly, considering that all the detected cases of COVID-19 and deaths in the state are travel-related, it appears that this integration and early preparedness have prevented the establishment of community transmission of COVID-19 in South Kordofan.

These outcomes need not remain isolated. As humanitarian actors, particularly those working in the WASH and health sectors, begin to break down institutional walls and find ways to integrate programmes, the outcomes in both fields will reach more people and increase the health of individuals, families, and communities living in complex humanitarian contexts.

Monitoring, evaluation, and learning

In reflecting on the work done on monitoring, evaluating, and learning in the WASH field, it is clear that we have come a long way. Since 2016 the joint monitoring programme (JMP) for water supply and sanitation by the WHO and UNICEF has become the official UN mechanism for monitoring progress toward SDG 6 (WHO and UNICEF, n.d.). Since the 1990s, there have also been more efforts to improve the monitoring of humanitarian response activities, including WASH, to ensure response effectiveness and enhance accountability (GWC, 2019; WHO and UNICEF, 2017). In 2021, Ricau et al noted that monitoring is essential to tracking progress and showing the impact of WASH services, and guides resource allocation. They noted further that monitoring data required a 'clear protocol to support data collection, entry, and reporting; the use of appropriate tools and methodologies, including outcome and output results; trained data collectors to support data standardization, consistency, and reliability over time; and sufficient data to ensure statistical significance'. However, in humanitarian contexts obtaining and providing this level of data are complicated and not always available. As we have mentioned before, the size, complexity, and duration of humanitarian emergencies are growing, and the needs are becoming harder to fund and meet. D'Mello-Guyett et al (2018) noted that there is a need for 'stronger evidence on what works to guide more effective and efficient investment and to achieve better health and social outcomes'. Joint coordination is required to fill knowledge gaps and improve WASH services.

Although there is considerable agreement on the value of overlap between the WASH and health sectors, there are still gaps in understanding and room to improve. Monitoring, evaluation, and learning represent not only an area for improvement but also an opportunity to begin integration between the WASH and health sectors. In the WASH field, monitoring is still focused more on 'what' services and hardware were provided and far less on the impact of WASH intervention on the health of those served. Deola et al (2021) noted that 'the humanitarian WASH sector is not yet equipped with coherent or effective systems to measure or evaluate the causal effects, outcomes or impacts of its activities'. This discrepancy, the authors argued, often stands in the way of effective advocacy of the value and impact of WASH services in humanitarian contexts, which in turn can stand in the way of funding needs. In a 2015 systematic study of WASH evaluation and reporting, Ramesh et al (2015) highlighted some key gaps in monitoring, evaluation, and learning in the WASH sector, recommending that future reporting should focus more on jointly reporting on public health and water quality outcomes and track the 'effects of WASH interventions on non-diarrheal diseases (e.g., trachoma, vector-borne disease)', among other recommendations. Further recommendations included a more significant push for collaboration between WASH and health responders, which we also argue for here.

Conclusion: low-hanging fruit and ways forward

Although there have been signs of progress in the last few years, closing gaps is essential as WASH and health practitioners aim to meet the needs of more frequent, protracted crises. Even though the connections between the WASH and health sectors are clear, as discussed above, organizations, including the WHO, continue calls to integrate better, stating that '[i]ntegrat[ing] WASH into regular health sector planning, budgeting, and programming, including COVID-19 response is key' (WHO, 2020). The same report went on to note that there are significant gaps in most countries' abilities to report on basic WASH services in health care facilities, which should be a priority worldwide as the humanitarian and development community seeks better integration between WASH and health.

Even with recent success in collaboration and integration efforts between WASH and health actors, there is a significant lack of research and monitoring showing the effectiveness of WASH programming in addressing health outcomes in humanitarian settings. In an older 2015 study, Ramesh et al found that, 'while evidence exists on the effectiveness of WASH interventions in relation to water quality or other WASH indicators, there remain significant gaps in knowledge with regards to the impact of WASH in interventions in relation to health outcomes in humanitarian crises' (Ramesh et al, 2015). The lack of quantifiable research around the impact of WASH services on reducing infection rates and risk remains a clear gap (Esteves and Cumming, 2016). To date, we have also been unable to find clear connections between WASH and health beyond qualitative evidence in humanitarian contexts. There is a growing need to improve WASH measurement standards to focus more on outcomes and impacts and less on water quality and provision of services. This change will require a particular shift in WASH practitioners' thinking as they look to not only integrate WASH services with health programming but update monitoring, evaluation, and learning to better show results. Such results will also significantly impact fundraising efforts for WASH services worldwide, which are consistently underfunded (Sorensen and Snel, 2020; Snel and Sorensen, 2021; Deola et al, 2021). Bridging WASH funding gaps is vital to the success of health outcomes. As humanitarian crises become longer and more complex, and displace larger numbers of people, the success of health outcomes will become harder to achieve, especially as humanitarian WASH funding continues to lag behind. Integration of services, innovation in technologies, and bridging the humanitarian and development divide become essential solutions to the complex humanitarian problems currently existing and those in the future.

The protracted nature of recent decades' humanitarian crises suggests that innovation is required to meet growing needs. These innovations will require greater collaboration between WASH, health, and government actors (Kendall and Snel, 2016), and the incorporation of new technologies that bring efficiency, impact, and reduce the cost of service, as well as focus on sustainable solutions that specifically aim for long-term WASH and health outcomes in humanitarian contexts (Deola et al, 2021).

The COVID-19 pandemic highlighted not only the value of greater integration between WASH and health actors, particularly in humanitarian contexts, but also critical weaknesses, particularly the crucial gap in safe, effective, and sustainable WASH services in health care facilities. Addressing these deficiencies will require a greater commitment from humanitarian and development funders as well as governments (Kanyangarara et al, 2021). The problems lie in the WASH and health sectors, where integration opportunities are often missed, leading to the spread of treatable diseases. Noting this failure, Deola et al (2021) stated that 'over the last decade, the humanitarian community's public health responses to displacement emergencies have struggled to provide life-saving relief at the same time as addressing the underlying causes of infectious disease'. Integrating the WASH and health sectors is essential to addressing the cause and effect of infectious diseases in humanitarian and development contexts. The COVID-19 pandemic explicitly highlights the need to cast off the traditional short-term, lifesaving focus on humanitarian crises and to start viewing these contexts with a united vision, using long-term systems approaches.

As Parikh et al (2020) so eloquently stated, 'the COVID-19 pandemic is exposing inequalities, it reminds us that the cure will reside in the political will to ameliorate the underlying conditions that have made societies vulnerable to pandemics and other disasters'. In the end, the focus of both humanitarian and development interventions is not only to improve the health, safety, education, and economic potential of individuals, families, and communities, but to empower their wellbeing moving into the future. With that vision of our purpose, coordination and integration of services become paths of empathy and empowerment for those served instead of burdens and inconveniences on those serving.

Notes

1. Marïelle Snel is the Senior Global Humanitarian WASH advisor for Save the Children International, however the opinions addressed in this chapter are expressly her own and do not represent Save the Children in any way.
2. The minimum usage of water is 40 litre per patient per day.
3. The hygiene kits include a plastic bucket with lid (1); plastic cups-500 mils (2); laundry soap-250 gram (18 pieces); bathing soap (18 pieces); bleach (2 bottles); jerry can 20 litres (2); aqua tabs (2 packs); plastic kettle (2 pieces); packaging bag (1); plastic container 5 litres (1); solar touch light (1) and potties (1)

References

Abdelaziz, Y.Z. and G. Arthurson, H. West, A. Torres. 2021. 'WASH responses to COVID-19 in Ethiopia, Somalia and South Sudan.' *Forced Migration Review* 67 (July): 29–33.

Alawa, J. and N. Alawa, A. Coutts, R. Sullivan, K. Khoshnood, F.M. Fouad. 2020. 'Addressing COVID-19 in humanitarian settings: a call to action.' *Conflict and Health* 14 (1): 64. <https://doi.org/10.1186/s13031-020-00307-8>

Ali, Y. and A. Ahmed, E.E. Siddig, N.S. Mohamed. 2022. 'The role of integrated programs in the prevention of COVID-19 in a humanitarian setting.' *Transactions of The Royal Society of Tropical Medicine and Hygiene* 116 (3): 193–96. <https://doi.org/10.1093/trstmh/trab119>

CDC. 2022. 'Global WASH fast facts.' 1 June. <https://www.cdc.gov/healthy-water/global/wash_statistics.html>

Cortez, E.A. and L. van Blerk. 2021. 'The impact of COVID-19 on older refugees.' *Forced Migration Review* 67 (July): 36–38.

Deola, C. and S.Y.A. Khan, A. Torres, E. Kearney, R. Schweitzer. 2021. 'Breaking down silos: integrating WASH into displacement crisis response.' *Forced Migration Review* 67 (August): 4–7.

D'Mello-Guyett, L. and T. Yates, A. Bastable, M. Dahab, C. Deola, C. Dorea, R. Dreibelbis et al. 2018. 'Setting priorities for humanitarian water, sanitation and hygiene research: a meeting report.' *Conflict and Health* 12 (1): 22. <https://doi.org/10.1186/s13031-018-0159-8>

Esteves, J. and O. Cumming. 2016. 'The impact of water, sanitation and hygiene on key health and social outcomes: review of evidence.' UNICEF. <https://www.lshtm.ac.uk/sites/default/files/2017-07/WASHEvidencePaper_HighRes_01.23.17_0.pdf>

GWC. 2019. 'Delivering humanitarian WASH at scale, anywhere and any time: road map for 2020–2025.' WASH Cluster.

Howard, G. and R. Calow, A. Macdonald, J. Bartram. 2016. 'Climate change and water and sanitation: likely impacts and emerging trends for action.' *Annual Review of Environment and Resources* 41 (1): 253–76. <https://doi.org/10.1146/annurev-environ-110615-085856>

IISD. 2014. 'WHO, UN-water report finds investing US$1 in WASH delivers US$4.3 return.' 20 November. <http://sdg.iisd.org/news/who-un-water-report-finds-investing-us1-in-wash-delivers-us4-3-return>

Jeffries, R. and H. Abdi, M. Ali, A.T.M.R.H. Bhuiyan, M. El Shazly, S. Harlass, A. Ishtiak, et al. 2021. 'The health response to the Rohingya refugee crisis post August 2017: reflections from two years of health sector coordination in Cox's Bazar, Bangladesh.' *Plos One* 16 (6): e0253013. <https://doi.org/10.1371/journal.pone.0253013>

Jones, N. and M. Bouzid, R. Few, P. Hunter, I. Lake. 2020. 'Water, sanitation and hygiene risk factors for the transmission of cholera in a changing climate: using a systematic review to develop a causal process diagram.' *Journal of Water and Health* 18 (2): 145–58. <https://doi.org/10.2166/wh.2020.088>

Kanyangarara, M. and S. Allen, S.S. Jiwani, D. Fuente. 2021. 'Access to water, sanitation and hygiene services in health facilities in sub-Saharan Africa 2013–2018: results of health facility surveys and implications for COVID-19 transmission.' *BMC Health Services Research* 21 (1): 601. <https://doi.org/10.1186/s12913-021-06515-z>

Kendall, L. and M. Snel. 2016. 'Looking at WASH in non-household settings: WASH away from the home information guide.' IRC.

Mara, D. and J. Lane, B. Scott, D. Trouba. 2010. 'Sanitation and health.' *Plos Medicine* 7 (11): e1000363. <https://doi.org/10.1371/journal.pmed.1000363>

McGowan, C.R. and L. Baxter, C. Deola, M. Gayford, C. Marston, R. Cummings, F. Checchi. 2020. 'Mobile clinics in humanitarian emergencies: a systematic review.' *Conflict and Health* 14: 4. <https://doi.org/10.1186/s13031-020-0251-8>

Mooijman, A. and M. Snel, S. Ganguly, K. Shordt. 2010. Strengthening water, sanitation and hygiene in school: a WASH guidance manual with a focus on South Asia. The Hague, the Netherlands: IRC International Water and Sanitation Centre. <https://www.susana.org/_resources/documents/default/2-1404-mooijman-2010-strengthening.pdf>

Pacheco, E-M. and I. Bisaga, R.S. Oktari, P. Parikh, H. Joffe. 2021. 'Integrating psychosocial and WASH school interventions to build disaster resilience.' *International Journal of Disaster Risk Reduction* 65 (November): 102520. <https://doi.org/10.1016/j.ijdrr.2021.102520>

Parikh, P. and L. Diep, J. Gupte, M. Lakhanpaul. 2020. 'COVID-19 challenges and WASH in informal settlements: integrated action supported by the sustainable development goals.' *Cities* 107 (December): 102871. <https://doi.org/10.1016/j.cities.2020.102871>

Ramesh, A. and K. Blanchet, J.H.J. Ensink, B. Roberts. 2015. 'Evidence on the effectiveness of water, sanitation, and hygiene (WASH) Interventions on health outcomes in humanitarian crises: a systematic review.' *PloS One* 10 (9): e0124688. <https://doi.org/10.1371/journal.pone.0124688>

Ricau, M. and L. Lacan, E. Ihemezue, D. Lantagne, G. String. 2021. 'Evaluation of monitoring tools for WASH response in a cholera outbreak in northeast Nigeria.' *Journal of Water, Sanitation and Hygiene for Development* 11 (6): 972–82. <https://doi.org/10.2166/washdev.2021.056>

Romanello, M. and A. McGushin, C. Di Napoli, P. Drummond, N. Hughes, L. Jamart, H. Kennard, et al. 2021. 'The 2021 Report of the Lancet countdown on health and climate change: code red for a healthy future.' *The Lancet* 398 (10311): 1619–62. <https://doi.org/10.1016/S0140-6736(21)01787-6>

Schmitt, M.L. and O.R. Wood, D. Clatworthy, S. Faiz Rashid, M. Sommer. 2021. 'Innovative strategies for providing menstruation-supportive water, sanitation and hygiene (WASH) Facilities: learning from refugee camps in Cox's Bazar, Bangladesh.' *Conflict and Health* 15 (1): 10. <https://doi.org/10.1186/s13031-021-00346-9>

Shammi, M. and M.R. Robi, S.M. Tareq. 2020. 'COVID-19: socio-environmental challenges of Rohingya refugees in Bangladesh.' *Journal of Environmental Health Science & Engineering* 18 (2): 1709–11. <https://doi.org/10.1007/s40201-020-00489-6>

Snel, M. and N. Sorensen. 2021. Bridging the WASH humanitarian–development divide: building a sustainable reality. Rugby UK: Practical Action Publishing Ltd. <https://practicalactionpublishing.com/book/2577/bridging-the-wash-humanitariandevelopment-divide>

Sorensen, N. and M. Snel. 2020. 'The new reality: perspectives on future integrated WASH.' *Waterlines* 39 (4): 277–92. <https://doi.org/10.3362/1756-3488.20-00007>

UNICEF and WHO. 2021. The measurement and monitoring of water supply, sanitation and hygiene (WASH) affordability: a missing element of monitoring of sustainable development goal (SDG) targets 6.1 and 6.2. New York: United Nations Children's Fund (UNICEF) and the World Health Organization (WHO). <https://washdata.org/sites/default/files/2021-05/unicef-who-2021-affordability-of-wash-services-full.pdf>

Walton, D. and M. van Aalst. 2020. Climate-related extreme weather events and COVID-19: a first look at the number of people affected by intersection disasters. Geneva: IFRC. <https://www.ifrc.org/sites/default/files/Extreme-weather-events-and-COVID-19-V4.pdf>

WHO. 2020. Global progress report on water, sanitation and hygiene in health care facilities: fundamentals first. Geneva: World Health Organization.

<https://washdata.org/sites/default/files/2020-12/WHO-UNICEF-2020-wash-in-hcf.pdf>

———. 2022a. 'Drinking-water.' 21 March. <https://www.who.int/news-room/fact-sheets/detail/drinking-water>

———. 2022b. 'When the water stops flowing in humanitarian emergencies.' Bulletin of the World Health Organization 100 (7): 418–19. <https://doi.org/10.2471/BLT.22.020722>

WHO and UNICEF. 2017. Progress on drinking water, sanitation and hygiene: 2017 update and SDG baselines. Geneva: World Health Organization (WHO) and the United Nations Children's Fund (UNICEF). <https://data.unicef.org/resources/progress-drinking-water-sanitation-hygiene-2017-update-sdg-baselines>

———. 2021. Progress on household drinking water, sanitation and hygiene 2000-2020: five years into the SDGs. Geneva: World Health Organization (WHO) and the United Nations Children's Fund (UNICEF).

———. 2022. Progress on WASH in health care facilities 2000-2021: special focus on WASH and infection prevention and control (IPC). Geneva: World Health Organization (WHO) and the United Nations Children's Fund (UNICEF). <https://data.unicef.org/resources/jmp-wash-in-health-care-facilities-2022>

———. n.d. 'About the JMP.' <https://washdata.org/how-we-work/about-jmp>

CHAPTER 4

WASH–nutrition integration: for vulnerable populations affected by conflict, climate change, and the COVID-19 pandemic

Jovana Dodos and Bram Riems

Links between WASH and nutrition

Despite significant progress made over the past decade, undernutrition in all its forms remains one of the greatest public health challenges and development concerns. The joint malnutrition estimates released in April 2021 are alarming: globally, 149.2 million children under five (CU5) are suffering from stunting (defined as low-height-for-age), 45.4 million CU5 are affected by wasting (defined as low-weight-for-height), of which 13.6 million are severely wasted – these children require urgent treatment and care to survive (UNICEF et al, 2021). The economic crisis and disruptions to food supply chains and health systems related to the COVID-19 pandemic have likely exacerbated these figures, meaning that there could be 15 times more wasted children than estimated, an additional 2.6 million stunted children, and 168,000 additional child deaths (Osendarp et al, 2021). The burden of undernutrition disproportionally falls on the children living in low-and-middle income countries (LMICs) across Asia and Africa (UNICEF et al, 2021).

Nearly half of all deaths in CU5 can be attributed to undernutrition (GNR, 2020). Undernourished children are more susceptible to repeated bouts of enteric and respiratory diseases, and to more severe and prolonged infections. Therefore, they are at greater risk of dying from common infections, such as diarrhoea. Frequent illnesses, in return, cause poor nutritional intake and reduced nutrient absorption. Children are thus locked into a vicious circle of recurring sickness and further deterioration of their nutritional status (Dewey and Mayers, 2011; ACF, 2017b). In the long term, the human and economic consequences of undernutrition are enormous, as they fall the hardest on poor women and children. Chronically undernourished children are more prone to suffer from delayed mental development and poor school performance and are at risk of losing more than 10 per cent of their lifetime earnings potential (ACF, 2014; The World Bank, 2005). The economic cost of undernutrition, in terms of lost national productivity and economic growth, is estimated at 3 to 16 per cent of gross domestic product (The World Bank, 2021).

The determinants of undernutrition are complex, and nutritional status is dependent on a broad range of diverse and interconnected factors. At the most immediate level, undernutrition is the outcome of inadequate dietary intake and disease (UNICEF, 2020a). Its underlying determinants encompass food insecurity, inadequate feeding and care practices, and an unhealthy environment, including inadequate access to water, sanitation, and hygiene (UNICEF, 2020a; ACF, 2017b). All these factors result in increased vulnerability to shocks and long-term stresses. The basic determinants of undernutrition are rooted in poverty and involve interactions between social, political, demographic, and economic conditions (ACF, 2017b).

Poor WASH conditions facilitate ingestion of faecal pathogens, which can lead to diarrhoea, helminth infections, and environmental enteric dysfunction (EED), 'an incompletely defined syndrome of inflammation, reduced absorptive capacity, and reduced barrier function in the small intestine' (Crane et al, 2015). These directly affect the body's ability to resist and respond to sickness, decreasing immunity, affecting the absorption of nutrients, and causing diversion of energy and nutrients from growth to the immune system to fight the infection (ACF, 2017b; Petri et al, 2008). Other water and sanitation-related illnesses, such as malaria, dengue, leishmaniosis, trypanosomiasis, yellow fever, together with chronic poisoning due to chemical contaminants in drinking water, can also contribute to the deterioration of nutritional status (see Figure 4.1).

The argument for improving WASH for nutrition is based on the hypothesis that better WASH conditions improve nutritional status through the prevention of infection and disease. It is precisely because WASH can prevent a range of water- and sanitation-related diseases, and because these in turn are an important but not the only cause of undernutrition, that the direct effects of improved WASH on nutritional status are difficult to measure. Indeed, disease is an intermediary factor on the causal pathway, and often, as is the case for EED, asymptomatic. This also implies that the hypothesis mentioned above needs to be tested much more systematically before the mechanisms between WASH conditions and practices, infection, and undernutrition, can be fully understood.

There are also indirect, non-biological links between WASH and nutritional status, referring primarily to a wide variety of social-economic factors, such as access and affordability of WASH services, education, and poverty. Absence of safe drinking water on premise or close to the home, for example, may have indirect effects on disease and nutrition. People are often left with no other choice but to drink unsafe water from unprotected sources, exposing themselves to contracting water-borne diseases, or to travel long distances every day to collect water. A disproportional burden of water-fetching falls on women and young children, especially girls (UNICEF, 2016a). Time wasted on water collection translates into decreased productivity, lower school attendance, and less time for childcare and household chores. Inadequate childcare is one of the underlying causes of undernutrition (ACF, 2017b).

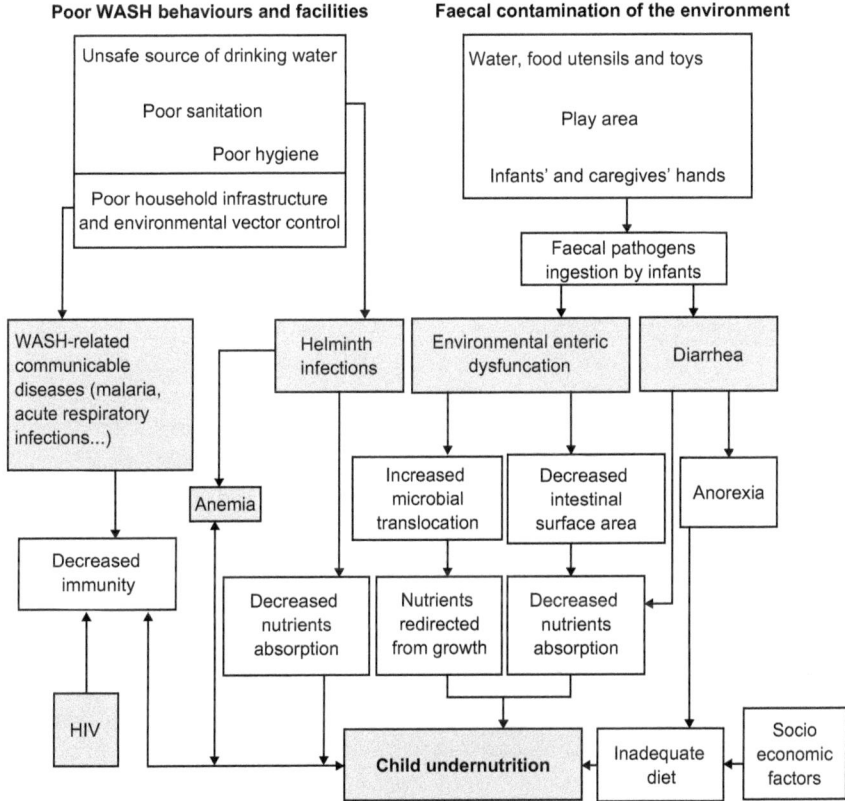

Figure 4.1 Key pathways from poor WASH to undernutrition

Source: ACF (2021) WASH 'Nutrition operational note'. Adapted from Rakotomanana H. and J.J. Komakech, C.N. Walters, B.J. Stoecker. 2020. 'The WHO and UNICEF joint monitoring programme (JMP) indicators for water supply, sanitation and hygiene and their association with linear growth in children 6 to 23 months in East Africa'. *International Journal of Environmental Research and Public Health* 17(17): 6262.

Available evidence suggests that WASH conditions often play a major role in determining nutritional status across multiple settings. Findings from participatory nutritional causal analyses or Link NCAs (ACF, 2015b), which are used to analyze complex, dynamic, and locally specific causes of undernutrition, show that the association between WASH and undernutrition is well recognized by communities themselves. WASH-related risk factors, such as open defecation practices in the community, unhygienic environments (including inadequate waste management), inconsistent access to safe drinking water, insufficient domestic water supply, and poor hygiene practices, are consistently identified as one of the main causes of undernutrition by the communities (Dodos et al, 2017).

There is moderate evidence that treating household drinking water has a positive effect on treatment duration (shorter) and recovery rates (higher)

of acute malnutrition (Stobaugh et al, 2020). Access to safe drinking water at home is of particular importance during the outpatient treatment of children with acute malnutrition in both its forms – moderate acute malnutrition (MAM) and severe acute malnutrition (SAM) – due to their increased vulnerability to water-borne diseases and infections. If contracted, infectious diseases like diarrhoea increase the risk of mortality in malnourished children and reduce the efficacy of nutritional treatment (Doocy et al, 2018). Recent studies have demonstrated that household WASH interventions implemented in conjunction with community management of acute malnutrition (CMAM) programmes have the potential to decrease the time-to-recovery and improve overall recovery rates and absolute weight gain of admitted children (Altmann et al, 2018). As indicated by Okotch et al (2020), point-of-use water treatment interventions may even have a sustained effect on preventing both diarrhoea occurrence and acute malnutrition six months after successful discharge from the CMAM programme. Further research on the effectiveness of a simple WASH kit on recovery from severe acute malnutrition is ongoing.[1]

Evidence also suggests that improved sanitation may decrease stunting. For example, a longitudinal study conducted in Peru showed that inadequate disposal of sewage, and poor water sources and storage accounted for a one-centimetre height deficit in children aged 24 months when compared to their counterparts living with better sanitation and water conditions (Checkley et al, 2004). Similar results were found in a multiple-country study, which demonstrated that diarrheal diseases, caused by poor sanitation, accounted for 25 per cent of stunting in children up to 24 months (Checkley et al, 2008). Meanwhile, an observational study in rural Bangladesh found that young children living in environmentally clean households had lower levels of parasitic infection, improved measures of gut function, and improved growth compared with similar children living in contaminated environments (Lin et al, 2013).

India's national Total Sanitation Campaign (TSC) found that, on average, the TSC increased height-for-age z-scores by approximately 0.2 standard deviation (Spears, 2012). In light of the spill-over effect of open defecation, these findings appear to support community- rather than individual-oriented sanitation interventions. These results were echoed by the findings from the study conducted by Quattri et al (2014), suggesting that community-level, unimproved sanitation contributes to stunting in rural Vietnam and Lao PDR, regardless of whether a child's household uses improved toilets. Similarly, children younger than two years of age living in community-led total sanitation (CLTS) villages in Mali were found to be taller and less likely to be stunted than those in the control group, suggesting that approaches involving the whole community, such as CLTS, may be effective in preventing growth faltering (Pickering et al, 2015). Thus, policies, programmatic interventions, and incentives would best focus on communitywide (rather than household) outcomes and behavioural change (Quattri et al, 2014). Despite these encouraging results, other studies have found no effect of improved sanitation on stunting (Contreras et al, 2021; Kwong et al, 2020; Wolf et al, 2019). There is a growing consensus that reducing human exposure to faecal pathogens requires not only communitywide sanitation coverage, but also improved service levels and addressing the multiple exposure pathways.

Good hygiene practices, particularly handwashing with water and soap, and other health behaviours, such as latrine use and removal of animal faeces from living spaces, are vital barriers to the spread of diarrheal, respiratory, and possibly other infectious diseases, as they prevent pathogens from reaching the domestic environment and food, and their subsequent ingestion. Several observational studies across multiple settings reported that poor hand hygiene of caretakers and/or unhygienic feeding practices are significantly associated with increased risk of diarrhoea and acute malnutrition (Dodos et al, 2018; Ambadekar et al, 2017; Ayana et al, 2015; Agustina et al, 2013). Good hygiene behaviours are influenced by individual and societal knowledge, and attitudes and beliefs regarding hygiene, as well as dependent on the availability, accessibility, and quality of WASH services, such as handwashing facilities (Curtis et al, 2011). Thereby, the two principal strategies of hygiene interventions in nutrition programming focus on behaviour-change communication and marketing, and the provision of WASH hardware – the enabling environment for hygiene promotion.

Households are where young children and their caretakers spend a lot of time. Infants and young children crawl, play, and are fed in the domestic environment. This usually means continuous exposure and daily ingestion of faecal pathogens early in life, in particular during the first 1,000 days (from conception until the age of two), which are a critical window for a child's growth and development. It has been hypothesized that the exposure to sanitation-related diarrheal and intestinal parasitic infections in the first 1,000 days of a child's life may cause irreversible, long-term damage to a child's health (Ravi and Singh, 2016). Consequently, WASH interventions should be designed to interrupt the primary faecal-oral transmission pathways specific to this critical window, which are mainly related to infant feeding practices and feeding environments, and age-related practices, such as hand-mouth activity, chewing on play objects, crawling on contaminated soil or among domestic animals and so on (Kwong et al, 2020; Dominguez, 2017; Ngure et al, 2014).

In the past years, a more specific, age-targeted approach has been widely promoted – BabyWASH, which does not replace general household WASH interventions that do have the potential to reduce overall contamination of the household environment, but complements them with interventions tailored to very young children. BabyWASH is designed to protect maternal and newborn health during the first 1,000 days by interrupting the faecal-oral transmission pathways, and reducing the onset and frequency of enteric infections. Some evidence indicates that WASH interventions are more effective in improving childhood nutrition in children under two compared with interventions targeting CU5 (Gizaw et al, 2019), reconfirming the relevance of BabyWASH.

While the potential effect of WASH on nutrition, in particular linear growth, is determined by age and type of intervention, singular interventions are unlikely to improve the nutrition status of children (Gizaw et al, 2019). Water, sanitation, and hygiene are closely linked, and keeping someone in good health depends on each of these components individually, as well as on the many interactions between them. For example, personal hygiene depends on water availability; access to water facilitates use of sanitation services; unhygienic latrines lead to an increase in number of flies and mosquitoes and threaten the quality of nearby water sources. In contexts where faecal-oral diseases spread through multiple transmission pathways and where environmental conditions favour the spread of communicable diseases (for example, in emergencies, epidemics, and crowded settlements such as refugee camps,) single interventions will probably have minimal benefit. In these contexts, it is highly unlikely that treatment of drinking water or handwashing or food safety or sanitation alone can prevent the occurrence and spread of faecal-oral diseases and consequently reduce the risk of undernutrition.

Field actors should therefore aim to address the most important transmission pathways if they aim to see an effect on undernutrition. The guiding principle of the transformative WASH approach is that – in any context – a comprehensive package of WASH interventions tailored to address the local exposure landscape and enteric disease burden is needed (ACF, 2021; Cumming et al, 2019). This implies understanding the multiple and multifaceted socio-economic, cultural, and environmental factors contributing to enteric infections, and their interconnectedness.

For instance, the role of the private sector, caregivers' motivation and perceived self-efficacy for improving hygiene levels around children, local preferences for cooking and eating practices, the presence of animal faeces in household, or mouthing all may present an increased risk of faecal exposure to infants and act as key pathways to undernutrition during the 1,000-days window of opportunity. A comprehensive package of WASH interventions should therefore aim to address all context-specific transmission pathways and lower the level of faecal contamination in the environment substantially enough to reduce infection and influence children's growth and nutritional status.

WASH, nutrition, and conflict

Peace and stability are essential for good nutrition. Yet war, different forms of political insecurity and crisis leading to mass population movements and climate-related disasters continue to affect an increasing number of countries. The World Bank estimates that around two billion people live in countries affected by fragility, conflict, and violence (IDA, 2021).

Violent conflicts and displacements are major drivers of hunger (Loewenberg, 2015) and tend to increase malnutrition and hunger-related mortality, especially among women, children, and infants (Brown et al, 2021).

There is a general consensus that hunger and conflict reinforce each other, creating a vicious circle: conflicts are one of the main causes of severe food insecurity; and food insecurity, in return, creates conditions conducive to the outbreak or spread of conflict (ACF et al, 2018). Conflict and food system fragility are therefore mutually linked, and often exacerbated by environmental shocks caused by climate change. The unfortunate reality is that, in many regions already susceptible to food insecurity (e.g. the Sahel or the Horn of Africa), conflict and climate events co-occur, acting as risk multipliers. The affected populations are consequently facing the triple burden of conflict, climate change, and malnutrition.

Numerous reports from war-torn settings illustrate the impact of conflict on the nutritional status of affected populations. For example, in 2017, 20 million people across four countries – South Sudan, Somalia, Yemen, and North-East Nigeria – faced famine, largely driven by conflict (ACF et al, 2018). In South Sudan, civil war and currency decline caused food prices to spike, making food unaffordable for people even in peaceful zones (Loewenberg, 2015). More recently, famine was declared in northern parts of the country, and 1.4 million of CU5 were expected to be acutely malnourished (OCHA, 2021). In Nigeria, due to violence and mass displacement caused by the Boko Haram in 2016, it was estimated that, on average, 134 children in Borno state would die every day from issues related to malnutrition (UNICEF, 2017). In Yemen, the disruption of the inflow of food and fuel that resulted from the violence and restrictions on imports paralyzed the delivery of basic services across the country, leaving almost half of CU5 chronically malnourished (UNICEF, 2016b).

Conflicts affect local livelihoods, impair productive and agricultural activities, and limit access to safe foods and basic services. Food shortages and limited access to adequate food are a major concern for populations living in conflict zones, which makes them highly dependent on food imports. At the same time, countries may encounter difficulties in importing food because of sanctions, and face food price inflation as a result of scarcity. The mass displacement of populations fleeing violence and looking for peace and security also contributes to the failure of local food markets as there simply are no people to buy or sell local produce. Even where demand still exists, the costs and risks of transporting produce to markets in conflict-affected areas can be prohibitively high (ACF et al, 2018). Hence, food and nutrition insecurity become increasingly worse in conflict situations (Caroll et al, 2017) and, together with destructions of health, water and agricultural infrastructure, decline in critical health services, poor WASH conditions, outbreaks of infectious diseases, violence, and poverty, contribute to a high level of malnutrition in all its forms.

Coping strategies commonly used by populations in fragile and conflict-affected contexts include prioritizing food quantity over quality, reducing portion sizes and frequency of meals, spending less on food, and borrowing food (Ghattas et al, 2014). Conflict-related circumstances can lead to a lower probability and shorter duration of breastfeeding, and replacing breastfeeding with formula-feeding. Studies report that, in conflict settings with a serious deterioration of WASH infrastructure (e.g. Iraq, Yemen) and compromised access to safe water, formula distributions were 'a major contributing factor to infant malnutrition, morbidity and mortality' (Diwakar et al, 2019). This is because formula was often prepared with dirty water and in unhygienic conditions.

UNICEF (2021) highlights that, in many conflicts around the world, more children die from diarrheal diseases linked to unsafe water and sanitation than from direct violence. Along with food and shelter, it is therefore evident that ensuring access to basic WASH services in conflicts is of crucial importance for preventing outbreaks of WASH-related diseases and improving the overall health of women and children.

But preventing infection and disease that potentially lead to malnutrition is only part of the solution. Health care facilities and community nutrition centres struggle to function when access to safe WASH is compromised by damaged infrastructure and disrupted services. Many malnourished children caught up in conflict cannot access the essential nutrition treatment and quality health care they need, hindering their ability to recover from malnutrition and increasing their risk of dying from SAM.

The conflict in Yemen, for example, greatly disrupted the delivery of basic child nutrition and health services. Hospitals, other health care facilities, and water and sanitation infrastructure were especially hard hit. The facilities that have remained operational have been facing serious challenges, such as lack of access to safe water and insufficient water supply, fuel for generators, or medical supplies (The World Bank, 2022). Insufficient access to safe drinking water has led to the largest outbreak of cholera and diphtheria in recorded history (WHO, 2017), further deteriorating the nutritional status of affected populations and perpetuating the risk of mortality from malnutrition and disease.

Providing safe drinking water, sanitation and hygiene services through improving or rehabilitating infrastructure, trucking water to refugee settlements and health care facilities, distributing hygiene kits, raising awareness of good sanitation and hygiene practices, protecting and promoting safe and appropriate infant and young child feeding practices and so on, are life-saving, nutrition-sensitive interventions that should be tailored to the social context of areas experiencing conflict (and not simply replicated as a standard package of relief interventions in every emergency).

Contextualized solutions for ensuring access to safe WASH in times of conflict should pave the way for other vital interventions, such as health, nutrition, education, and protection from violence, coercion, and deliberate deprivation. Given the limited evidence base currently available, it is not possible to reach definitive conclusions with regard to the effect of WASH interventions on preventing malnutrition and growth deficiencies in children in conflict-affected settings.

All regions of the world are experiencing, and will continue to experience, the effects of climate change with varying magnitude and consequences. These effects, such as higher temperatures, rising sea levels, variation in precipitation, ecosystems at risk, and more frequent, intense and unpredictable extreme weather events (e.g. drought and flooding), impact nutrition in various ways, including food security, quantity and quality of water, environmental hygiene, care and feeding practices, and disease prevalence.

Water and food security are key challenges under climate change as both are highly vulnerable to continuously changing weather patterns. With the most optimistic projected +2°C global average temperature increase, it is probable that the rate of undernourishment among the sub-Saharan African population will increase by 25–35 per cent by 2050 (ACF, 2015a), and that freshwater resources will substantially decline by the end of 21st century (Misra, 2014). Climate change is already affecting the four dimensions of food security: the physical availability of food, its economic and physical accessibility, its use, and the stability of these three dimensions over time (FAO, 2007). The implications of this development extend across all determinants of nutritional status. Be it too much water through flooding from heavy storms, or too little water in the form of prolonged and severe droughts, extreme weather events are impacting the availability of water and soil moisture, which can critically affect crop yields, food prices, household food security, and livelihood opportunities. Climate change also alters seasonal patterns, which are often a good predictor of peaks in acute malnutrition caseloads as shown by the Feinstein Centre and FAO (Young at al, 2019).

Major variations in temperatures, precipitation patterns, and humidity are expected to expand breeding opportunities for insects, bacteria, and other germs, and shift the range and incidence of vector-borne diseases, such as malaria (The World Bank, 2012). Evidence suggests that malaria may increase the incidence and severity of malnutrition and impair weight gain, while malnutrition may increase the risk of malaria infection (Oldenburg et al, 2018). More frequent droughts lead to water shortages, particularly for human and domestic use. When water becomes scarce, good hygiene practices, such as handwashing with water and soap, become more and more difficult to maintain, increasing the risk of infection and disease. On the other hand, (recurrent) flooding events compromise sanitation infrastructure. This increases environmental contamination and incidence of water-related illnesses, such as cholera, typhoid, and diarrhoea, all of which have the potential to lower nutritional status.

Women are more vulnerable to the effects of climate change than men – mainly because they constitute the majority of the world's poor and are more dependent for their livelihood on natural resources that are threatened by climate change (UN Women, 2022). Climate change also puts further strain on the already heavy workload of women, especially those engaged in water collection, negatively impacting their ability to provide proper care to infants and young children and heightening the risk of undernutrition (ACF, 2015a). Lastly, climate change is exacerbating recognized influencers of conflict, such

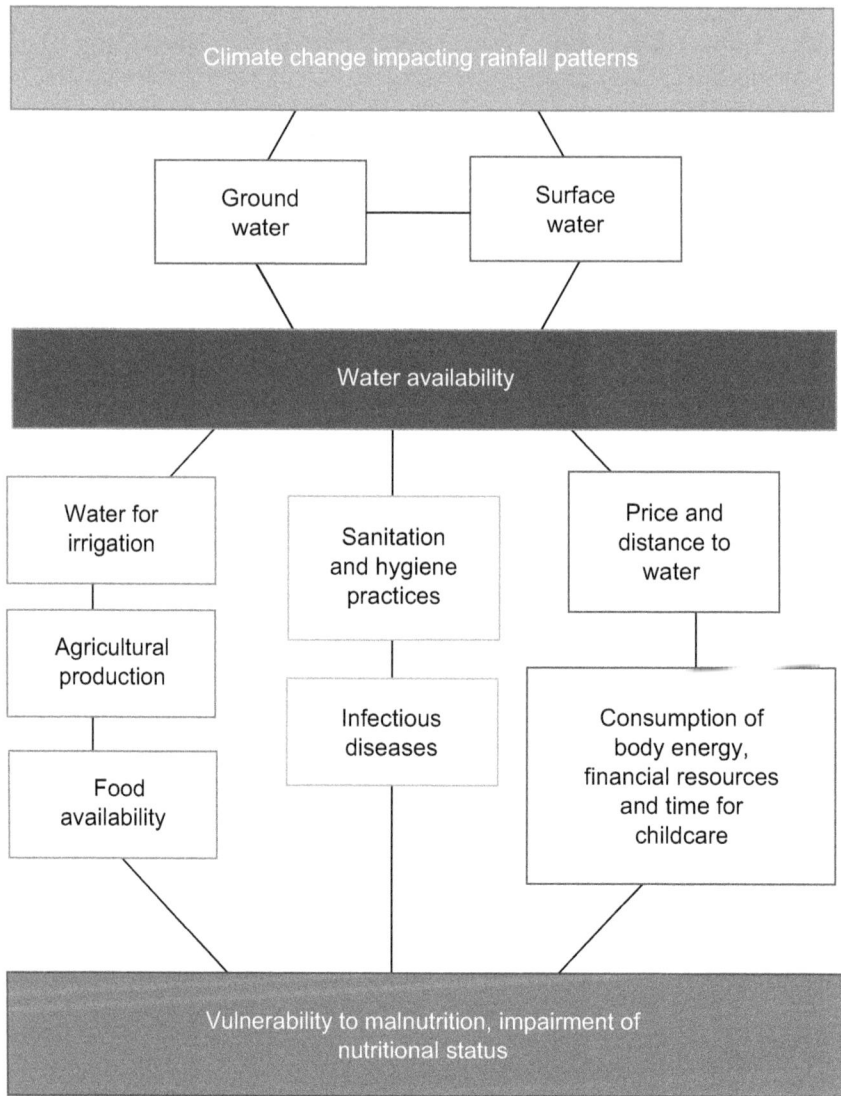

Figure 4.2 Linkages between climate change, water availability and nutritional status
Source: Action Contra la Faim, Alain Ricardo Patlan Hernandez. Early warning on nutrition and health crisis – Southern Madagascar. UNC Water and Health Conference 2020.

as competition over increasingly scarce water resources, which may increase the risk of migration and displacement (Hsiang et al, 2011), nutritional vulnerability, food insecurity, and hunger. Countries already affected by conflict, pollution, deforestation, and other challenges are likely to suffer the most. The most vulnerable and the most affected are, and will continue to be, those who depend on natural resources, as well as women and children who depend for survival mainly on subsistence farming or small-scale food production, water harvesting and related activities.

The research project 'Hydronut', implemented by ACF in southern Madagascar, provides a good illustration of the links between climate change, WASH (in particular water availability), and nutrition. Madagascar is one of the most vulnerable countries in the world to climate change and extreme weather events, such as cyclones, floods, and droughts. In the past two decades, the south of the country has been affected by droughts, whose severity has increased since 2015 with the El Niño phenomenon. Populations' dependence on rain-fed agriculture and extensive livestock farming makes them highly susceptible to climate variability.

The principal hypothesis tested though this research project was that climate change has triggered negative effects on nutritional and health indicators through reduced water resources. Hydro-climatic data (rainfall, groundwater, vegetation) and nutrition data (number of admissions to nutrition treatment centres, number of screened children with acute malnutrition) were collected between January 2014 and March 2019. Data interpretation and preliminary results indicate a strong inter-annual heterogeneity of groundwater recharge, and correlation between groundwater recharge and water quality. Groundwater recharge strongly depends on rainfall patterns and extreme weather events (cyclones and tropical storms). By cross-referencing these data with admissions to health centres, ACF also reported a correlation between rainfall and acute malnutrition prevalence, or in other words, a deficit of rainfall and its negative effect on nutritional status nine months to one year later. Rainfall has a strong impact on groundwater levels and crop production, which in turn determine people's ability to access water and food – and thus contributes to poor nutritional outcomes (GEOECO, ACF, ASOS, 2020).

More research is needed to better understand how climate change affects the water cycle in a given area, in particular the links between rainfall, surface temperature and groundwater, surface run-off, evapotranspiration, and soil moisture, and how and when these affect food security and malnutrition. The temporal effects are especially important for policymakers, both for early warning as well as for adaptive programming.

WASH, nutrition, and the COVID-19 pandemic

Good nutritional status is an essential part of an individual's defence against disease. Malnutrition is strongly linked to adverse COVID-19 outcomes, including the increased risk of hospitalization and mortality (GRN, 2020). The COVID-19 pandemic and related economic, food, and health systems disruptions have exacerbated all forms of malnutrition worldwide, especially among the most vulnerable – the poor, women, children, and those living in fragile contexts and conflict-affected areas. Of particular concern is an increase in moderate or severe wasting among CU5 by a shocking 14.3 per cent, which is equivalent to an additional 6.7 million cases (Fore et al, 2020) and more than 10,000 additional child deaths per month during the first 12 months of the pandemic (Headey et al, 2020). A projected 2.6 million more children who received poor nutrition due to COVID-19 will face stunted growth that could limit their lifelong potential (Osendarp et al, 2021).

Measures taken by countries to fight against the COVID-19 pandemic, such as lockdowns and border closures, have restricted movements of people and essential goods, and have disrupted food and value chains (production, transportation, storage and sale of food), triggering shortages or a surge in food prices. Countries that are heavily dependent on food imports suffered the most. For example, in Nepal, 53 per cent of traders reported insufficient food availability on the markets in the first year of the pandemic; in Uganda, restrictions on cargo movements resulted in fewer food imports and an increase in food prices (Action Against Hunger, 2020).

In addition to changes in the availability and affordability of nutritious foods, COVID-19 mitigation measures also resulted in steep declines in households' income, and the combination of limited income-generating opportunities and rising food prices have undermined the purchasing power of poorer households. Global estimates from mid-2020 suggested that economic contractions and food supply chain disruptions had led to 95 million people falling into extreme poverty and had contributed to increased household food insecurity (GNR, 2020; Laborde et al, 2020). Affected populations have therefore adopted coping strategies that may compromise the nutritional status of children, and increase the incidence and severity of childhood illnesses, such as changing their consumption habits, moving towards cheaper foods with less nutritional value, or even skipping meals altogether (Action Against Hunger, 2020).

The COVID-19 pandemic has challenged the access to health, nutrition, social protection, and other essential basic services, including water and sanitation (Action Against Hunger, 2020; Akseer et al, 2020). This is particularly true for underserved communities in rural and remote areas. UNICEF reports from the early months of the COVID-19 pandemic suggest a 30 per cent reduction in coverage of essential nutrition services in LMICs, and declines of coverage of 75–100 per cent under lockdown contexts (UNICEF, 2020b), putting millions of children at risk from not receiving the essential treatment they need to survive. In its interim guidance document on the maintenance of essential health services in the COVID-19 context, the WHO acknowledged that, as health services diverted their attention and capacities to the needed COVID-19 response, the delivery of essential nutrition services were threatened, along with the surveillance of at-risk populations (WHO, 2020).

Movement restrictions and the lack of information on whether services were functioning safely, if at all, have also hindered people's ability to access basic services, including essential nutritional services. To illustrate this, in Burkina Faso, in April 2020, Action Against Hunger recorded a 70 per cent decrease in attendance rate in the programmes using ready-to-use therapeutic food for treatment of CU5 diagnosed with severe acute malnutrition, probably due to caregivers' inability to travel for the follow-up visits under movement restrictions. In the Central African Republic, there has been a decrease in the number of children undergoing active screening for MAM or SAM since March 2020, as these programmes require proximity between community health workers, caregivers, and children, raising the fear of COVID-19 transmission.

The access and provision of WASH services have been paramount to reducing the spread of COVID-19 by strengthening infection prevention and control measures in households and institutions, such as health care facilities. Ensuring frequent and proper handwashing, a major element of the WASH framework, has been one of the most critical measures for preventing transmission and protecting those with compromised immunity, such as the malnourished, given their increased vulnerability and higher risk of death or serious complications from COVID-19.

Yet, at the peak of the pandemic, billions of people worldwide, from communities to frontline health care workers, did not have access to a facility to wash their hands with water and soap; approximately one-quarter of the global population still used water collected from off-premises water sources, and millions were dependent on untreated surface water (UNICEF/ WHO, 2021). Households that rely on water fetching usually do not have water available for handwashing because the amount of water collected is often inadequate to meet all needs and is being prioritized for other chores (Stoler et al, 2020). Similarly, physical distancing may not be possible for those who rely on fetching or sharing water, since the process of fetching often involves queuing in close proximity (Stoler et al, 2020). Sharing latrines, which is common in informal settlements with communal toilets, may also serve as a transmission pathway for COVID-19, especially in the absence of adequate water and soap for hygiene purposes and inherent difficulties to practising physical distancing (Giné-Garriga et al, 2021). All this makes it hard to control the pandemic, and protect malnourished and vulnerable members of households from contracting COVID-19. Not surprisingly, the poorest households have received the COVID-19 shock on top of the existing lack of access to basic WASH services, leading to a further deterioration of their health and nutritional status, and increasing social inequalities.

Despite the unquestionable importance of good hygiene for controlling the COVID-19 pandemic, a comprehensive package of WASH interventions is needed to address all the barriers to frequent and proper handwashing, and generate a protective effect on those suffering from malnutrition. This also implies ensuring the provision of functional hand hygiene facilities at points of care to protect health care workers, caregivers, and malnourished children from COVID-19 transmission. Continuous provision of adequate and safe WASH services in health care facilities is critical for reducing the risk of COVID-19 and other diseases during inpatient care and management of SAM, as well as for infection prevention during follow-up visits as part of outpatient treatment of acute malnutrition.

Box 4.1 Case study: BabyWASH approach in Nigeria

Nigeria has the second highest prevalence of stunting (32 per cent in CU5) in the world (UNICEF Nigeria, 2021). In 2019, over 136,600 persons had been displaced in Yobe State alone, fleeing violence from non-state armed groups. Global acute malnutrition prevalence was above the emergency threshold (10.9-14.1 per cent), while inadequate access to safe water, sanitation, and hygiene was considered a major contributing risk factor to high malnutrition prevalence (ACF, 2017).

In 2018 and 2019, ACF implemented a BabyWASH approach in Nangere local government area, targeting 5,562 pregnant and lactating women (PLWs) with interventions at cash distribution points. These interventions included the provision of handwashing materials (soap and items for constructing a tippy tap), promotion of child WASH and nutrition practices, and the provision of complementary feeding items (child cup with lid, child bowl with lid, child spoon, child fork, and child play mat). Additional WASH activities, mainly borehole construction, CLTS and WASH in health facilities were conducted in those communities with the highest numbers of PLWs. After 18 months, ACF commissioned an external evaluation to document outcomes, challenges, and good practice, using a mixed-methods approach (household survey, key informant interviews, and focus group discussions). A non-intervention community in the same state, Tarmua, received cash distributions but none of the WASH activities, and was surveyed as a comparison group.

Data analysis showed there were significant differences in BabyWASH knowledge, attitudes, and practices between intervention and non-intervention communities: more PLWs believed that drinking water can transmit disease (64.7 per cent versus 51.1 per cent, $p<0.0001$), and that diarrheal disease is caused by unwashed fruit/vegetables, undercooked food, or contamination from soil or animal faeces. More PLWs in intervention communities washed their hands with soap and water (90.4 per cent versus 74.9 per cent, $p<0.0001$), and did this at all five critical times (36.5 per cent versus 21.9 per cent, $p<0.0001$). Reported use of BabyWASH items was high (82.5 per cent used the playmat and 91.3 per cent used child utensils at least once a day), and so was frequency of cleaning these items with soap and water. Children under two (CU2) in Nangere benefited from significantly better caretaker practices than CU2 in Tarmua: more children were breastfed (83.5 per cent versus 67.3 per cent, $p<0.0001$), slept under a mosquito net (67.5 per cent versus 56.6 per cent, $p=0.0001$), or were given zinc supplements (28.8 per cent versus 21.2 per cent, $p=0.0025$). There was no significant difference for exclusive breastfeeding. Respondents from Nangere were also more likely to clean water containers, to do so with soap, to cover all containers with a lid, and to treat their water all the time. Sanitation service levels were highly similar in both communities and the use of child potties was widespread.

In terms of health outcomes, significantly fewer caregivers in BabyWASH intervention areas reported that their children suffered from diarrhoea in the last two weeks (16.7 per cent versus 23.0 per cent, $p=0.0067$). Children in households with unimproved sanitation were more likely to have had a diarrhoea episode, especially if household members practised open defecation. The prevalence of MAM in Tarmua was significantly higher for the entire period of study, whereas prevalence of SAM was initially significantly higher in Nangere compared to Tarmua, but declined over the study period. By the end of the study period, SAM prevalence was found to be significantly lower in Nangere than Tarmua. While the statistical analysis was inconclusive – for example, the BabyWASH approach and specifically handwashing and use of items were not significant predictors of diarrhoea in CU2 – the approach did effectively change health-related practices and might have had an effect on SAM incidence in the entire area.

Recommendations and way forward

There is no silver bullet for integrating WASH with nutrition, and approaches must be context-specific. In countries or areas with (a history of) high malnutrition caseloads, WASH interventions should be designed to maximize their effect on undernutrition, either to prevent it, or to accompany treatment, or both. As such, they should aim to interrupt (multiple) transmission pathways to prevent faecal pathogens in the environment from entering the body and to reduce the risk of other WASH-related diseases impacting the nutritional status (e. g. acute respiratory infections, malaria, helminth infections).

Figure 4.3 shows different spheres around a child's life in which WASH interventions can maximize their effect on undernutrition. These spheres should also be understood within the broader context of an intervention, as well as the diversity and complexity of undernutrition determinants and multiple exposure pathways. In this regard, it is worth highlighting that singular WASH interventions are unlikely to be effective enough in reducing the exposure to faecal pathogens to make an impact on the nutrition status of children, especially in highly contaminated environments. Therefore, a comprehensive package of WASH interventions, tailored to address the local exposure landscape and enteric disease burden, should always be considered.

There is a growing consensus among both researchers and practitioners that contaminated soil, children's hands, food, and objects may be the primary pathways of faecal pathogen ingestion, especially during the first 1,000 days of life, justifying intervening along these pathways using a BabyWASH approach.

There are several common entry points for governments and development actors to take integrated WASH–nutrition action, especially in the areas where both WASH conditions and undernutrition are a concern. These recommendations are applicable to the contexts with disease outbreaks, such as COVID-19, and emergency/conflict situations, and can help shape integrated, multisectoral programming aiming to provide comprehensive solutions to climate change.

Figure 4.3 WASH interventions to maximize effect on the nutritional status of CU5
Source: ACF (2021) WASH 'Nutrition operational note'.

At the strategic level, linking the WASH and nutrition sectors can involve building an integrated strategy, which is produced in a collaborative way and based on a joint multisectoral analysis, planning, and strategic thinking. Several national governments in the Sahel (e.g. Mali, Burkina Faso) are setting the example. If developing an integrated strategy is not feasible, then ensuring that a strategy for one sector includes important crosscutting issues and specific objectives of another sector and identifies opportunities for integration (e.g. 1,000-days window) is the second-best option. This can mean integrating nutrition objectives in all WASH frameworks and strategies from the outset. It can also involve including WASH-related indicators and standards in nutrition and health frameworks and strategies.

Integration at the strategic level should extend to the programmatic level. Programmatic recommendations include:

- Joint situation analysis and planning. Conducting joint assessments by WASH and nutrition technical sectors is more likely to foster a comprehensive understanding of the situation and context-specific needs, and encourage an integrated response.
- Identifying programmatic joint opportunities based on context-specific nutritional needs and priorities as well as areas of common interest (e.g. undernutrition hotspots; 1000-days window of opportunity).
- Geographical co-location of WASH interventions in nutritionally vulnerable areas. The use of relatively low-cost and easy-to-apply mapping techniques to overlay various key indicators to better understand the relationship between WASH conditions and undernutrition rates can also help improve decision-making. Mapping can be used at any geographical level (household, community, district, region) as an assessment, programme design and/or monitoring tool, but primarily, it can help to ensure good geographical concentration of WASH projects in the areas with high prevalence of undernutrition.
- Incorporating WASH and nutrition indicators discussed and chosen jointly in the monitoring, evaluation, accountability and learning (MEAL) framework of integrated projects. Examples of indicators include: percentage of nutritional centres delivering the WASH minimum package; number of children admitted for SAM treatment having received a WASH minimum package of activities (WASH kit with key hygiene messages/behaviours recommended to parents/caregivers, and/or WASH activities at community level); percentage of nutritional centres with residual chlorine measured in the drinking water used for appetite tests.

The WASH'Nutrition strategy (GWC, 2012), initially designed by the west and central Africa WASH regional group in 2012 with the support of many partners, and its five main pillars (Figure 4.4) are especially relevant for humanitarian contexts.

The mother-child dyad = the mother-offspring unit

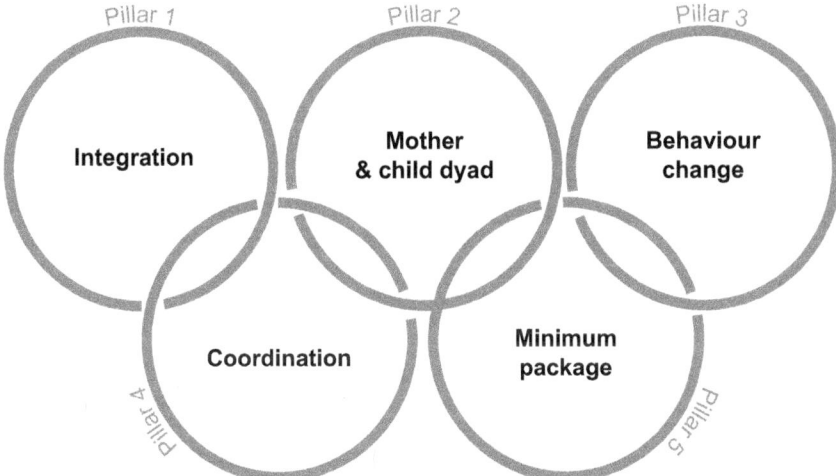

Figure 4.4 WASH nutrition strategy – the five main pillars
Source: ACF (2017b) WASH' Nutrition practical guidebook

Pillar 1 - Integration: improving coordination and enhancing partnerships to ensure the integration of health and nutrition goals in all WASH projects from the start.

Pillar 2 - Mother and child dyad: giving special attention to the mother and child couple in relation to the 1000-days window of opportunity, as the prevention of undernutrition during this period is crucial.

Pillar 3 - Behaviour change: emphasizes the importance of behaviour change, knowing that provision of hardware only (access to water and sanitation facilities) brings little benefit to health if it is not accompanied by suitable hygiene behaviours.

Pillar 4 - Coordination: ensuring proper coordination with other organizations and partners, as well as appropriate choices depending on the specific characteristics of each project.

Pillar 5 - Minimum package: implementing a set of measures needed to ensure that mothers/caretakers and children have access to safe water in sufficient quantities, are provided with adequate sanitation facilities, and can practise good hygiene at home. It contains a combination of WASH service delivery and promotion of good practices, both at the household and at the health facility level.

Note

1. The TISA trial – Senegal, see: <https://clinicaltrials.gov/ct2/show/record/NCT04667767>

References

Action Against Hunger. 2020. COVID-19 impact: the seeds of a future hunger pandemic? Fieldwork insight. <https://www.accioncontraelhambre.org/sites/default/files/documents/rapport-covid-en-mod.pdf>

ACF. 2017a. 'Nutrition causal analysis: Nigeria, Nangere LAG, Yobe state'. <https://www.linknca.org/etude/etat_de_yobe_nangere_lga.htm?lng=en&>

_____. 2017b. '"WASH" nutrition. A practical guidebook on increasing nutritional impact through integration of WASH and nutrition programmes. For practitioners in humanitarian and development contexts'. <https://www.actionagainsthunger.org/publication/2017/01/increasing-nutritional-impact-through-integration-wash-and-nutrition-programmes>

_____. 2015a. 'Who cares about the impact of climate change on hunger and malnutrition? A plea to the international community to ensure food and nutrition security for the most vulnerable in a changing climate'. <https://www.actioncontrelafaim.org/en/publication/who-cares-about-the-impact-of-climate-change-on-hunger-and-malnutrition>

_____. 2015b. 'Nutrition causal analysis guidelines'. Link NCA. <https://linknca.org/methode.htm>

_____. 2014. 'ACF international nutrition security policy. A common multisectoral understanding and approach to address undernutrition'. <https://www.actioncontrelafaim.org/en/publication/acf-international-nutrition-security-policy>

_____. 2021. WASH' nutrition. Compiled by A. Cassuto, in collaboration with WASH'Nutrition experts across the Action Against Hunger network. June. <https://www.actioncontrelafaim.org/wp-content/uploads/2021/10/2021-ACF-WASH-Nutrition-Operational-Note.pdf>

ACF, Concern Worldwide, Norwegian Refugee Council, Oxfam, Save the Children, World Vision. 2018. 'Conflict and hunger. How the UN and member states can help to break the cycle?' <https://www.actionagainsthunger.org/publication/2018/09/conflict-and-hunger-how-un-and-member-states-can-help-break-cycle>

Agustina, R. and T.P. Sari, S. Satroamidjojo, I.M. Bovee-Oudenhoven, E.J. Feskens, F.J. Kok. 2013. 'Association of food-hygiene practices and diarrhoea prevalence among Indonesian young children from low socioeconomic urban areas'. *BMC Public Health*. <http://www.ncbi.nlm.nih.gov/pmc/articles/PMC3813984>

Akseer N. and G. Kandru, E.C. Keats, Z.A. Bhutta. 2020. 'COVID-19 pandemic and mitigation strategies: implications for maternal and child health and nutrition.' *American Journal of Clinical Nutrition*. <https://academic.oup.com/ajcn/article/112/2/251/5860091>

Altmann, M. and C. Altare, N. van der Spek, J.C. Barbiche, J. Dodos, M. Bechir, M. Ait Aissa, P. Kolsteren. 2018 'Effectiveness of a household water, sanitation and hygiene package on an outpatient program for severe acute malnutrition: a pragmatic cluster-randomized controlled trial in Chad'. *The American Journal of Tropical Medicine and Hygiene* 98(4): 1005–12. <http://dx.doi.org/10.4269/ajtmh.17-0699>

Ambadekar N.N. and S.P. Zodpey. 2017. 'Risk factors for severe acute malnutrition in under-five children: a case-control study in a rural part of India'. *Public Health* 142: 136–143. <https://doi.org/10.1016/j.puhe.2016.07.018>

Ayana, A.B. and T.W. Hailemariam, A.S. Melke. 2015. 'Determinants of acute malnutrition among children aged 6–59 months in public hospitals, Oromia region, West Ethiopia: a case–control study'. *BMC Nutrition* 1: 34. <https://doi.org/10.1186/s40795-015-0031-9>

Brown. M.E. and K. Grace, T. Billing, D. Backer. 2021. 'Considering climate and conflict conditions together to improve interventions that prevent child acute malnutrition'. *The Lancet Planetary Health* 5(9): e654-e658. <https://doi.org/10.1016/S2542-5196(21)00197-2>

Carroll, G.J. and S.D. Lama, J.L. Martinez-Brockman, R. Pérez-Escamilla. 2017. 'Evaluation of nutrition interventions in children in conflict zones: a narrative review'. *Advances in Nutrition* 8(5): 770–779. <https://doi.org/10.3945/an.117.016121>

Checkley, W. and R.H. Gilman, R.E. Black, L.D. Epstein, L. Cabrera, C.R. Sterling, et al. 2004. 'Effect of water and sanitation on childhood health in a poor Peruvian peri-urban community'. *The Lancet* 363(9403): 112–118. <https://doi.org/10.1016/S0140-6736(03)15261-0>

Checkley, W. and G. Buckley, R.H. Gilman, A.M. Assis, R.L. Guerrant, S.S. Morris, K. Mølbak, et al. 2008. 'Multi-country analysis of the effects of diarrhoea on childhood stunting'. *International Journal of Epidemiology* 37(4): 816–830. <https://doi.org/10.1093/ije/dyn099>

Contreras J. and M. Islam, A. Mertens, A.J. Pickering, L.H. Kwong, B.F. Arnold, J. Benjamin-Chung, et al. 2021. 'Longitudinal effects of a sanitation intervention on environmental fecal contamination in a cluster-randomized controlled trial in rural Bangladesh'. *Environmental Science & Technology* 55(12): 8169–8179. <https://doi.10.1021/acs.est.1c01114>

Crane, R.J. and K.D. Jones, J.A. Berkley. 2015. 'Environmental enteric dysfunction: an overview'. *Food and Nutrition Bulletin* 36(1): S76–S87. <https://doi.org/10.1177/15648265150361S113>

Cumming, O. and B.F. Arnold, R. Ban, T. Clasen, J. Esteves Mills, M.C. Freeman, B. Gordon, et al. 2019. 'The implications of three major new trials for the effect of water, sanitation and hygiene on childhood diarrhea and stunting: a consensus statement'. *BMC Medicine* 17(1): 173. <https://doi.10.1186/s12916-019-1410-x>

Curtis, V. and W. Schmidt, S. Luby, R. Florez, O. Touré, A. Biran. 2011. 'Hygiene: new hopes, new horizons'. *The Lancet Infectious Diseases* 11(4): 312–321. <https://doi.10.1016/S1473-3099(10)70224-3>

Dewey, K.G. and D.R. Mayers. 2011. 'Early child growth: how do nutrition and infection interact?' *Maternal and Child Nutrition* 7(Suppl 3): 129–42. <http://dx.doi.org/10.1111/j.1740-8709.2011.00357.x>

Diwakar, V. and M. Malcolm, G. Naufal. 2019. 'Violent conflict and breastfeeding: the case of Iraq'. *Conflict and Health* 13(61). <https://doi.org/10.1186/s13031-019-0244-7>

Dodos, J. and C. Altare, M. Bechir, M. Myatt, B. Pedro, F. Bellet, J. Lapegue, J. Peeters, M. Altmann. 2018. 'Individual and household risk factors of severe acute malnutrition among under-five children in Mao, Chad: a matched case-control study'. *Archives of Public Health* 76(35). <https://doi.org/10.1186/s13690-018-0281-5>

Dodos J. and B. Mattern, J. Lapegue, M. Altmann, M.A. Aissa. 2017. 'Relationship between water, sanitation, hygiene, and nutrition: what do Link NCA nutrition causal analyses say?' *Waterlines* 36(4). <https://doi.10.3362/1756-3488.17-00005>

Dominguez, E.I. 2017. BabyWASH and the 1,000 days: a practical package for stunting reduction. Action Against Hunger. <https://www.actionagainsthunger.org/publications/babywash-and-1000-days/>

Doocy, S. and H. Tappis, N. Villeminot, A. Suk, D. Kumar, S. Fazal, S. Pietzsch. 2018. 'Point-of-use water treatment improves recovery rates among children with severe acute malnutrition in Pakistan: results from a site-randomized trial'. *Public Health Nutrition* 21(16): 3080–90. <http://dx.doi.org/10.1017/S1368980018001647>

FAO. 2007. 'Climate change and food security: a framework document'. <https://www.fao.org/3/i0145e/i0145e00.pdf>

Fore, H.F. and Q. Dongyu, D.M. Beasley, T.A. Ghebreyesus. 2020. 'Child malnutrition and COVID-19: the time to act is now'. *The Lancet* 396(10250): 517–518. <https://doi.org/10.1016/S0140-6736(20)31648-2>

GEOECO, ACF, ASOS. 2020. 'Le projet hydronut. Amélioration du système d'alerte précoce et renforcement de la résilience des populations fragiles face aux crises nutritionnelles et sanitaires liées au changement climatique au Grand Sud de Madagascar'. <https://fondation.actioncontrelafaim.org/projets/le-projet-hydronut>

Ghattas H. and A.J. Sassine, K. Seyfert, M. Nord, N.R. Sahyoun. 2014. 'Food insecurity among Iraqi refugees living in Lebanon, 10 years after the invasion of Iraq: data from a household survey'. *British Journal of Nutrition* 112: 70–9.

Giné-Garriga, R. and A. Delepiere, R. Ward, J. Alvarez-Sala, I. Alvarez-Murillo, V. Mariezcurrena, H. Göransson Sandberg, P. Saikia, P. Avello et al. 2021. 'COVID-19 water, sanitation, and hygiene response: review of measures and initiatives adopted by governments, regulators, utilities, and other stakeholders in 84 countries'. *Science of the Total Environment* 795. <https://doi.org/10.1016/j.scitotenv.2021.148789>

Gizaw, Z. and A. Worku. 2019. 'Effects of single and combined water, sanitation and hygiene (WASH) interventions on nutritional status of children: a systematic review and meta-analysis'. *Italian Journal of Pediatrics* 45(1): 77. <https://doi.org/10.1186/s13052-019-0666-2>

Global Nutrition Report (GNR). 2021. <https://globalnutritionreport.org/reports/2021-global-nutrition-report>

GWC, 2012. '"WASH in Nut" strategy'. <https://www.humanitarianresponse.info/en/operations/west-and-central-africa/document/wash-nut-strategy>

Headey, D. and R. Heidkamp, S. Osendarp, M. Ruel, N. Scott, R. Black, M. Shekar, H. Bouis et al. 2020. 'Impacts of COVID-19 on childhood malnutrition and nutrition-related mortality'. *The Lancet*. 396(10250): 519–521. <https://doi.org/10.1016/S0140-6736(20)31647-0>

Hsiang, S. and K. Meng, M. Cane. 2011. 'Civil conflicts are associated with the global climate'. *Nature* 476: 438–441. <https://doi.org/10.1038/nature10311>

IDA. 2021. 'Conflict and fragility'. <http://ida.worldbank.org/theme/conflict-and-fragility>

Kwong, L.H. and A. Ercumen, A.J. Pickering, J.E. Arsenault, M. Islam, S.M. Parvez, L. Unicomb et al. 2020. 'Ingestion of fecal bacteria along multiple pathways by young children in rural Bangladesh participating in a cluster-randomized trial of water, sanitation, and hygiene interventions (WASH benefits)'. *Environmental Science & Technology* 54(21): 13828–13838. <https://doi.10.1021/acs.est.0c02606>

Laborde, D. and C. Smaller, J. Porciello. 'What would it cost to avert the COVID-19 hunger crisis?' Cornell University. <https://hdl.handle.net/1813/70172>

Lin, A. and B.F. Arnold, S. Afreen, R. Goto, T. Huda, R. Haque, R. Raqib, et al. 2013. 'Household environmental conditions are associated with enteropathy and impaired growth in rural Bangladesh.' *The American Journal of Tropical Medicine and Hygiene* 89(1): 130–137. <https://doi.org/10.4269/ajtmh.12-0629>

Loewenberg, S. 2015. 'Conflicts worsen global hunger crisis'. *The Lancet* 386 (10005): 1719–1721. <https://doi.org/10.1016/S0140-6736(15)00734-5>

Misra, A.K. 2014. 'Climate change and challenges of water and food security'. *International Journal of Sustainable Built Environment* 3(1): 153–165. <https://doi.org/10.1016/j.ijsbe.2014.04.006>

Ngure, F.M. and B.M. Reid, J.H. Humphrey, M.N. Mbuya, G. Pelto, R.J. StoltzfusJ. 2014. 'Water, sanitation, and hygiene (WASH), environmental enteropathy, nutrition, and early child development: making the links'. *Annals of the New York Academy of Sciences* 1308: 118–128. <https://doi.org/10.1111/nyas.12330>

Okotch, K., Gadir, E. Elsimat, A., Gonzalez, L., Heeger, J. and Dodos, J. 2020. <file:///C:/Users/M.Snel/Downloads/10_3362_1756_3488_19_00014.pdf>

OCHA. 2021. 'South Sudan inter-agency response update'. <https://reliefweb.int/sites/reliefweb.int/files/resources/south_sudan_response_achievements.pdf>

Oldenburg, C.E. and P.J. Guerin, F. Berthé, R.F. Grais, S. Isanaka. 2018. 'Malaria and nutritional status among children with severe acute malnutrition in Niger: a prospective cohort study'. *Clinical Infectious Diseases* 67(7): 1027–1034. <https://doi.org/10.1093/cid/ciy207>

Osendarp, S. and J.K. Akuoku, R.E. Black, D. Headey, M. Ruel, N. Scott, M. Shekar et al. 2021. 'The COVID-19 crisis will exacerbate maternal and child undernutrition and child mortality in low- and middle-income countries'. *Nature Food* 2: 476–484. <https://doi.org/10.1038/s43016-021-00319-4>

Petri, W.A. and M. Miller, H.J. Binder, M.M. Levine, R. Dillingham, R.L. Guerrant. 'Enteric infections, diarrhea, and their impact on function and development'. *Journal of Clinical Investigation* 118(4): 1277–90.

Pickering, H.D. and C. Lopez, M. Coulibaly, M.L. Alzua. 2015. 'Effect of a community-led sanitation intervention on child diarrhoea and child growth in rural Mali: a cluster-randomised controlled trial'. *The Lancet Global Health* 3(11): e701-e711. <https://doi.org/10.1016/S2214-109X(15)00144-8>

Quattri, M. and S. Smets. 2014. 'Lack of community-level improved sanitation causes stunting in rural villages of Lao PDR and Vietnam'. Loughborough University. Conference contribution. <https://hdl.handle.net/2134/31106>

Ravi, S. and R. Singh. 2016. 'Nutrition in India: targeting the first 1,000 days of a child's life'. Policy brief. <https://www.brookings.edu/wp-content/uploads/2016/10/20161023_policybrief_2.pdf>

Spears, D. 2012. *Effects of rural sanitation on infant mortality and human capital: Evidence from india's total sanitation campaign.* Princeton University, USA. <https://www.susana.org/en/knowledge-hub/resources-and-publications/library/details/1767#>

Stobaugh, H.C. and A.R. Patlán-Hernández, M. José, J. Lapègue, A. Angioletti, D. Pantchova, M.L. De Rubeis et al. 2020. 'Impacts of WASH on acute malnutrition: from available scientific evidence to informed action'. Action Against Hunger. <http://research4action.org/wp-content/uploads/2020/09/GB-R4ACT-Final-Report-V092020.pdf>

Stoler, J. and W.E. Jepson, A. Wutich. 2020. 'Beyond handwashing: water insecurity undermines COVID-19 response in developing areas'. *Journal of Global Health* 10: 10355. <https:// doi.org/10.7189/jogh.10.010355>

The World Bank. 2022. 'Health and WASH services reaching most vulnerable yemenis despite difficult context'. <https://www.worldbank.org/en/country/yemen/brief/health-and-wash-services-reaching-most-vulnerable-yemenis-despite-difficult-context>

_____. 2021. The World Bank and Nutrition. Overview. [Press release] <https://www.worldbank.org/en/topic/nutrition/overview#1>

_____. 2012. 'Turn down the heat: why a +4°C warmer world must be avoided. A report for the World Bank by the Potsdam Institute for Climate Impact Research and Climate Analytics'. Washington, DC: The World Bank

_____. 2005. 'Repositioning nutrition as central to development'. <https://doi.org/10.1596/978-0-8213-6399-7>

UNICEF. 2021. 'Water under fire volume 3: attacks on water and sanitation services in armed conflict and the impacts on children'. <https://www.unicef.org/media/98976/file/Water%20Under%20Fire%20%20Volume3.pdf>

_____. 2020a. 'UNICEF conceptual framework on the determinants of maternal and child nutrition, 2020. A framework for the prevention of malnutrition in all its forms'. <https://www.unicef.org/media/91741/file/UNICEF-Nutrition-Strategy-2020-2030-Brief.pdf>

_____. 2020b. Situation tracking for COVID-19 socio-economic impacts. <https://data.unicef.org/resources/rapid-situation-tracking-covid-19-socioeconomic-impacts-data-viz>

_____. 2017. 'Nearly 1.4 million children at imminent risk of death as famine looms in Nigeria, Somalia, South Sudan and Yemen'. <https://www.unicef.org/turkey/en/press-releases/nearly-14-million-children-imminent-risk-death-famine-looms-nigeria-so malia-south>

_____. 2016a. 'Collecting water is often a colossal waste of time for women and girls'. [press release] <https://www.unicef.org/press-releases/unicef-collecting-water-often-colossal-waste-time-women-and-girls>

_____. 2016b. 'Children on the brink: the impact of violence and conflict on Yemen and its children'. <https://www.unicef.org/yemen/reports/children-brink>

UNICEF Nigeria. 2021. 'Nutrition programme'. <https://www.unicef.org/nigeria/nutrition>

UNICEF and WHO. 2021. 'State of the world's hand hygiene: a global call to action to make hand hygiene a priority in policy and practice'. New York: UNICEF.

UN Women. 2022. 'Explainer: how gender inequality and climate change are interconnected'. 28 February. <https://www.unwomen.org/en/news-stories/explainer/2022/02/explainer-how-gender-inequality-and-climate-change-are-interconnected>

WHO. 2020. 'Maintaining essential health services: operational guidance for the COVID-19 context: interim guidance'. 1 June. Geneva: WHO. <https://www.who.int/publications/i/item/WHO-2019-nCoV-essential_health_services-2020.2>

———. 2017. 'Diphtheria – Yemen'. Disease outbreak news. <https://www.who.int/emergencies/disease-outbreak-news/item/22-december-2017-diphtheria-yemen-en>

Wolf, J. and R. Johnston, P.R. Hunter, B. Gordon, K. Medlicott, A. Prüss-Ustün. 2019. 'A faecal contamination index for interpreting heterogeneous diarrhoea impacts of water, sanitation and hygiene interventions and overall, regional and country estimates of community sanitation coverage with a focus on low- and middle-income countries'. *International Journal of Hygiene and Environmental Health* 222(2): 270–282. <https://doi.10.1016/j.ijheh.2018.11.005>

Young, H. and A. Marshak, A. Venkat. 2019. 'Twin peaks: the seasonality of acute malnutrition, conflict, and environmental factors'. <https://fic.tufts.edu/publication-item/twin-peaks-the-seasonality-of-acute-malnutrition-conflict-and-environmental-factors>

CHAPTER 5
Integrated WASH and shelter

Susannah Webb

Introduction

> *Improved shelter conditions can save lives, reduce disease, increase the quality of people's lives, help mitigate the impact of climate change ... and ... contribute to the achievement of the sustainable development goals. (GWC coordinator, Global Shelter Cluster annual meeting 2020)*

After making the above statement at the Global Shelter Cluster's (GSC) annual meeting in October 2020,[1] the Global Health Cluster (GHC) coordinator stressed the need for greater collaboration between WASH actors to improve wellbeing outcomes for people affected by humanitarian crises. The session's overall message was that adequate housing is not just a human right in and of itself, it also facilitates the achievement of many other human rights, including access to health, water, and sanitation and education. The GWC coordinator echoed this call for greater sectoral coordination at the GSC's open session on 'Integrated shelter and WASH' in June 2021.[2] Action point 3.4 of the WASH sector's 2020–2025 road map on multisectoral collaboration was brought to the attention of the attending group of mainly shelter and settlements[3] practitioners. This led to discussion of the opportunities for increased integration and collaboration between WASH and shelter actors. In this high-level meeting, it was clear that shelter and WASH clusters[4] are positive, in principle, about exploring further integration. In September 2022, both clusters came together in an online learning event, Working Together, to discuss how integrated working can benefit wellbeing and health for people living through crises (Webb, 2022).

What does integration mean?

There is already alignment between both clusters' ambitions to work towards sustainable outcomes and engage with the humanitarian–development–peace nexus whilst continuing to respond to global challenges at scale and being mindful of the need to mainstream gender, protection, the environment, and other cross-cutting issues. So why is shelter and WASH integration not routine in humanitarian settings? What does 'integration' really mean for both sectors? Snel and Sorensen (2021) define integrated WASH as programming that 'focuses on the nexus between WASH and nutrition, education, livelihoods, child protection, agriculture and food security'. Shelter is not listed as a sector relevant to an approach that 'enables more people to gain access to improved services'. This seems wrong-headed; perhaps the wider impact of shelter assistance is not recognized by WASH and other humanitarian actors or taken for granted?

Despite both WASH and shelter clusters agreeing with the principle of greater integration, there is probably more appetite for, and experience with, 'complementary' rather than truly 'integrated' ways of working. Therefore, further investigation into the possibilities of shelter/WASH integration at the global cluster level as well as at the levels of policymakers within INGOs, programme managers and implementers within INGOs and NGOs, and other stakeholders is timely. The donors who sanction and finance particular humanitarian interventions are crucial stakeholders. Integration already happens – some examples are examined below – and it is likely that there is scope for doing more while also ensuring that the technical expertise of each sector is not compromised. While the Venn diagram of shelter and WASH needs and activities has commonalities and interesting intersections, there are also significant differences between the sectors' programming objectives, ways of working, and operational teams. These need greater mutual understanding. At the core of any further integration must be the aim of making beneficial changes for the affected communities recovering after crises.

What are the gaps?

During and after humanitarian crises, affected populations are frequently forced to live in inadequate housing, without safe and dignified access to sanitation and in settings with compromised environmental health. If we want to understand reasons for inadequacies in living conditions following disasters and conflict-related displacement, and answer basic questions such as 'why are there shelters without latrines?', we need to understand better whether some answers lie in better integration between shelter and WASH. At the heart of this exploration of integration among these two sectors is the shared desire to achieve long-term wellbeing outcomes. People's living conditions during displacement have a comparable (or greater) impact on their physical and mental wellbeing as the initial trigger of that crisis or disaster (Webb and Weinstein Sheffield, 2021); shelter and WASH together can have a huge impact on living conditions in humanitarian settings and beyond. In addition, the two sectors can identify 'easy wins' for the short and medium term.

Adequate housing, shelter, and WASH

There are many different types of shelter assistance provided by a range of international, national, and local NGOs in a wide spectrum of emergency, transitional, and protracted situations, with 17.5 million people reached, in responses where a cluster or cluster-like mechanism was active in 2021

(GSC, 2021b) First-line Shelter emergency responses commonly consist of distributions of tarpaulins/tents and other non-food items (NFIs). Some responses to disaster and displacement result in tented camps, which may last for many years, even decades, transitioning into informal or formal permanent settlements. Increasingly, shelter responses also consist of unconditional or conditional cash/vouchers, materials with technical assistance/training, rental support, or other indirect assistance with accommodation.[5] Increasing numbers of displaced people are in urban settings, often in multi-household and/or rented accommodation. Like the WASH and other sectors, the shelter sector is grappling with how to bridge the emergency to development nexus. Perhaps this is encapsulated in the challenges of managing exit strategies after humanitarian engagement, operating in protracted crises, and enabling a transition from 'shelter' to 'housing' (see, for example, Bamforth and Urquia, 2018).[6] Similarly, the WASH sector faces challenges in transitioning from humanitarian action to sustainable long-term water and sanitation provision (Snel and Sorensen, 2021). Several conditions must be met before particular forms of shelter can be considered to constitute 'adequate housing', according to the following criteria specified in UN Habitat's Right to Adequate Housing fact sheet (UN Habitat, 2009):

- security of tenure;
- availability of services;
- materials;
- facilities and infrastructure;
- affordability;
- habitability;
- accessibility;
- cultural adequacy.

Out of these, facilities and infrastructure and habitability are particularly pertinent to shelter, WASH and health, because they focus on aspects such as safe drinking water, adequate sanitation, energy provision, and protection against threats to health and structural hazards, among others. Clearly, meeting these criteria in humanitarian settings is challenging, yet it must be the goal of governments and other actors, such as humanitarian agencies.

The aspects of adequate housing that relate most closely to the expertise of shelter and WASH actors (water and sanitation facilities and habitability) and contribute to health and psychosocial wellbeing are the focus of this chapter, which also touches on wider aspects of environmental health (Prüss-Üstün et al, 2016).

WASH and shelter's contributions to health and wellbeing

A focus on physical and mental health and wellbeing outcomes in humanitarian assistance makes the links between shelter and WASH clear and, indeed, impossible to ignore. Applying an understanding of environmental health, and the points of connection between health, sheltering, and WASH. For example, risks in humanitarian contexts such as overcrowding and inadequate sanitation contribute to communicable and non-communicable diseases. In the context of increasing displacement and both conflict and disaster-related shelter needs (OCHA, 2022)[7], both shelter and WASH sectors should consider how incorporating household- and settlement-level environmental health and wellbeing outcomes into shared objectives can effectively and efficiently address these needs. Strategies that centre on physical and mental health and wellbeing outcomes can start to bridge emergency response, early recovery, and indeed contribute to the sustainable development goals (SDGs).

Public health has always been at the heart of humanitarian WASH activities. In recent years, Shelter actors have become more aware of the impact of people's shelters, or (albeit temporary) homes on their health. Indeed, recent research has led to greater understanding of the connections between humanitarian sheltering activities and health (Webb et al, 2020; Weinstein Sheffield and Webb, 2021), and health is one of the current strategic priorities of the GSC (GSC, 2018).

Having a safe and secure home is key to post-crisis recovery; there is a growing body of literature and understanding about the 'wider impacts' of shelter assistance (Interaction, 2020).

> *The primary objectives of shelter and settlements assistance are to safeguard the health, security, privacy and dignity of families and communities affected by crises. Beyond lifesaving, shelter and settlements assistance is fundamental in rebuilding the psychological, social, livelihood and physical components of life. (GSC, 2021a)*

Adequate living conditions for displaced populations, in conjunction with other public health interventions, can help to protect people from preventable illnesses. Respiratory infections, like pneumonia and tuberculosis; water- and vector-borne diseases, like cholera, diarrhoea, and malaria; and non-communicable cardiovascular conditions are all related to inadequate living conditions. These include overcrowding, exposure to indoor and outdoor air pollution, temperature extremes, and inadequate water and sanitation. Protection from disease vectors, decent air quality, effective waste management, access to clean water, washing facilities, and household toilets are integral to healthy homes. There is increasing recognition within the GSC and its partner organizations of the role of safe and healthy living conditions for mental health and wellbeing. Daily stressors related to the burdens of disease, inadequate and unsafe toilets and washing facilities, and the associated risks of increased gender-based violence are considerable (Webb and Weinstein Sheffield, 2021). Healthy homes and communities contribute to many SDGs, including those related to education and the environment.

One house, one toilet: an achievable aim?

SDG 6.2 is to 'achieve access to adequate and equitable sanitation and hygiene for all and end open defecation' by 2030. In 2020, just over half (54 per cent) of the world's population had access to safely managed sanitation. Around six per cent do not have any sanitation facilities at all (Ritchie and Roser, 2021). Access to household toilets was at a low level globally 30 years ago, but there has been considerable progress through the Millennium Development Goals, now the SDGs (Ritchie and Roser, 2020). Household norms and expectations have, rightly, changed. Meeting the ambition of household latrines in humanitarian settings requires both shelter and WASH specialist expertise, including expertise in construction safety, to operate in a more coordinated, and ideally integrated, way.

The provision of latrines with household accommodation should ideally become the norm in humanitarian programming (whilst understandably this is rarely a priority in the emergency phase of a rapid-onset crisis). This relates closely to menstrual hygiene management (MHM), which has become an integral component of WASH in recent years and has a direct impact on women and girls' wellbeing. The acceptable level of 'adequate' provision varies considerably between countries and regions; there are stark differences in provision of household latrines between, for example, humanitarian settings in the Middle East and sub-Saharan Africa.

Refugee camps in Jordan demonstrate how shelter and WASH actors can work together to improve provision of sanitation over time. By 2018, most shelters in Zaatari camp had access to their own water tank (filled every two or three days from a piped water supply) and some had a household toilet instead of communal sanitation facilities. In informal tented 'camps' in Lebanon, which have policy restrictions on permanent construction, improvements over time to household toilets served by regular tank desludging demonstrate what is possible even within a densely built environment. Necessary modifications to shelters do require careful attention to construction site safety, and therefore resources must be allocated for technical assistance that can guide adherence to standards.

These challenges should not preclude household-level toilets or even assisted self-build latrines[8] and other community-based programming, if training and awareness-raising are built into those programmes to ensure community responsibility and clear accountability. In fact, there is a great opportunity, especially when promoting self-recovery (GSC, 2022) approaches to shelter assistance, to see the shelter/house and latrine/toilet as a package. The affected population engaging in self-recovery programming in partnership with humanitarian actors need the means to build toilets, and this ambition necessarily cuts across sectors, clusters, and donors.

'One house, one toilet', which has the potential to have positive physical and mental health outcomes for households and communities, requires a change in mindset and attitude towards public health risk by the WASH sector in particular. If women and girls, especially, are not using communal latrines in mass displacement settlements due to the significant cultural and safety barriers they face, ways must be found to enable the provision of more acceptable facilities. A new focus on how to deal with faecal sludge management at household level is required, requiring engagement with households and communities for the management of public health risks.

How can integrated, multisectoral programming succeed?

WASH knowledge and expertise at settlement and household level is integral to the ambition of facilitating better, safer, dignified and healthier homes during and following humanitarian crises (Webb, 2022). Within the shelter sector, it is already recognized that integrated programming is one of the 'essentials' of good programming. Of the nearly 300 shelter projects included in the biannual collection of case studies produced by the International Organization for Migration (IOM) on behalf of the GSC, many report a degree of integration with other sectors, including WASH, and this is more likely to be presented as a strength than a weakness (see, for example GSC, 2021b). The GSC (2021a) distils the 12 key recurring messages learnt from this significant bank of case studies and concludes that shelter projects must explore the opportunities that can arise from integrated support, including integration with WASH. So why is this not routine?

Barriers to integrated WASH/shelter programming

Barriers to effective integrated WASH and shelter projects and programmes exist at a variety of levels, and have implications for strategic planning within organizations, future funding applications, and project set up and closure. Mapping these barriers is the first stage of addressing them. Many of them are structural, relating to the 'humanitarian architecture' and coordination system at different stages of programme and project cycles. Others are related more to individuals and organizational structures within humanitarian agencies.

Priorities at different phases of emergency responses
The biggest humanitarian needs and interventions do not necessarily occur at the same time or place. Shelter interventions, especially distributions of lifesaving tarpaulins and NFIs and the creation of camps are, of necessity, implemented at the first stage of an emergency. Funding and implementation of longer-term (transitional and recovery) shelter projects is less common. In contrast, the provision and ongoing maintenance of safe water supplies, community-level sanitation, and sewage works require longer-term engagement by WASH actors, in partnership with local government actors in certain settings.

> *Shelter is often done in one hit. WASH is continuous. (Shelter practitioner)*

Sector-specific language and terminology
The language used by the different sectors can be a barrier to integration; the meanings and use of terms such as 'settlement' and 'area-based' are not universal within the humanitarian sector, which often remains removed from the language of 'development'.

> *Terminology such as 'settlement approach' can over-complicate and get in the way. It's what many local level NGOs and CSOs do anyway – the private sector has to deal with the big picture routinely. Humanitarians are behind the curve. (Senior humanitarian practitioner with both shelter and WASH experience)*

Gaps and blurred boundaries between siloed sectors
Whilst the siloed nature of the humanitarian architecture is often cited as a barrier to integrated working, the precise location of sector 'boundaries' can also be unclear, leading to overlaps, gaps, and inefficiencies in responses. For example, there is a lack of clarity on which sector 'owns' issues/activities such as surface water drainage, vector control at settlement and household level, and cooking, fuel, and related indoor air quality. Household items such as stoves and hand-washing stations are not firmly related to specific sectors yet are relevant to several. Such confusion leads to inefficiencies in interventions and in community and household messaging: one senior shelter technical advisor reported that 'stoves and kitchen kits are generally under the shelter "portfolio" – yet boiling as a household-level water purification activity is part of WASH. We need the skills our WASH colleagues, particularly hygiene promoters, have'.

Household-level sanitation and other characteristics of shelters impacting health are additional gaps/blurred areas. The COVID-19 pandemic highlighted that the four walls of people's houses/shelters were the primary source of protection against COVID, but also a source of other concerns and risks, such as overcrowding and gender-based violence, exacerbated for many in prolonged enforced lockdowns. Humanitarian and development actors are now more aware of the need for multisectoral efforts to fight communicable and non-communicable diseases and risks to mental health through more attention to the built environment and the nature of programming (see, for example, Webb and Weinstein Sheffield, 2021; Webb, 2022).

Agency specialisms/ institutional internal silos
Different organizational barriers to integrated programming need to be navigated internally at head office, country office, and partner organizations.

- Head office/policy level: humanitarian agencies tend to specialize in a particular sector or sectors, which can be a barrier to integrated programming.

  > *To compete for 'market share', NGOs specialize but this does not necessarily work in responses where operations are spread over large*

areas and multiple NGOS are competing. Is anyone competent to deliver in all sectors? If not, how is this coordinated? (Humanitarian practitioner with shelter and WASH experience)

There are several contrasting ways that humanitarian organizations are structured internally, with associated pros and cons; some specialize in both WASH and shelter, either separately or in more integrated ways. Organizations with WASH and shelter as core competencies, like the Norwegian Refugee Council and CARE International, can, at least theoretically, work together 'in-house', yet this may not happen routinely. At ICRC, construction, shelter, and water are in one 'block', making integrated working more possible or harmonious. In some large agencies, such as the IFRC, the operational plans group WASH and health together, leaving shelter in a separate structure. This was also the case at UNHCR, which now structures WASH alongside shelter in their headquarter advisory structure, rather than with health. Save the Children International has technical advisors mandated to oversee the separate shelter and WASH sectors under the 'construction' umbrella, which allows a certain level of integration.

Individual, team, and senior management structures and relationships can control whether lines of communication are open and effective between WASH and shelter teams at global and regional levels. There may be few opportunities for separate departments to share ideas. Integrated programme development and advocacy at head office (as well as field level) can be restricted by the need to identify colleagues with relevant experience across both shelter and WASH portfolios. There are certainly concerns about 'merging' teams – one senior shelter advisor explained that '[i]t is extremely hard to find colleagues with expertise that goes across the wide range of activities, themes, and modalities that a full shelter and full WASH portfolio have. Merged sectors or core competencies work better during emergencies or first line responses, but innovation and more sophisticated programming might be compromised'.

- Country office specialisms/experience: within INGOs, specific country offices tend to specialize in particular sectoral responses due to a combination of the prevalent types of disaster in a region (for example recurrent tropical storms affecting Pacific islands mean that there is expertise in shelter responses but less experience with WASH) and the experience of individuals within those offices. This is self-perpetuating: once an office or humanitarian team has experience in a certain type or sector of response, they are likely to apply for funding for similar projects in the future. There are sometimes perceptions about the ease or cost of certain types of response (for example that shelter interventions are expensive) that are barriers to those individuals or teams launching activities in an unfamiliar territory. The humanitarian programme

managers at the top of the advisory ladder at a country office level tend to have either a shelter or a WASH background and consequently have limited knowledge about the other sector.
- Team make-up: both shelter and WASH have technical and 'soft' components that can be both useful and problematic for integrated responses, and teams may struggle to include the balance of expertise needed for successful integrated programmes. Many teams lack expertise that combine shelter and WASH experience/technical knowledge. There has been a gradual expansion of sectors' components, which can put pressure on team members. For example, WASH hygiene promoters can be expected to give advice on latrine construction in the field. Some WASH technical experts and engineers have no training on design. Shelter now has a significant component of housing, land, and property (HLP) interventions, and a shelter response may well consist of rental support and/or advocacy rather than reconstruction. This breadth of specialist capabilities has implications for existing teams, even without agencies attempting to further integrate 'traditional' shelter and WASH components.

Hardware-based activities, such as construction or installation of infrastructure, often hold a higher value within agencies than 'soft' activities, such as community engagement and information sharing, and are consequently awarded additional attention, resources, and appreciation. A senior shelter advisor of one INGO, which systematically advocates for access to latrines at household level, highlighted that shelter teams are perceived as the constructors or engineers of the agency. Capacity-building is necessary to bolster the 'soft' components of project design and implementation in order to be able to promote and model further integration.

Community mobilization and hygiene promotion need to be valued as highly as the other technical aspects of programmes and therefore included into project design (theory of change, indicators, IEC resources, budgets, and HR resources). (Senior shelter advisor)

Donors
People do not live in sectoral silos, yet funding for humanitarian (and development) activities are frequently siloed, which feeds through into proposal writing and programme design. This can lead to decidedly sub-optimal outcomes for public health, such as this example observed recently in central Africa:

The transitional shelters had no household-level or community-level latrines included because it wasn't included in the [donor] design and [the donor] didn't like that, as an issue. The country office probably didn't have the capacity to be able to say, 'actually, we need to have household-level or community-level latrines included'. (Senior shelter advisor)

118 ADDRESSING CONFLICT, COVID-19, AND CLIMATE CHANGE

Donors' and agencies' branding can be a barrier to 'un-siloing' even NFI responses. Donors' attitudes towards multisectoral proposals vary. Whilst donors may encourage integrated activities in their guidance, the practical reality of constructing proposals linked to two sectors is challenging. Perhaps there are opportunities for proposals that are multisectoral, yet a lack of confidence from overstretched practitioners that these will be accepted may prevent busy practitioners from attempting this.

Box 5.1 Case study: Challenges of integrated shelter and WASH proposal-writing in Malawi

Catholic Relief Services (CRS)

Acknowledgment: Jamie Richardson

CRS's Homes and Communities programme in Malawi aims for holistic post-flood responses in contexts of recurrent seasonal flooding and endemic poverty. Programming, using a self-recovery approach, aims to give equal weight to safety and health considerations of post-disaster rebuilding, with objectives of long-term health and wellbeing outcomes. Programming therefore requires integration of WASH and shelter expertise to advise and support householders recovering their homes after flooding.

CRS also aims to support communities to build resilience to future disasters. As part of the programme, CRS is developing a builders' training curriculum that incorporates 'healthy housing' designs, materials, and techniques as well as those related to safe flood- and storm-resilient construction. These housing elements may include insect mesh at windows, improved flooring, and household latrines, as well as raised plinths to protect from flooding. Advice and information on maintenance are also included in messaging for householders.

The country programme team, supported by senior shelter advisors from the global programme, are committed to integrating latrine provision into their designs for affordable post-disaster reconstruction. However, they face barriers to this when applying for funding from some donors for projects focused on recovery housing, for example in the aftermath of cyclones Idai in 2019 and Ana in 2022. Donor requirements can add considerable burdens and costs to proposals when guidance on both shelter and WASH elements of proposed projects need to be followed.

CRS welcomes integrated approaches to achieve 'healthy home' outcomes, yet the humanitarian architecture and donors' sectoral boundaries can be cumbersome and costly, impacting the number of households supported. Despite donors and sectors encouraging coordination and integration, donors can simultaneously create obstacles to that, especially as agencies try to achieve cost-effective and efficient responses. If there was wider donor and sector recognition that adequate housing should for example, by default, include household sanitation, then integrated programming would be easier and more cost-effective.

If we said that basic household sanitation is integrated into a shelter, then we should not have to add WASH as a sector, as it is in there already. There will of course be times when there are WASH-focused project activities, but many aspects of healthy design should be integrated as a default. (Jamie Richardson)

The pressure of 'cross-cutting' issues

The humanitarian system has many demands for the integration of cross-cutting issues. Asking individuals, agencies, and clusters to consider further integration and operational change can be unwelcome.

> *The pressure to integrate cross-cutting issues (gender, disability, protection…) means that the time and capacity that would be needed to take a step back and plan for inter-sector programming is hard to come by. Getting beyond positive noises at cluster annual meetings will be challenging. (Shelter practitioner)*

Coordination pressures
Shelter and WASH actors do not often sit down together, at least in the early phases of cluster activation and responses. It is already difficult for cluster coordinator multisector meetings to be anything more than basic information exchange. Only occasionally, and often linked to individual experience and personal connections, can bi- or tri-sector plans be made. Whilst there is often agency willingness in principle to plan shelter/WASH integrated activities, this is much harder to translate into responses due to system complexities and the burden and chaos of crisis situations.

Camp management, through the CCCM cluster, is the strongest coordination mechanism at the 'settlement' level, but it is not relevant in many responses. Yet many site- or settlement-level considerations for both shelter and WASH are also of relevance to health, protection, and other actors: site selection and planning are important for the achievement of public health objectives such as the prevention of disease outbreaks; sites prone to flooding can expose people to injury or death and contribute to asset loss; sites with poorly located communal toilets may exacerbate protection risks, such as gender-based violence, or create the risk of physical injury if water delivery trucks and pedestrians are not well separated.

Politics: emergency shelter and 'house building'
In many crisis settings, including in protracted displacement contexts related to the ongoing Syrian conflict, there are additional significant barriers to the creation of adequate living conditions. As explored through the case study in Northwest Syria (see box 5.2), political considerations make it hard for any humanitarian organization to implement interventions that can be seen as promoting permanent housing with the WASH infrastructure that this entails. Especially in conflict contexts, access to land is fundamental for lifesaving shelter and water. However, WASH and shelter sectors approach the need for land in different ways, necessitating dealing with different authorities and ministries, using different contractors with different timescales and priorities of interventions. There are also implications for HLP issues connected to restrictions by local authorities regarding the excavation and construction necessary for latrines. These are perceived to be more permanent than tents, which are therefore more easily tolerated. For example, in Tigray in 2021, tents and tarpaulins were deployed by shelter actors in rapid interventions to people displaced by escalating conflict. Building water infrastructure using boreholes, which can alter relationships with other land users, such as herders, takes longer and requires different interactions with landowners by WASH

specialists. These issues therefore require due diligence and advocacy within often politically challenging contexts.

Lack of guidance for shelter/WASH integration
The lack of guidance for integrated programming, for example the inclusion of toilets in transitional and recovery dwellings, stems in part from a historical legacy and Sphere's emergency focus. The Sphere Standards indicators, for example, still speak mainly about communal toilets: 'Ratio of shared toilets: Minimum 1 per 20 people, Distance between dwelling and shared toilet: Maximum 50 metres' (Sphere Association, 2018). While Sphere indicators are intended for the immediate crisis, there are no follow-up indicators for the longer term, for shelter at least. With so many people living in protracted settings, either in camps or in urban areas, updated guidance is needed. Working towards the SDGs under national systems, rather than towards humanitarian indicators, should be the focus where post-crisis settlements remain.

Different delivery modalities of WASH and shelter activities
Shelter and WASH typically operate through very different modalities and have a contrasting interface with households. As a generalization, WASH operates through service providers/contractors to deliver water supplies, sanitation, and solid waste management via boreholes, water trucking, desludging, and so on. Planning and delivery are more likely to be executed at settlement level and require close involvement with municipalities. Shelter actors are more likely to operate at the household level, particularly in camp settings, where shelter is provided at a household level and latrines on a much more communal basis. Some organizations have found it hard to shake this inheritance, especially if they are more focused on short-term responses. The recent emphasis on self-recovery approaches within the shelter sector has also necessitated working with families and builders for technical support and training. What is the equivalent for WASH?

Even when both operate at household level, shelter and WASH teams often work through different community committees and focal points. Consequently, for households, it can be confusing and hard to access the assistance they need. Indicators used for programme and project monitoring and evaluation are commonly output-related and therefore singular to sectors. Similarly, communications and complaints mechanisms are often separated by sector.

Although both shelter and WASH sectors conduct distributions of NFIs, these tend to be sector-specific NFI packages with sector-specific targeting and reporting requirements. This is a barrier to more efficient and user-friendly joint distributions or even multisector packages. One practitioner explained that, in a long-term response in Somalia, top-up NFI distributions could usefully include tarpaulins, which householders find invaluable for maintaining and upgrading their shelters. Tarpaulins can also be used to enclose latrines and showering areas and help to eliminate the accumulation of stagnant water and associated reproduction of disease vectors. However, according to one donor's rules, plastic sheeting had to be removed from the emergency shelter-NFI package, unless it was included in a full shelter programme, with messaging on its correct use.

Operationalizing integrated shelter/WASH programming

There is clearly a need to be realistic regarding shelter/WASH integration in emergency, early-recovery, and longer-term programming contexts. Programme context, phase and changing priorities will define what is appropriate and possible. Within camp settings, in the emergency phase, the current cluster approach is pragmatic and can be logical for operational reasons. However, as such settings become more protracted, as so many do, the continued sectoral siloing of responses is less useful and can miss putting people's lived realities and priorities at the heart of programmes.

Certain contexts make shelter/WASH integration more logical and feasible, such as post-disaster situations with high levels of devastation of the built environment and overlapping requirements for WASH and shelter (e.g. following an earthquake or cyclone). It is increasingly understood that urban responses should move away from siloed activity, despite continued requirements for sectoral response plans. Much work is already being done to create shared operating procedures for housing and site improvements, particularly in urban areas. Integrated programming can include, for example, support to landlords to upgrade sanitation provision that will enable displaced people to occupy unfinished or substandard top floors of houses and multi-household buildings.

Market-based programming and the use of cash, with and without conditionality and restrictions, can cut across sectors. Cash and vouchers as an assistance modality is in alignment with, for example, community-led and self-recovery approaches to shelter (and other humanitarian) support, which aim to foreground affected populations' agency and choice as they recover from crises. If people can choose to spend cash grants on a range of options, including WASH and shelter materials or upgrades, this will also be beneficial to overall recovery.[9] Cash conditions can be 'smarter' and align with building resilience to climate change. For example, repairs for roofs can also include rainwater harvesting technology, which contributes to WASH facilities at household level. Programming needs to be flexible: if families have opportunities to identify their own priorities, some might choose rooftop water tanks, some private toilets, depending on the setting and existing services. However, some WASH experts might be unwilling to loosen 'control' of the provision of sanitation, due to concern over public health implications.

> How can WASH cede control of toilets? To a certain extent the shelter sector has liberated itself from 'delivery of products', e.g. from directly building a transitional shelter to provision of materials, advice, guidance. I think that the WASH sector needs to let go of its quality control and

enable households to deliver their own toilets or shared toilets ... Can we work towards a 'household materials package', which includes the means to create a shared latrine? Then the WASH sector needs to work on the faecal sludge management side of things. (Practitioner with experience of both WASH and shelter)

Box 5.2 Case study: 'Dignified shelter solutions' in Northwest Syria

CARE Turkey

Acknowledgment: Joud Keyyali

Regarding internally displaced persons (IDP) and refugee camps as settlements can prompt holistic thinking and programming, with expertise from both shelter and WASH jointly contributing to dignified shelter solutions even in complex conflict settings, such as Northwest Syria. Assessments show that most IDPs in Northwest Syria live in inadequate, non-durable, and unsafe shelters, usually in damaged houses or collective centres, hosting with other families, or in informal settlements lacking adequate access to water and sanitation services. Around 1.7 million IDPs live in 1,400 unplanned sites where approximately 900,000 people live in tents or other makeshift shelters, years after initial and subsequent displacement. Not all sites are monitored by the camp management sector. The most vulnerable, such as women and children, located in informal settlements, multi-occupancy buildings, and damaged residential buildings, are most in need of shelter and WASH support; financial constraints restrict the ability of IDPs to repair or upgrade shelters themselves. Overcrowding, lack of privacy, and being forced to share shelters with non-family members can increase protection risks for the most vulnerable, particularly gender-based violence risks for women and girls. Overcrowding can also create health risks, particularly given the COVID-19 pandemic.

For INGOs operating in Northwest Syria, there are persistent political and logistical issues over humanitarian border crossings and the procurement of materials other than cement blocks, and fears about formalizing the outcome of conflict, forced evictions, and displacement through allowing 'permanent' dwellings. UN policy used not to promote block houses with latrines, although cluster strategy has shifted over time and donors are also moving towards funding such construction. Working within the political and logistical constraints, some INGOs, including CARE International, are implementing pilot projects to produce 'dignified shelter solutions', using new designs of shelter units that incorporate private latrines and showers, with the WASH infrastructure that these entail at household and settlement level. In addition, INGOs are implementing shelter rehabilitation and upgrade interventions, for example adding household toilets to existing basic household units, levelling up tents with blocks and concrete to create a flat base for a kitchen and toilet, creating connections with settlement level drainage and sewage, and gravelling main roads within sites. Holistic programming that addresses inadequacies in living conditions can also allow construction risks, and public health and environmental issues to be addressed effectively.

In order to design, finance, and implement such household and settlement interventions, some INGOs have integrated shelter and WASH expertise. One such example can be seen in case study A.25 in *Shelter Projects 8th Edition* (GSC, 2021b). CARE International works with local implementing partners, coordinating activities remotely from Turkey. CARE tries to run shelter interventions hand in hand with WASH, understanding the acute need and the great impact of integrated interventions on people's lives. The programme's theory of change states that these integrated shelter/WASH activities, including improving household access to clean water, toilets, and good hygiene

(Continued)

Box 5.2 Continued

practices, will increase resilience and allow displaced and vulnerable people to recover from the shock of conflict and displacement. CARE's country office in Turkey has one WASH and shelter department, so activities that would often be separated are being managed and monitored by the same project manager through one grant. Other grants have both WASH and shelter components, but integration stems more from organizational effort rather than donors' requirements.

CARE monitors affected populations' satisfaction with their interventions and evaluates whether basic needs are met via well-established monitoring, evaluation, accountability, and learning (MEAL) practices. In addition, CARE is exploring ways of measuring intervention success in terms of long-term impact on IDPs' health and wellbeing. For example, qualitative research using interviews and focus group discussions gives some insights into the impact of household toilets within rehabilitated shelters. 'Mohamed' was forced to leave his home in southern Idlib and initially found shelter in Northwest Syria for himself, his wife and two children in a livestock stall. He did some minor repairs and turned the basic shed into what he called a house. CARE supported Mohamed by upgrading this shelter using a contractor: walls were repaired, doors and windows were installed, a kitchen workspace and cupboards were added. CARE also provided the shelter with a water tank and a latrine connected to a cesspit. The impacts of these upgrades are significant, as this statement from Mohamed shows:

'My son, when he saw the toilet, he could not believe his eyes. He ran to his mother and said, "Mom, mom, they built us a toilet!" Seeing my son this happy was incredible, I can't describe it. He is happy with a toilet. The place turned from a livestock stall into a house, our house'.

The humanitarian outlook: the greatest risks related to shelter

The compounding risks associated with the cross-cutting issues of climate change, COVID, and conflict can be addressed with sustainable shelter/WASH responses, linked, ideally, with resilience-building and disaster preparedness activities.

Shelter and climate change

In the context of climate change, progress towards healthier homes is increasingly important. People are forced to flee flooding, drought, environmental degradation, and resource-based conflicts, triggering complex emergencies and shelter and protection needs. These trends and their intersection with rapid urbanization, especially in Africa, will result in higher risk of ill health, also damaging mental health and wellbeing. Thirteen of the twenty countries most vulnerable to climate change[10] also had a global humanitarian appeal in 2021, and the majority of these have an active conflict. Displaced people, whether living in informal urban dwellings, rented properties, informal camps/settlements on agricultural land, or formal camps are likely to be more vulnerable to health challenges brought about by climate change, such as increased exposure to vector-borne disease and non-communicable conditions triggered by extreme temperatures (Romanello et al, 2021). Inadequate shelter, overcrowding, and poor access to services compound the threats to physical and mental health related to climate change. It is forecast that climate change will bring more extreme weather events; storms and floods in turn impact water quality and availability for households. Extreme heat (and cold) and heat/humidity events increase the need for better insulation of roofs and walls.

The traditional approach of shelter programming has been to prioritize safety when 'building back better' after disasters triggered by hazards such as earthquakes, floods, and storms. The need to build back healthier as well as safer is now also being considered in the shelter sector (Weinstein Sheffield and Webb, 2021). The GSC is also addressing the need to focus on the environmental impact of its responses and how to incorporate climate change considerations into programming (GSC, 2022). Climate change prompts a wider-angle lens on what resilience and preparedness activities need to entail, if physical and psychosocial wellbeing outcomes are put at the centre of humanitarian programming. Increased need and squeezed humanitarian funding point to a need for all humanitarian actors to 'do more with less', which suggests that efforts towards efficient integrated responses are worth pursuing.

Shelter and COVID

The COVID-19 pandemic focused attention on the impact of living conditions on physical and mental health and wellbeing and exacerbated conflict and vulnerabilities (Hilhorst and Mena, 2021). Humanitarian actors are increasingly aware of the impact that COVID has had on protection issues for refugees and internally displaced people, particularly on women and girls, through higher rates of gender-based violence. These issues are often exacerbated by overcrowding and lack of control over living conditions. Throughout the early stages of the pandemic, the shelter sector pivoted rapidly towards health outcomes, in addition to its usual protection focus. Agencies working in displacement settings acted to decongest settlements and reduce overcrowding within shelters to limit transmission of the virus, in addition to planning and building isolation areas and medical facilities, often in partnership with health and WASH actors. The GSC produced guidance on operational priorities for mitigating COVID risks for affected populations and practitioners (GSC, n.d.). However, in many settings, such as the Democratic Republic of the Congo and the Tigray region in Ethiopia, COVID is low on people's priority list, given other immediate threats to their safety, livelihoods, nutrition, and so on.

Shelter and living condition issues illuminated by the pandemic that are also of relevance for WASH actors to consider include:

- air quality and overcrowding within different types of emergency and longer-term shelter;
- widespread regulations requiring refugees and IDPs to 'stay at home' when they are living in inadequate shelter. These are challenging for humanitarian organizations and more challenging for the IDPs to adhere to;

- the need for handwashing for people coping with limited water supplies, a lack of washing facilities in the home, communal latrines, and so on;
- the mental health aspects of inadequate living conditions, including unsafe access to washing facilities and latrines.

The necessary attention on living conditions and their connections with health must not be lost as the current COVID pandemic wanes. Other infectious and non-infectious diseases require joined-up attention from shelter, WASH, and health actors with humanitarian and development mandates.

Shelter and conflict

This chapter does not allow space to explore in detail the particular challenges of shelter responses in conflict settings, most of which also face the WASH sector (UNICEF, 2019). Many of these are discussed in the shelter sector's 'Roadmap for Research' (Parrack et al, 2021). WASH is not mentioned specifically as an issue in the literature on conflict and shelter. However, there are issues that involve pressure on scarce resources and community cohesion/coexistence that also have a WASH element. Post-conflict settings where humanitarian and development actors are facing the need for significant reconstruction, especially in cities, mean that shelter and WASH actors will inevitably need to work together. Housing reconstruction is recognized as a complex undertaking, which, if carried out without full consideration of the context, can undermine governance structures and exacerbate social exclusion (Barakat and Zyck, 2011). When conflict results in displacement, especially for prolonged periods, engaging representatives from the host community in discussions about shelter and WASH interventions and throughout their implementation may help to legitimize the presence of the displaced community, improve housing outcomes, and lead to better support for vulnerable households.

Moving forward with integrated shelter and WASH

Using an environmental health lens that brings together shelter and settlement, WASH, and public health considerations when planning interventions to support people recovering from crises can have multiple benefits. The recovery of shelter after disaster is foundational (Khan et al., 2021). Within the shelter sector, a current trend is for greater awareness of the wider impacts of Shelter programming and the ways in which good quality shelter and adequate housing can contribute to, for example, people's livelihoods, children's education, and community health and wellbeing. Improving understanding of these wider impacts is one of the strategic priorities of the GSC and logically suggests holistic programming that includes integrated WASH and shelter. Given the differences between traditional modalities and scope of WASH and shelter activities, priority areas for future integrated programming can usefully be identified.

Promoting shelter and WASH integration also requires a word of caution. Agencies and their humanitarian teams still need the technical skill sets that experienced practitioners and departments have built up over time and in certain contexts. Shelter and WASH first-line assistance can be delivered with merged teams. However, when guidance on integrated programming is developed, teams' capacities and workloads should be kept in mind. There is a risk that, in merging shelter and WASH teams, assistance may be limited to a basic level, and opportunities to develop more sophisticated programming in one or the other sector may be missed. This risk can be managed by careful attention to the make-up of programming and implementing teams, as one senior shelter advisor explains: 'Integration doesn't mean everybody has got to be a sort of "Jack or Jill of all trades". Make sure that we've got the right expertise to support whatever we're doing.'

It is also important to recognize the different perspectives of humanitarians and affected populations about priorities around their living conditions. A recent WASH gap analysis revealed a mismatch (see Aldaour, 2022) and the same could probably be said for priorities around shelter activities, highlighting the need for humanitarian action that puts the voice and agency of affected populations at the centre.

Priorities and 'easy wins'

Simple changes to programming can give greater efficiency in both emergency and longer-term responses:

- Multisectoral assessments allow for multisectoral NFI kits and are also vital for cross-sector referral. The Beirut blast demonstrated that working with tenants and landlords made possible repairs and upgrades to the physical infrastructure, as well as child protection and health referrals (Rule, 2020).
- Multisector NFI distributions to meet multisector needs effectively and efficiently in immediate emergency settings and as top-ups in extended situations are possible, although these require greater flexibility from common donor conditions.
- Cash and voucher assistance can play a role in connecting shelter and WASH activities. Within the current cluster system, a cash working group is often convened following joint assessments to seek sectoral inputs. At that point, opportunities for integrated projects can be explored. At the moment, cash tends to be conditioned to sectors or completely multipurpose, with related problems of reporting on outcomes by sector. 'Smart conditionality' of cash could be related to healthier home and public health aspects.

- Sectoral expertise can be brought together over combined messaging (for example structural safety in rebuilding alongside hygiene promotion) and referral pathways. Help desks, one-stop-shops and 'urban hubs' are all ways of making 'healthy home' information available outside the status-quo of siloed sectors.
- Converting existing NGO staff training manuals to form new integrated resources would certainly take time but is feasible.

We went through all of the WASH training materials ('soft' training on creating context-specific messaging) and just added shelter in ... It was surprisingly easy. (Senior shelter manager)

Longer-term ambitions

A longer-term ambition is to put overall wellbeing outcomes at the heart of integrated programming. Neither WASH nor shelter single-sector outcomes should drive MEAL processes. The development of higher-level outcome monitoring and evaluation is key to a change in mindset that will drive changes in programming (Kelling, 2021; Webb, 2022).

There is a trend now for more measurement, more outputs/results, rather than outcome indicators. These are basically just following an input all the way through, and not actually caring about whether people are still alive by the end of it as long as you distributed your bucket or whatever. That really doesn't help and maybe that's something to focus on – integrated programming from the outcome point of view and looking at ways that we can try and do programming that focuses on the agency of households. (Senior construction advisor)

An article on breaking down silos and integrated WASH (Deola et al, 2021), which did not, incidentally, focus on integration with shelter, suggests that the WASH and shelter sectors are facing similar struggles regarding evidence (data that can inform decisions and improve programming) and measuring outcomes: 'Unlike the health sector, the humanitarian WASH sector is not yet equipped with coherent or effective systems to measure or evaluate the causal effects, outcomes or impacts of its activities.'

For a new emphasis on higher-level multisectoral outcomes to be planned and achieved, there needs to be strong critical thinking and an operational (and policy) attempt to break down the common separation between technical and MEAL teams within both sectors. The sectors/clusters can perhaps grapple with these challenges together at global and organization levels.

Global-level initiatives:

- Advocacy around the opportunities of more integrated programming, using success stories that show ways forward. A thematic compilation of lessons learnt from integrated shelter/WASH projects would be useful to disseminate good practice and experience gained over many years by some agencies and individuals.

We're not blazing new ground in terms of integration; we tend to forget some of the lessons that we've learned in the past. (Practitioner with shelter and WASH experience)

- Donor-focused advocacy. Some donors' current sectoral divisions are a driver of continued compartmentalization of programming.

It's insane if you've got [a donor] where they have a set of indicators for shelter and a set of indicators for WASH, doubling the amount of reporting that you're going to have to do if you try and bundle those sectors together. But maybe you have to go through all the pain in order to have some projects that you can demonstrate integrated programming? (Shelter practitioner and academic researcher)

- An inter-cluster working group with an environmental health/wellbeing remit to push forward the goal of developing relevant and practical guidance The shelter, WASH, and mental health and psychosocial support (MHPSS) learning event in September 2022 included discussion of the possibilities of such a working group (Webb, 2022). The sector leads were in broad agreement of the value of cross-cluster collaboration, yet it is hard to clamber over the boundaries between busy silos. If formed, an inter-cluster working group would be a suitable forum to tackle the many unanswered questions:
  - Where does sector integration happen already and with what impact?
  - What would a minimum integrated 'shelter/WASH package' look like in different phases of response and in different contexts?
  - What indicators should be used to evaluate outcomes of integrated projects?
  - How does shelter and WASH integration align with trends within the humanitarian sector for area-/settlement-based approaches, cash programming and self-recovery?

Operational-level initiatives:
- Shelter and WASH practitioners have complementary skills and capacities. Typically, those with civil engineering and/or architecture backgrounds have similar expertise around construction and sanitation. WASH teams are more likely to contain communication and behavioural change specialists. Sharing 'hard' and 'soft' skills, expertise, and experience between currently separate shelter and WASH teams at different organizational levels will be valuable.
- Putting local implementing partner organizations in the driving seat of programming initiatives and connecting better with public health and other developmental actors necessarily lessens the divide between shelter and WASH.

- Community-led programming, such as shelter self-recovery programming, forces a renewed focus on affected populations' lived experiences, priorities, and plans. Households may wish to prioritize healthier home aspects of their recovery.

    If we come at it at a community level and are using participatory tools which prompt people to consider all aspects of their lives, then automatically we will come up with integrated solutions. (Practitioner with experience of both shelter and WASH)

- While the increase in crises in urban and peri-urban settings has prompted better coordination between clusters and multiple other stakeholders, agency and individual experience of area-based approaches is in its infancy.[11] Such approaches necessitate collaboration between humanitarian actors, public works departments, private sector actors, and others. Greater experience with the Settlements Approach may lead to different levels of coordination and integration between shelter and WASH actors.

Conclusion

The intersecting and compounding crises of the 3Cs increase the importance of tackling the existing links between inadequate living conditions and health for those in humanitarian settings. WASH and shelter actors have a shared responsibility for creating an enabling environment for environmental health in emergency and recovery contexts. Shelters/houses and sanitation facilities must incorporate disaster-risk reduction, resilience and climate change adaptation, and mitigation for sustainable futures. For example, activities such as rainwater harvesting are prompted by resilience thinking as well as achieving a better water supply through improving drainage, reducing flood risk, and allowing irrigation for household and community planting, which all contribute towards sustainable environments and wellbeing. Air quality and vector control are issues that can be tackled at settlement and household level by integrated programming.

The shelter sector should be recognized more widely as a crucial pillar of public health and wellbeing alongside WASH in acute emergencies, recovery, and protracted situations. A renewed focus on environmental health in humanitarian response can help connect the fundamental pillars of public health: health, WASH, and shelter. Wellbeing is at the centre of dignified living conditions, which also align with global humanitarian priorities such as protection and gender. Growing connections between shelter and MHPSS point a way forward for a focus on wellbeing outcomes of programming and can include WASH too. An operational approach that brings together normally siloed sectors in order to achieve wellbeing outcomes aligns with humanitarian mandates and development goals. Both shelter and WASH have important roles to play: the positive impacts of healthier homes will contribute to recovery and therefore bridge the humanitarian–development–peace nexus. A new coordinated approach to displaced people's housing and sanitation needs, guided by environmental health, will prompt better long-term outcomes and contribute to the achievement of the SDGs. Both shelter and WASH sectors can work more closely together to facilitate post-crisis adequate housing, a human right that must provide more than four walls and a roof.

Appendix I Note on methodology and authorship

The main author of this chapter is Susannah Webb, although significant contributions were made by many others, listed below.

The original outline of this chapter was informed by an unpublished article on the links between shelter, WASH, and environmental health, co-written by Susannah Webb, Niall Roche and Emma Weinstein Sheffield in 2021 as part of the 'Self-Recovery from Humanitarian Crisis' research project (see www.self-recovery.org). Further material was gathered between October 2021 and April 2022 through literature review but primarily through (mainly online) interviews and discussions with WASH and shelter practitioners. Collectively, they hold great experience in programme design and implementation and in sector and cluster coordination. Participants were asked to identify opportunities for shelter and WASH activities to contribute to public and environmental health and wellbeing in humanitarian settings and to reflect on their own experiences of barriers to integration of shelter and WASH. Quotations in the text are attributed to individuals' main professional experience/role without identifying their current or previous employers. I am grateful for their time and valuable contributions to this chapter. The topic certainly prompted enthusiastic discussion and revealed some frustrations with the status quo and the barriers to holistic programming, as revealed by the quotation below.

> *Sorry for offloading: it's like a therapy session! (Shelter and settlements senior manager)*

Contributors

Emma Weinstein Sheffield
Niall Roche
Jamie Richardson, CRS
Joseph Ashmore, IOM
Joud Keyyali, CARE Turkey
Miriam Lopez Villegas, NRC
Richard Luff
Liz Palmer, Save the Children International
Nick Brooks, CARE International
Charles Parrack, Oxford Brookes University

Sarah Wierszycki
Bill Flinn, CARE International UK
Rick Bauer
Amelia Rule, NRC
Elizabeth Babister, Habitat for Humanity
Fiona Kelling

Notes

1. GSC annual meeting 'Ignite' open session in October 2020 consisted of a panel discussion including the leads of the Shelter and Health clusters. For more information and a recording of the meeting: <https://www.sheltercluster.org/global-shelter-cluster-annual-meeting/events/gsc-online-meeting-2020-ignite-talk>
2. For a recording of the GSC annual meeting's open session in June 2021: <https://www.sheltercluster.org/global-shelter-cluster-online-meeting-2021/events/open-space-session-10-integrated-WASH-and-shelter>
3. Hereafter, reference to the Shelter and Settlements sector is abbreviated to Shelter.
4. Clusters are groups of humanitarian organizations, both UN and non-UN, in each of the main sectors of humanitarian action. They are designated by the Inter-Agency Standing Committee (IASC) and have clear responsibilities for coordination. <https://www.humanitarianresponse.info/en/coordination/clusters/what-cluster-approach>
5. For more information on the range of shelter implementation modalities and assistance options (direct and indirect) see <https://sheltercluster.org/resources/page/more-just-roof>
6. Language is tricky and confusing to those not working in humanitarian sector. 'Shelter' and 'latrines' are referred to when 'houses' and 'toilets' would be usual in development and general settings.
7. In 2022, 274 million people will need humanitarian assistance and protection. OCHA Humanitarian Overview 2022 projections were, however, made before the Ukraine crisis unfolded in early 2022. <https://reliefweb.int/report/world/global-humanitarian-overview-2022>
8. Richard Luff (independent WASH consultant) presented 'A different approach to refugee latrines' at the online UNHCR WASH officer training on 3 November 2020. He used the example of Rohingya refugee camps in Bangladesh, where communal latrines do not meet the privacy needs of women and girls.
9. In 2017, the Global WASH and Shelter Clusters issued a joint advocacy note on the use of cash. However, it did not consider integrated use of cash. See <https://www.sheltercluster.org/sites/default/files/docs/wash_shelter_cash_advocacy_paper_-_final_version.pdf>
10. The ND-GAIN country index summarizes a country's vulnerability to climate change <https://gain.nd.edu/our-work/country-index/rankings/>

11. Within the shelter sector, guidance on the settlements approach was published and disseminated in 2021: <https://www.sheltercluster.org/settlements-approaches-urban-areas-working-group/documents/settlement-approach-guidance-note>

References

Aldaour, R. 2022. 'Poo, periods and priorities: what does research tell us about the different views of practitioners, populations and academics about WASH?' [blog post]. 5 April. <https://oxfamapps.org/fp2p/poo-periods-and-priorities-what-does-research-tell-us-about-the-different-views-of-practitioners-populations-and-academics-about-wash>

Bamforth, T. and M. Urquia. 2018. 'Divided we fall: coordination and collaboration in humanitarian shelter and settlements response'. *The State of Humanitarian Shelter and Settlements 2018*. <https://sheltercluster.org/resources/pages/state-humanitarian-shelter-and-settlements>

Barakat, S. and S.A. Zyck. 2011. 'Housing reconstruction as socio-economic recovery and state building: evidence from southern Lebanon'. *Housing Studies* 26(1): 133–154. <https://doi.org/10.1080/02673037.2010.512750>

Deola, C. and S. Ahmad Khan, A. Torres, E. Kearney, R. Schweitzer. 2021. 'Breaking down silos: integrating WASH into displacement crisis response'. *Forced Migration Review* 67 (July). <https://www.fmreview.org/issue67/deola-khan-torres-kearney-schweitzer>

GSC. 2022. 'Pathways home: guidance for supporting shelter self-recovery'. <https://sheltercluster.org/recovery-community-practice/documents/pathways-home-guidance-supporting-shelter-self-recovery>

_____. 2022. 'Greening the humanitarian shelter and settlements response' [web page]. <https://sheltercluster.org/ar/node/22172>

_____. 2021a. 'Shelter projects essentials'. <http://www.shelterprojects.org/essentials.html>

_____. 2021b. *Shelter Projects*. 8th edition. <http://shelterprojects.org/editions.html#8thedition>

_____. 2018. 'Strategy 2018–2022'. <https://www.sheltercluster.org/strategy-2018-2022/documents/gsc-strategy-2018-2022-executive-summary>

_____. n.d. 'COVID-19 and shelter' [web page] <https://sheltercluster.org/response/covid-19-and-shelter>

Hilhorst, D. and R. Mena. 2021. 'When COVID-19 meets conflict: politics of the pandemic response in fragile and conflict-affected states'. *Disasters* 45: S174–S194. <https://doi.org/10.1111/disa.12514>

Interaction. 2020. 'More than four walls and a roof' [blog post] 3 March. <https://www.interaction.org/blog/more-than-four-walls-and-a-roof>

_____. 2020. 'The wider impacts of humanitarian shelter and settlements assistance'. <https://www.interaction.org/wp-content/uploads/2020/03/1.-Wider-Impacts-of-Shelter-Key-Findings_Final1.pdf>

Kelling, F. 2021. 'What impact?' In: GSC. *Shelter Projects*. 8th edition <http://shelterprojects.org/shelterprojects8/ref/B03-whatimpact180821.pdf>

Khan, S., Lopez-Villegas, M., Flinn, B. and Moles, O. 2021. 'All the ways home'. In: *Shelter Projects*. 8th edition. <http://shelterprojects.org/editions.html#8thedition>

OCHA. 2022. 'Global humanitarian overview 2022'. <https://reliefweb.int/report/world/global-humanitarian-overview-2022>

Parrack, C. and R. Evans, J. Ashmore, A. Piccioli, M. Urquia, B. Moore, J. Richardson. 2021. 'Exploring the role of shelter and settlements in conflict and peacebuilding'. In: InterAction. *Roadmap for Research*. <https://www.interaction.org/wp-content/uploads/2021/06/Roadmap-for-Research_96ppi.pdf>

Prüss-Üstün, A. and J. Wolf, R. Bos, M. Neira. 2016. 'Preventing disease through healthy environments: a global assessment of the burden of disease from environmental risks'. World Health Organization. <https://www.who.int/publications/i/item/9789241565196>

Ritchie, H. and M. Roser. 2021. 'Clean water and sanitation'. OurWorldInData.org. <https://ourworldindata.org/clean-water-sanitation>

Romanello, M. and A. McGushin, C. Di Napoli, P. Drummond, N. Hughes, L. Jamart et al. 2021. 'The 2021 report of the *Lancet* Countdown on health and climate change: code red for a healthy future'. *The Lancet* 398(10311): 1619–1662. <https://doi.org/10.1016/S0140-6736(21)01787-6>

Rule, A. 2021. 'Beirut blast: 5 lessons from CARE's emergency shelter advisor' [blog post]. 16 November. <https://insights.careinternational.org.uk/development-blog/beirut-blast-5-lessons-from-care-s-emergency-shelter-advisor>

Sphere Association. 2018. *The Sphere Handbook*. Rugby: Practical Action Publishing. <https://spherestandards.org/handbook-2018/>

Snel, M. and N. Sorensen. 2021. *Bridging the Humanitarian–Development Divide*. Rugby: Practical Action Publishing.

UN Habitat. 2009. 'The right to adequate housing factsheet 21'. <https://www.ohchr.org/EN/Issues/Housing/Pages/AboutHRandHousing.aspx>

UNICEF. 2019. 'Water under fire'. <https://www.unicef.org/stories/water-under-fire>

Webb, S. 2022. 'Working together'. <https://sheltercluster.org/resources/pages/shelter-and-health>

Webb, S. and E. Weinstein Sheffield. 2021. 'Mindful sheltering: recognising and enhancing the impact of humanitarian shelter and settlements on mental health and psychosocial well-being'. <https://www.sheltercluster.org/sites/default/files/Mindful%20Sheltering_0.pdf>

Webb, S. and E. Weinstein Sheffield, B. Flinn. 2020. 'Towards healthier homes in humanitarian settings: proceedings of the multi-sectoral shelter & health learning day 14th May 2020'. Oxford: Oxford Brookes University and CARE International UK. <https://sheltercluster.s3.eu-central-1.amazonaws.com/public/Towards%20Healthier%20Homes%20in%20Humanitarian%20Settings.%20CARE%20CENDEP%20August%202020.pdf>

Weinstein Sheffield, E. and S. Webb. 2021. 'A healthier home is better home'. In: GSC. *Shelter Projects*. 8th edition. <http://shelterprojects.org/editions.html#8thedition>

CHAPTER 6
Integrated WASH and education

Anne Corwith, PhD and Erin Sorensen, PhD

Introduction

The WASH and education sectors in humanitarian response and international development have long recognized the need for safe access to water and sanitation services in schools to promote child safety, health, learning, and wellbeing. UNICEF and the International Water and Sanitation Centre (IRC) began implementing school sanitation and hygiene education programmes in 1998 (Mooijman et al, 2004). The 2002 World Summit on Sustainable Development plan of implementation for poverty alleviation linked the importance of providing safe drinking water and sanitation facilities to education facilities (Mooijman et al, 2004). The sustainable development goals (SDGs) carry forward the need for WASH in schools in both SDG 4 and 6. Specifically, SDG 4, which is focused on quality education, states in target 4.a to 'build and upgrade education facilities that are child, disability and gender sensitive and provide safe, non-violent, inclusive and effective learning environments for all' and indicator 4.a.1 looks at the 'proportion of schools with access to … (e) basic drinking water, (f) single-sex basic sanitation facilities, and (g) basic handwashing facilities' (UNICEF and WHO, 2018b). Additionally, SDG 6, which is focused on clean water and sanitation for all, states that 'by 2030, achieve universal and equitable access to safe and affordable drinking water for all' and 'by 2030, achieve access to adequate and equitable sanitation and hygiene for all and end open defecation, paying special attention to the needs of women and girls and those in vulnerable situations'' (UNICEF and WHO, 2018b). On the humanitarian side, the *Sphere Handbook: Humanitarian Charter and Minimum Standards in Humanitarian Response* (2018) bases access to clean water, sanitation, and hygiene on the shared principles of humanity, and the rights of people impacted by disasters to 'life with dignity, the right to protection and security, and the right to receive humanitarian assistance on the basis of need'. These humanitarian and development principles, goals, and standards indicate the importance of providing adequate WASH in education as a priority for both health and learning.

Much has been stated regarding the importance of WASH in education in helping to prevent disease transmission, promote nutrition, prevent dehydration, increase gender and child safety, address menstrual hygiene management (MHM), and promote access to education – including for children with disabilities (UNICEF, 2019b). WASH and education have two parts, the 'hardware', which refers to the actual WASH facilities and resources at a school location, and the 'software', which is the practice of good hygiene at school and the inclusion of WASH curriculum in the classroom (Snel and Sorensen, 2021). The hardware and software sides of WASH in schools work together to help provide clean and accessible WASH facilities and ensure proper hygiene and sanitation behaviours. The global community knows the benefits and importance of including WASH facilities, information, and practices at education facilities to help promote child health and learning.

However, education and WASH integration primarily focuses on short-term indicators of access, the prevalence of supplies, facilities, and basic education. For example, the joint monitoring programme (JMP) indicators for WASH provision in schools, which are patterned after the SDG 4 indicators (UNICEF and WHO, 2018a), are to measure the proportion of schools with any:

- water, sanitation, and handwashing facility;
- improved water, sanitation, or handwashing source;
- basic water, sanitation, or hygiene service.

Although over twenty years have passed since international efforts were galvanized to improve access to WASH in schools, the JMP has found that many schools still do not have access to basic WASH services. Globally, as of 2018, 31 per cent of schools have no or limited access to safe drinking water, 35 per cent of schools have limited or no access to basic sanitation services, and 47 per cent of schools have limited or no access to hygiene facilities (UNICEF and WHO, 2018b). These are significant gaps to fill in regarding adequate WASH facilities in schools if the SDGs are to be reached by 2030. Access is even more dire for students in schools in fragile and low-resource contexts (UNICEF, 2019b).

While the basic provision of WASH services and education in schools is crucial, the focus on access alone is limited in scope and does not consider the longer-term elements of sustainability and resilience of WASH in schools over time. When one considers approaching WASH and education through the lens of the humanitarian–development–peace (triple) nexus, there is a wealth of untapped opportunity. In this chapter, we explore how WASH and education have worked together to address the challenges of the 3Cs: the COVID-19 pandemic, climate change, and conflict. Additionally, we illustrate how WASH and education integration can better operate over the triple nexus through increased inclusion of transitional and long-range indicators to reflect the overall development required for resilient and sustainable systems, focusing on training and workforce development (maintenance, emergency preparedness, and health), promoting community involvement (voice and resources), and inviting and listening to the perspectives of children (psychosocial and education).

Literature review

Improved WASH systems in school facilities increase access to education, and education in WASH behaviour enhances students' abilities to attend school and stay safe while promoting their psychosocial development (Mooijman et al, 2010; Pacheco et al, 2021). In countries faced with underdevelopment and exposure to crises, the lack of services and education creates challenges that the triple nexus attempts to overcome. We focus on three areas that present both unique and overlapping challenges: the COVID-19 pandemic, climate change, and conflict.

COVID-19, WASH, and education

Although the link between WASH and education has long been recognized as necessary, the COVID-19 pandemic underscored the importance of adequate and accessible WASH facilities and hygiene measures to keep schools open and to maintain safety. To prevent the spread of the pandemic, UNICEF recognized that school lockdowns would 'probably be the first measure taken by local authorities to protect students and their teachers' (UNICEF, 2020). Unfortunately, the pandemic presented a combination of challenging circumstances with the risk of mass infection if schools were left open at the height of the pandemic. However, the consequences of closing schools have been significant (UNICEF and WHO, 2020). School closures due to the pandemic have had a highly negative effect on children's learning outcomes and wellbeing, with some sources citing up to a year of learning loss for only three months of school closure (Nugroho et al, 2020).

Recognizing the impacts of school closures, some parents, teachers, and administrators called for schools to reopen. As pressure built, vaccinations became available, and infections and deaths started to decline, schools looked to reopen. Global guidance on school reopening criteria often revolved around following proper personal and group health measures, promoting cleanliness of school environments, and providing necessary WASH facilities to help stop the spread of disease (Save the Children, 2020).

However, in a world where 30–50 per cent of schools do not have access to basic WASH services, such guidance could not be followed. UNICEF and the WHO (2020) found that 'in the 60 countries identified as having the highest risk of health and humanitarian crisis due to COVID-19, one in two schools lacked basic water and sanitation services and three in four lacked basic hand washing services at the start of the pandemic'. Although WASH in schools is crucial to students' access to safe and clean learning environments, the pandemic revealed the global inequities in access to safe, accessible, and sustainable WASH facilities in schools. In response to these inequities in WASH provision, integration between multiple sectors of child safety, health, education, facilities, and others has been essential to promoting widespread access to WASH programming in schools. As indicated by UNICEF in a COVID-19 guidance note on WASH and education (2020), '[i]n all education settings, the COVID-19 emergency response requires a triangulated approach to inform ..., educate ..., and provide the needed resources'.

Most of the key guidelines for WASH in schools when reopening post-COVID focused on helping educate students and school personnel about hand hygiene, providing hand hygiene stations at schools and on school buses, handwashing frequency, and disinfecting the school environment daily (Bolton, 2021). Schools in low-income settings without adequate WASH resources were provided with a host of solutions for providing no-touch handwashing facilities (Bolton, 2021; Coultas et al, 2020). These COVID guidelines and resources were developed using an integrated approach between the health, education, and WASH sectors to help get kids back to school. Integration and collaboration between various sectors have been crucial to providing WASH services in schools in response to the global pandemic and ensuring the safe reopening of schools for children globally.

Climate change, WASH, and education

Where the COVID-19 pandemic illustrated the need for existing education systems to respond quickly and flexibly to fast-changing circumstances and pressures, the impacts of climate change represent aspects of slow-onset crises that provide the ability to plan, mitigate, and prepare before the world faces significant impacts. As a result, climate change response features more of the elements of the development side of the humanitarian and development nexus. Climate change poses a substantial physical and environmental threat to the future of our planet, and those effects are felt keenly in the education and WASH sectors. 'A child who lacks access to safe ... WASH services is more vulnerable to climate and environmental hazards, shocks and stresses' (UNICEF, 2021). The environmental changes and natural disasters caused by climate change, such as increased flooding (Tabari, 2020), water scarcity, and extreme temperatures (Howard et al., 2016), and environmental migration (Rigaud et al, 2018), all affect children and youth's access to education, stability, and reliable WASH facilities. Climate change events directly impact WASH services by contaminating water sources, damaging and destroying school infrastructure, depleting water, breaking down of waste disposal services, and spreading disease.

Worldwide tracking shows that disaster events have increased fivefold over the past 50 years and are on course to increase as climate change continues to pose significant threats to education and WASH services (Tabari, 2020; World Meteorological Organization, 2021). Drought and tropical cyclones are identified as the deadliest disasters; however, flooding is associated with 44 per cent of all disasters (World Meteorological Organization, 2021). As of 2021, roughly 330 million children are highly exposed to riverine flooding, and 240 million children are highly exposed to coastal flooding (UNICEF, 2021). Additionally, 920 million children are highly exposed to water scarcity and 600 million to vector-borne diseases (UNICEF, 2021). Flooding, in particular, poses one of the most substantial threats to WASH and education, as it can damage or destroy water supply and sanitation systems, leading to a lack of access to WASH services at a time when clean and dependable water supply and sanitation are already hard to come by. Water and sanitation services 'are complex systems that require technical expertise and resources to maintain and restore when service is disrupted' (Associated Programme on Flood Management, 2015). Flooding has been shown to increase the spread of water-borne and infectious diseases through water contamination and mass population displacement (Howard et al, 2016). The WHO 'estimates that climate change will cause an additional 48,000 diarrheal deaths in 2030' (Howard et al, 2016).

Although the natural disasters resulting from climate change often constitute a humanitarian crisis, the approach to addressing climate change in WASH and education is often focused more on development and prevention, such as focusing on building resilient WASH facilities and providing climate change education. To adequately address the challenges of climate change for WASH and education, international organizations recognize the need for a 'multisectoral approach, integrating stakeholders from a variety of agencies (environment, water and sanitation provision, education, health, transport, infrastructure, etc.) which collaborate and communicate effectively to mitigate and manage risk' (Associated Programme on Flood Management, 2015). A grand challenge, such as climate change, requires a grand solution that works at every level and incorporates integration between sectors. WASH services must address climate resilience and sustainability, and schools must educate about climate change.

While things may look bleak, actions to help address these challenges are being considered and implemented. It has been found that 'investments that improve access to resilient ... WASH services can considerably reduce overall climate risk for 415 million children' (UNICEF, 2021). Therefore, the WASH and education sectors have focused on building WASH facilities that are resilient to natural disasters, such as flooding or tropical storms, and having plans to address problems when they do arise, such as water contamination or broken facilities. Additionally, 'investments that improve educational outcomes can considerably reduce overall climate risk for 275 million children' (UNICEF, 2021). For example, educating children about climate change, about how to respond to a natural disaster, and about proper hygiene and sanitation in such events can go a long way to help mitigate impacts and prevent the spread of disease. Education also can help children and families more readily adapt to various changing circumstances caused by climate change.

Conflict, WASH, and education

There is a symbiotic relationship between conflict and the basic services of education and WASH. The unequal distribution or lack of access to public services such as clean water, sanitation, and education in communities can cause and contribute to increased tensions among groups (UNICEF, 2019b). In contrast, the stable provision of quality education and access to clean water and sanitation help societies thrive and prosper. The UN Agenda for Humanity links the 2030 SDGs to the UN's agenda to sustain peace. The Agenda consists of five core principles (OCHA, 2019):

1. Prevent and end conflicts
2. Respect rules of war
3. Leave no one behind
4. Work differently to end need
5. Invest in humanity

The approaches that bridge the triple nexus set out to prevent conflict or incorporate conflict-sensitive programming to 'do no harm' (UNICEF, 2019b). When services are lacking or begin to deteriorate, it generates a downward spiral. 'When basic service delivery is halted or quality is diminished, the generations that do not receive those services carry the impacts for the rest of their lives in detriments to physical and psychosocial health, forgone education and limited job opportunities' (UN and World Bank, 2018). The prevalence of violent conflict can be sudden, intermittent, and protracted, each time causing significant loss of human and economic capital (UN and World Bank, 2018).

In 2020, one in six children were impacted by global conflict, resulting in around 452 million children facing interruptions to their education (Kamøy et al, 2021). The Global Coalition to Protect Education from Attack (GCPEA) 2020 report indicated that the overall number of attacks on education facilities declined between 2015 and 2019. However, new conflict areas emerged, resulting in interruption of schooling, displacement of students, and destruction of facilities. Current conflicts have shifted away from interstate conflicts between countries to intrastate conflicts between armed groups within countries and cross-borders, with civilian populations and infrastructure being targeted (UN and World Bank, 2018). In many cases, a strategy of violent conflict is intentionally targeting education facilities and water and sanitation systems (UNICEF, 2019a). Recent research has shown that the average length of conflict is longer, upwards of 17 years, and the reconstruction of facilities can take up to 30 years (UN and World Bank, 2018). As a result, crises are compounded by the reality that children impacted by conflict are more likely to die from diarrhoeal diseases from drinking unclean water or not having access to proper sanitation facilities (UNICEF, 2019a).

Conflict can cause large refugee populations to seek safety elsewhere. Expanding water inaccessibility and the impacts of climate change can also cause significant relocation to already inhabited, sometimes overcrowded areas, overwhelming existing infrastructure and increasing tensions between refugee populations and host communities (UNICEF, 2019b). 'Deterioration and destruction of WASH systems and water insecurity are increasingly widespread causes of social, economic and political instability, threatening the survival, health, and development of children and their communities, and peace and development at all levels' (UNICEF, 2019b).

In response to the impact of conflict on education, in 2015 the international community established the Safe Schools Declaration to protect the lives of the school community and its infrastructure from damage and destruction. One hundred and fourteen countries signed the Declaration to prevent or mitigate attacks on education facilities (GCPEA, 2020). Conflict-sensitive approaches to education have been developed to be taught in schools, and increased collaboration between WASH and education sectors has been encouraged. New sources and techniques for funding have been developed and instituted to ensure that education and WASH are provided from the immediate outset of humanitarian response through the establishment of temporary learning sites and corresponding WASH facilities. The lack of WASH in schools poses a security risk for children, as it means they have to leave school property to use the latrine or obtain water. It also limits education access for adolescent girls as they seek to manage menstrual hygiene (UNICEF, 2019a). In response to the significant influx of refugees, international collaboration, policy development, and funding have helped host communities to incorporate refugee students into host country education facilities.

Bridging the humanitarian–development–peace nexus

By highlighting the role WASH and education integration has in responding to the 3Cs, we now provide examples of how this integration can function over the triple nexus by presenting case studies on the development of frequent monitoring and longer-range indicators, training, community involvement, and the critical representation of children.

Monitoring, evaluation, and longer-term indicators

Monitoring, evaluation, and indicators need to be expanded to include short-term, transitional, and longer-term horizons, and should include qualitative as well as quantitative data. A school WASH monitoring and evaluation plan is key. Although it is essential to have access to facilities and basic hygiene information, the current JMP indicators only assess whether WASH services are accessible 'at the time of the survey' (UNICEF and WHO, 2018a). However, what indicators exist to ensure that WASH services remain accessible and functional and are utilized during the other days of the year when there are no surveys? If there are no plans to clean and maintain WASH facilities, those services can be rendered useless over time or stop functioning altogether (Zomerplaag and Mooijman, 2005). This can be especially true if the operation, maintenance, and cleaning of WASH facilities are left to school teachers and administrators, thus adding to their already full and busy schedules. Monitoring and evaluation indicators that involve the voices of children as well as teachers, administrators, and staff provide information on whether or not the facilities are meeting the needs of those who regularly use those facilities and who are impacted by the quality of the services available (D'Adamo, 2021).

In order to enhance the sustainability and resilience of school WASH systems, transitional and longer-term indicators need to be utilized. Current indicators need to be expanded to include budgeted funds for repairs and maintenance, salary for dedicated staff to manage facilities, and the creation of capital budgets for future improvements to facilities. Longer-term indicators should measure the development of skilled and semi-skilled workers in both the software and hardware of WASH systems instead of depending on training school staff. Lastly, indicators should include measuring the incidences of violence over WASH systems, and the existence and testing of emergency plans for including WASH facilities in temporary learning centres. These indicators go beyond measuring the existence of WASH access in schools and instead help to ensure ethical, sustainable, and resilient WASH services in a school for the long term.

Box 6.1 Case examples

WASH indicators must assess more than access to school WASH facilities. The Cox's Bazar WASH Sector Hygiene Promotion Strategy Guiding Framework (D'Adamo, 2021) is an example of a programme that incorporated indicators assessing the usability and safety of WASH and gathered feedback from the users when developing the indicators. In 2020, the Inter-Sector Coordination Group, supported by UNICEF, conducted a ten-month study to gather and consolidate three years of lessons learnt in the WASH sector in Cox's Bazar. Starting in 2017, over 740,000 Rohingya fled Myanmar, creating the Cox's Bazar refugee settlement. Over 120 documents and 160 persons, 47 per cent female, were consulted to generate the Framework. Although the education sector was not included in the Framework due to logistic challenges caused by COVID-19, the recommendations apply to educational facilities and the community at large. The research showed that monitoring and evaluation measurements should include cleanliness, smell, water-testing, security, and privacy, which includes the ability to lock doors, doors that provide sufficient coverage, sufficient lighting in latrines, lighting in hallways or pathways leading to or from WASH facilities, as well as whether or not WASH facilities are located within the walls of the school facility (D'Adamo, 2021). These indicators highlight that WASH access in schools is about more than just having drinking water and latrines available and that the safety and usability of WASH facilities are also important.

An example of key transitional and longer-term WASH indicators is presented by a US-based non-profit organization, Friendly Water for the World, which was established in 2010 to support WASH projects in upwards of 17 countries. In recognition of its tenth anniversary, it conducted a self-reflection and identified five lessons that are represented in its three longer-term indicators (Friendly Water for the World, n.d.):

1. 'Does it fulfill its mission of training and equipping communities in sustainable village-scale technologies to safe-guard, conserve and expand essential resources?
2. Is the program community-led and community-accepted?
3. Are the program outputs and outcomes sustainable?'

In order to meet the indicators, Friendly Water for the World develops a warranty and maintenance plan with the community (Friendly Water for the World, 2021). These indicators have been applied to Friendly Water for the World's programmes constructing rainwater catchment tanks built by local masons with locally made bricks at primary schools, increasing water accessibility and security. During COVID-19, the organization helped a community develop locally made soap, obtain government approval, and distribute it to schools. Friendly Water for the World approaches each project as a community investment process with the goal of long-term sustainability and improvement over time.

Training

As argued above, meeting short-term WASH indicators requires expanding and developing interim and long-term indicators for WASH access in schools, including constructing WASH facilities and maintenance. The focus of significant WASH programmes within education falls on the software side in teaching basic hygiene, handwashing, latrines usage, proper MHM with dignity, and the importance of clean water. However, education's role in the WASH sector can be much broader. It provides the opportunity to enhance the triple nexus through technical and vocational training (TVET) in water and sanitation systems management and maintenance, systems emergency preparedness and response, and long-term health, nutrition, and environmental factors. Focusing on training individuals to be prepared to address problems with WASH facilities in schools so that schools can remain open in an emergency can help ensure longer-term sustainability and resiliency of WASH services in schools. It is insufficient for teachers to be solely responsible for the care and maintenance of school WASH facilities, because they already have many other responsibilities.[1] Having trained community members with the knowledge and experience to help address problems can help ensure the continuous accessibility and usability of WASH facilities. Furthermore, ensuring both men and women have access to training increases knowledge and awareness of gender-related concerns. In particular, Oxfam's WASH Social Architecture approach engages women architects and engineers in the construction and management of WASH facilities to improve access for girls and women (D'Adamo, 2021).

TVET opportunities that are made available during crises can be transitioned and incorporated into formal education programmes and professionalization in establishing water systems, building cisterns, water harvesting, and liquid and solid waste management, and should include information on construction, maintenance, repair, and alternative emergency systems (Heidebrecht and Hase, 2017). Approaches by the German Agency for International Cooperation (GIZ) indicate that there are several options for TVET for WASH services, depending on the context and size of the population:

- 'independent training in specific water and wastewater occupations;
- basic training in skilled occupations (electricians, fitters, plumbers, etc) with advanced, modular qualifications in water supply and wastewater disposal;
- modular further training' (Heidebrecht and Hase, 2017).

Having adequate training and education to manage and maintain WASH services is crucial, as 'the lack of skills and knowledge among employees in the informal sector are often the cause of high water losses (through leakages) and of inappropriate and environmentally hazardous disposal of wastewater' (Heidebrecht and Hase, 2017). When designing TVET training for implementation and the possible incorporation into formal education systems, the

> **Box 6.2** Case examples
>
> Since the 2011 civil war erupted in Syria, Jordan's schools and communities along the border have been overwhelmed with refugees, further burdening Jordan's already weak WASH infrastructure. In April 2017, 657,000 Syrian refugees were registered with the Jordanian government, with, at minimum, an equal number of refugees being unregistered (Heidebrecht and Hase, 2017). In response, from 2016 to 2019, the GIZ implemented its Vocational Training and Skill Enhancement for Jordanians and Syrian Refugees in the Water Sector (VTW) programme to provide skilled and semi-skilled training in water quality and wastewater treatment. Upwards of 700 Jordanian and Syrian males and females received training and advice on employment and income opportunities in the water sector. In 2017, the GIZ also recommended the creation of vocational training in the refugee camp setting, recognizing that the average length refugees may remain in camps is greater than 20 years, and WASH systems needed to be installed, serviced, and maintained (Heidebrecht and Hase, 2017).

following should be taken into account: '1) close cooperation between the state and the private sector; 2) on the job learning; 3) social acceptance of standards; 4) training of vocational teachers and instructors; 5) institutionalized research and advice' (Heidebrecht and Hase, 2017). Besides increasing the pool of skilled workers who can address WASH issues within a country,[2] the knowledge and training in the field provide lifelong employability and reduces poverty, leading to increased stability (Heidebrecht and Hase, 2017). The GIZ points out that TVET needs to go hand-in-hand with investments in infrastructure, and, in addition to technicians in WASH, the field generates growth in related occupations, such as construction, information technology, administration, and finance.

Overall, the links between education and WASH indicate that more must be done to increase the availability of training in water and sanitation to develop the workforce and provide employment opportunities, especially for youth. Integrating TVET in WASH within the triple nexus would help increase communities' ability to mitigate the impacts of conflicts and crises, while enhancing peace and stability.

Community

One of the main drivers of sustainability in international humanitarian and development work is community ownership by engaging the school's community as leaders in identifying and addressing the WASH needs of its educational facilities. Communities impacted by disasters are the most able to respond immediately when crises strike. The Agenda for Humanity called for increasing the capacity of local communities by giving 'greater voice, choice and agency to affected people' (OCHA, 2019). It may seem obvious that community members impacted by the construction, implementation, and funding of school WASH facilities should be involved in the decision-making. However, it is often the case that, due to expediency, funding, or oversight, critical voices are not included, such as marginalized groups, children with disabilities, girls and boys, mothers, and teachers. It is not only necessary that communities have a voice in addressing WASH needs, but that they are supported in identifying local resources and the means to immediately respond when crises hit, as well as engage in their own development (UNICEF, 2011). The Associated Programme on Flood Management (2015) acknowledges the need for a participatory approach from the community and a multisectoral approach to addressing flood vulnerabilities. Additionally, Friendly Water for the World describes in its *5 Lessons Learned* that not engaging 'the community and invit[ing] participation ... completely fails to leverage the talent, desire, and dignity of the people living there' (Friendly Water for the World, n.d.).

Communities must take ownership and be invested in structuring and maintaining WASH at their schools, especially when it comes to longer-term investment, capital improvements, and emergency planning. Experience with centring community-based service providers locally may protect communities from the political and financial drivers of conflict (UNICEF, 2019b).

The aspect of local funding for sustainability and resilience is often ignored. Although significant efforts have been made to increase international humanitarian and development aid, the support for education and WASH functions is significantly underfunded (OCHA, 2019; WHO, 2017). With the increase in incidents of climate disasters, conflict, and pandemics, the expectation for humanitarian and development aid to address the global need is unlikely and donors remain risk-intolerant (OCHA, 2019). Even with efforts to localize aid through pooled funding and cash transfers, significant challenges exist between international actors and stakeholders on the ground (OCHA, 2019). Funding continues to be approached from the top down, instead of the bottom up,. The approach to funding should start from the local context by assessing the resources, training, and knowledge available for WASH within schools, and identifying the economic and resource capitals of the community (OCHA, 2019). Questions should cover aspects such as: what local materials are available to the community to construct and maintain facilities? How will the school budget for the construction, maintenance, supplies, and capital improvements of WASH facilities? What funding do emergency plans require, and how would funds be readily available in case of crisis to address WASH needs at the school? Many schools depend on funding from a district office and do not have ownership over their budget, funds, and planning. In some cases, the lack of localized, transparent funding can result in poor accountability for the contracted work for the school (UNICEF, 2011).

In many ways, the COVID pandemic has taught the importance of localization and relying on local communities to respond to crises. Instead of being able to send emergency responders and development personnel everywhere, international organizations had to provide guidance and allow communities to identify how best to respond given their unique and individual needs. During the pandemic, Save the Children and other organizations put together a 'Safe back to school: a practitioner's guide' (Save the Children, 2020) to help support education personnel and students to return to school. The guide

> **Box 6.3** Case examples
>
> Having a sense of community ownership and pride in local school WASH facilities and practices can help improve overall school WASH accessibility and cleanliness. In India, the state of Odisha implemented the Odisha Swachh Vidyalaya Puraskar (OSVP) award in 2019-20 to recognize schools that had implemented effective and clean WASH facilities and practices, and hopefully motivate other schools to do the same (UNICEF, Odisha and IRC, 2020). Across the state, community engagement has been essential in helping promote adequate and clean WASH facilities and practices in the roughly 58,000 schools. In particular, community involvement at the Dumerguda school, which won the OSVP award in 2019, helped provide essential upgrades to the school building and WASH facilities. Earlier, the community recognized the need for a new school building and helped raise funds to purchase property for the new school. Additionally, the community contributed labour and funds to help update the school so it had adequate WASH facilities. The community involvement and sense of community ownership of the Dumerguda school have had positive benefits in promoting WASH practices in the broader community and contributing to a sense of pride in what the community has done for its students.

provides advice and guidance for local communities to reference as they make decisions about reopening schools during the pandemic. It strongly encourages engaging the community in preparing schools for reopening, pooling resources, sharing information, and supporting children and youth in returning to school.

In addition to communities owning and recognizing WASH in schools, it is also crucial for communities to be leaders in identifying local resources for WASH and areas for improvement. One WASH in education resource that includes and engages communities is the WASH self-assessment process, which has been developed by the German WASH Network (Stockholm World Water Week, 2019). Utilizing the self-assessment method, schools conduct their own assessments of WASH facilities and indicators, which helps create ownership and makes the school aware of its current status of WASH. It was found that when schools collected and owned their own WASH data they became aware of things that needed attention. They also had the power to set their priorities and make decisions for the next steps. The data helped school leaders plan and make changes while informing the community how to budget for, plan, manage, and update school WASH facilities. While not perfect, the self-assessment process has helped promote better managed and improved school WASH facilities in Bangladesh, Uganda, Pakistan, Philippines, Cambodia, and Ethiopia.

Children

When involving the community in WASH in education, all voices need to be represented, especially those of the children and youth who regularly use the facilities and learn the material in class. The importance of including children and youth in the provision of WASH and education cannot be overemphasized when it comes to addressing longer-term sustainability and resilience. Previous WASH programmes that did not incorporate children's perspectives and input resulted in wrong-sized facilities and the discontinuation of hygiene practices. Additionally, 'children have a different view of the world than adults and therefore experience the use of facilities differently' (Zomerplaag and Mooijman, 2005). Children may be afraid of things adults have not considered or may have ideas for solutions that adults have not thought of.

Additionally, including children in designing and implementing WASH can help encourage them to use the facilities (and use them correctly) and help designers consider the unique needs of children, as well as those with disabilities. Education provided to children about proper hygiene, especially during times of crisis, can enhance their knowledge and ability to survive, and allow them to share this knowledge with their siblings, parents, and community. Ensuring that children, and especially girls, are equally represented in the establishment of WASH in education enhances their psychosocial development in knowing how to care for themselves and keep clean. Incorporating broader aspects of WASH enhances the information and engagement of children, such as learning how to reduce, recycle, and reuse, and establishing 'eco-clubs' to develop school and community projects, including water use and school gardens.

Zomerplaag and Mooijman (2005), working with the IRC International Water and Sanitation Centre and UNICEF, developed ten points for child-friendly hygiene and sanitation facilities in schools. They should:

1. be 'interactive' spaces that stimulate children's learning and development
2. be designed with the involvement of children, teachers, parents, and communities
3. provide lowest-cost solutions with no compromise on quality
4. have operation and maintenance plans
5. have appropriate dimensions and features for children
6. address the special gender-related needs and roles
7. do not harm the environment
8. encourage hygienic behaviour
9. offer enough capacity and minimal waiting time
10. have well-considered locations

These indicators all help ensure that children are involved in the implementation of WASH services and education, and recognize that children can be a big part of designing and developing facilities and education formats. Additionally, the 'Safe back to schools: a practitioner's guide' (Save the Children, 2020) mentions that child and youth participation is crucial in helping prepare schools to reopen after the COVID pandemic. Children have been known to be very effective at learning about WASH, using WASH facilities, and then mobilizing the community through sharing that knowledge and experience.

> **Box 6.4** Case examples
>
> Children can be a strong force for advocating and implementing WASH in schools and promoting WASH in the communities. One case example is the School-led Total Sanitation (SLTS) programme in Baijalpur village in Nepal (Mooijman et al., 2010). The SLTS programme was started in 2005 by UNICEF and the Water Supply and Sanitation Sub Divisional Office (WSSDO) to train teachers in WASH and provide materials for households to build latrines. The traction was slow initially, but a group of school children from Shree Pancha Primary School, with support from teachers and the community, began an SLTS club to lead a community sanitation drive. Once the SLTS club received training on sanitation and cleanliness, the children began to educate their families and community as well. This children-run initiative resulted in every home in the village having access to a latrine. The school headmaster said, 'We did all we could but it was ultimately the children ... who could better convince their parents' (Mooijman et al, 2010).
>
> Another programme, which emphasizes the importance of WASH practitioners first consulting the children as users, is Oxfam's Sani Tweaks (Gensch et al, 2022). Sani Tweaks is a communication tool that prioritizes user input in every stage of developing WASH facilities, such as design and location, operations and maintenance, and continued use. The Sani Tweaks model uses a 'consult, modify, consult' process to help WASH practitioners listen to the needs of the community, especially children, women, and girls who are more likely to stop using WASH facilities if they are unsafe or unclean (Oxfam, 2018). Tools like Sani Tweaks that prioritize gathering user feedback and implementing it can go a long way to helping communities and children feel heard and ensuring that facilities will be used.

Conclusion

WASH in education is crucial to providing access to safe and sanitary schools, and this need is supported by global imperatives in both international development (SDGs) and humanitarian response (SPHERE). In this chapter we explored how the WASH and education sectors have worked together to address the various challenges of the 3Cs. The COVID-19 pandemic, which required a primarily humanitarian and immediate response, highlighted the importance of working across multiple sectors (such as WASH, education, health, etc.) to quickly and flexibly maintain safe learning environments, and further revealed gross inequities in global WASH access. The challenges of global climate change, which requires a primarily development response, represents an opportunity to plan, mitigate, and prepare WASH services and education to build community resilience to future environmental shocks. As both a humanitarian and development response, conflict connects the triple nexus and is closely linked to WASH and education, as unequal distribution of water, sanitation, and education resources can fuel conflict. As illustrated through the challenges of the 3Cs, providing WASH facilities in schools and teaching children about safe hygiene practices are more complicated than simply providing access to WASH.

However, the primary focus of global WASH goals is on providing access to WASH facilities and educating children and communities on safe sanitation and hygiene. While access is necessary, the short-term focus on access does not adequately address longer-term needs to ensure the sustainability and resilience of WASH services. To help WASH and education bridge the triple nexus, we recommend that:

1. indicators need to expand beyond measuring access to include indicators that reflect the overall development required for resilient and sustainable systems;
2. TVET training and workforce development on the maintenance and upkeep of WASH services need to be prioritized;
3. the community needs to be engaged and have ownership of WASH facilities and education; and
4. children need to be valued as essential stakeholders in planning and implementing WASH programmes.

These methods to improve WASH and education services help bridge the short-term, transitional, and long-term focuses of the triple nexus and open the way to explore more innovative and equitable possibilities.

Notes

1. In discussing the integration of WASH and education, we need to be careful not to place undue burden on the education sector to teach and maintain everything. While schools can do a lot to reach a wide group of children, requiring teachers and schools to be primarily responsible to teach proper WASH practices and maintain school WASH facilities, in addition to their other responsibilities, can be asking too much. Finding ways to integrate WASH education into preexisting subjects and hiring trained individuals to manage WASH facilities in schools can help relieve some of this burden and allow teachers to focus on teaching.
2. Research published by the European Environmental Agency in 2014 indicates that 1,000 skilled workers are required in the water and sanitation sector for every 1 million of population in developed European countries (Heidebrecht and Hase, 2017, p. 24).

References

Associated Programme on Flood Management. 2015. 'Health and sanitation aspects of flood management'. *Integrated Flood Management Tools Series* 23

Bolton, L. 2021. 'WASH in schools for student return during the COVID-19 pandemic'. *K4D Helpdesk Report*. Institute of Development Studies.

Coultas, M. and R. Iyer, J. Myers. 2020. *Handwashing Compendium for Low Resource Settings: A Living Document*. 3rd ed. Brighton: IDS.

D'Adamo, M. 2021. 'WASH sector hygiene promotion strategy guiding framework'. *Cox's Bazar WASH Sector and Inter Sector Coordination Group*. <https://reliefweb.int/sites/reliefweb.int/files/resources/210422_coxs_bazar_wash_sector_hp_guiding_framework.pdf>

Friendly Water for the World. (2021). *Water Security. Friendly Water for the World Newsletter*. <https://app.getresponse.com/view.html?x=a62b&m=BSwb0m&u=wvvzj&z=EEqYCTv&o=pp_1>

_____. n.d. 'About us' [web page.] <https://friendlywater.org/about-us>

Gensch, R. and S. Ferron, P. Sandison, A. Bindel, A. Coerver, L. Cottafavi, K. Deniel, et al. 2022. 'Compendium of hygiene promotion in emergencies'. German WASH Network (GWN), Global WASH Cluster (GWC), Sustainable Sanitation Alliance (SuSanA) and International Federation of the Red Cross and Red Crescent Societies (IFRC). <https://www.emergency-wash.org/hygiene/files/WSH_hygiene_compendium_digital.pdf>

Global Coalition to Protect Education from Attack (GCPEA). 2020. 'Education under attack 2020: a global study of attacks on schools, universities, their students and staff, 2017–2019'. <https://protectingeducation.org/wp-content/uploads/eua_2020_full.pdf>

Heidebrecht, R. and I. Hase. 2017. 'Technical and vocational education and training in the water sector'. Deutsche Gesellschaft fur International Zusammenarbeit (GIZ). <https://en.dwa.de/files/_media/content/03_THEMEN/Bildung/giz2018-0209en-tvet-water-sector.pdf>

Howard, G. and R. Calow, A. Macdonald, J. Bartram. 2016. Climate change and water and sanitation: likely impacts and emerging trends for action. *Annual Review of Environment and Resources* 41: 253–76.

Kamøy, K. and P. Podieh, K. Salarkia. 2021. 'Stop the war on children: a crisis of recruitment'. Save the Children International. <https://resourcecentre.savethechildren.net/document/stop-the-war-on-children-a-crisis-of-recruitment/>

Mooijman, A. and K. Shordt, M. Snel. 2004. 'Symposium proceedings & framework for action. School sanitation & hygiene education symposium the way forward: construction is not enough'. IRC International Water and Sanitation Centre and Water Supply and Sanitation Collaborative Council. <www.ircwash.org/sites/default/files/Snel-2004-School.pdf>

Mooijman, A. and M. Snel, S. Ganguly, K. Shordt. 2010. *Strengthening Water, Sanitation and Hygiene in Schools: a WASH Guidance Manual with a Focus on South Asia*. IRC International Water and Sanitation Centre.

Nugroho, D. and C. Pasquini, N. Reuge, D. Amaro. 2020. 'COVID-19: how are countries preparing to mitigate the learning loss as schools reopen? Trends and emerging good practices to support the most vulnerable children'. *UNICEF Innocenti Research Brief*. <https://www.unicef-irc.org/publications/1119-covid-19-how-are-countries-preparing-to-mitigate-the-learning-loss-as-they-reopen.html>

OCHA. 2019. *Sustaining the Ambition: Delivering Change. Agenda for Humanity Annual Synthesis Report 2019*. <https://reliefweb.int/report/world/agenda-humanity-annual-synthesis-report-2019-sustaining-ambition-delivering-change>

Pacheco, E. and I. Bisaga, R. Oktari, P. Parikh, H. Joffe. 2021. 'Integrating psychosocial and WASH school interventions to build disaster resilience'. *International Journal of Disaster Risk Reduction*, 65(102520). <https://doi.org/10.1016/j.ijdrr.2021.102520>

Oxfam. 2018. 'Sani tweaks: best practices in sanitation'. <https://www.oxfamwash.org/en/sanitweaks>

Rigaud, K. and A. de Sherbinin, B. Jones, J. Bergmann, V. Clement, K. Ober, J. Schewe, et al. 2018. Groundswell: preparing for internal climate migration. World Bank. <https://openknowledge.worldbank.org/handle/10986/29461>

Save the Children. 2020. 'Safe back to school: a practitioner's guide'. Global Education Cluster. <https://resourcecentre.savethechildren.net/document/safe-back-school-practitioners-guide>

Snel, M. and N. Sorensen. 2021. *Bridging the WASH Humanitarian–development Divide: Building a Sustainable Reality*. Rugby: Practical Action Publishing.

Sphere Association. 2018. *The Sphere Handbook: Humanitarian Charter and Minimum Standards in Humanitarian Response*. Rugby: Practical Action Publishing. www.spherestandards.org/handbook

Stockholm World Water Week. 2019. 'The power of self-assessment: triggering action for WASH in schools'. Stockholm World Water Week conference. <https://programme.worldwaterweek.org/Content/ProposalResources/PDF/2019/pdf-2019-8515-1-SWWW_V6.pdf>

Tabari, H. 2020. Climate change impact on flood and extreme precipitation increases with water availability. *Scientific Reports* 10(13768): 1–10. <https://doi.org/10.1038/s41598-020-70816-2>

UNICEF. 2021. 'The climate crisis is a child rights crisis: introducing the children's climate risk index'. <https://www.unicef.org/media/105376/file/UNICEF-climate-crisis-child-rights-crisis.pdf>

_____. 2020. 'COVID-19 emergency preparedness and response WASH and infection prevention and control measures in schools'. Guidance note. <https://www.unicef.org/media/66356/file/WASH-COVID-19-infection-prevention-and-control-in-schools-20>

_____. 2019a. Water under fire: for every child, water and sanitation in complex emergencies. <https://www.unicef.org/media/51286/file/Water-under-fire-2019-eng%20.pdf>

_____. 2019b. 'Water under fire: emergencies, development and peace in fragile and conflict-affected contexts'. <https://www.unicef.org/media/58121/file/Water-under-fire-volume-1-2019.pdf>

_____. 2011. 'Compendium temporary learning spaces (TLS): design and practices in emergencies'. <https://resourcecentre.savethechildren.net/document/temporary-learning-spaces-tls-compendium-design-and-practice-emergencies>

UNICEF, Odisha and IRC. 2020. 'Water sanitation and hygiene in schools: a journey towards Swachh Odisha'. <https://www.ircwash.org/sites/default/files/water_sanitization_final_-_booklet.pdf>

UNICEF and WHO. 2020. 'Progress on drinking water, sanitation and hygiene in schools: special focus on COVID-19'. <https://www.unicef.org/media/74011/file/Progress-on-drinking-water-sanitation-and-hygiene-in-schools-focus-on%20covid-19.pdf>

_____. 2018a. 'Core questions and indicators for monitoring WASH in schools in the sustainable development goals'. <https://washdata.org/report/jmp-core-questions-monitoring-wash-schools-2018>

_____. 2018b. 'Drinking water, sanitation and hygiene in schools: global baseline report 2018'. Joint monitoring programme for water supply, sanitation and hygiene. <https://data.unicef.org/resources/wash-in-schools>

UN and World Bank. 2018. 'Pathways for peace: inclusive approaches to preventing violent conflict'. <https://doi.org/10.1596/978-1-4648-1162-3>

WHO. 2017. 'UN Water GLAAS 2017: financing universal water, sanitation and hygiene under the sustainable development goals'. <https://www.unwater.org/publications/un-water-glaas-2017-financing-universal-water-sanitation-hygiene-sustainable-development-goals>

World Meteorological Organization. 2021. 'WMO atlas of mortality and economic losses from weather, climate and water extremes (1970-2019)'. WMO-No. 1267. <https://library.wmo.int/doc_num.php?explnum_id=10989>

Zomerplaag, J. and A. Mooijman. 2005. *Child-friendly Hygiene and Sanitation Facilities in Schools: Indispensable to Effective Hygiene Education*. IRC International Water and Sanitation Centre and UNICEF.

CHAPTER 7
Child protection and WASH integration

Allison Jeffery

This chapter explores the key linkages between the WASH and child protection (CP) sectors and reflects upon how to fully integrate them to improve service delivery and quality. It summarizes the *Minimum Standards for Child Protection in Humanitarian Action* related to WASH and discusses the relationship with three key influencing factors: conflict, climate change, and COVID-19 (the 3Cs). The chapter considers Save the Children's WASH and CP work, as well as two case studies, one showing effective integration and one demonstrating some of the barriers to successful integration of these sectors. The chapter concludes with a discussion on the way forward and means of overcoming barriers to WASH and CP integration for future programmes.

Introduction to integrated CP and WASH

CP is the prevention and response to abuse, neglect, exploitation, and violence against children (The Alliance for Child Protection in Humanitarian Action, 2019). CP activities take place wherever children are at risk of or experiencing harm, including in developed, developing, and humanitarian contexts. Successful CP structures and programmes operate to support and strengthen four levels of intervention: the individual child, the family, the community, and the governmental or national system.

CP professionals identify vulnerable children and provide services at multiple levels of intervention to reduce, mitigate, and eliminate risks. Activities include comprehensive case management with referrals to specialized services; family-tracing and reunification for unaccompanied and separated children (UASC); safe and alternative family-based care for children without appropriate care; prevention and response to gender-based violence (GBV), child marriage, and child labour; reintegration and support to children formerly associated with armed forces and armed groups (CAAFAG); parenting without violence training programmes for caregivers; mental health-focused child- and youth-friendly spaces; and mainstreaming and integration with other sectors.

CP mainstreaming and integration is key to ensuring that all sectors' interventions take children's unique needs into account and that the programming is not only safe for children (child safeguarding) but also actively promotes

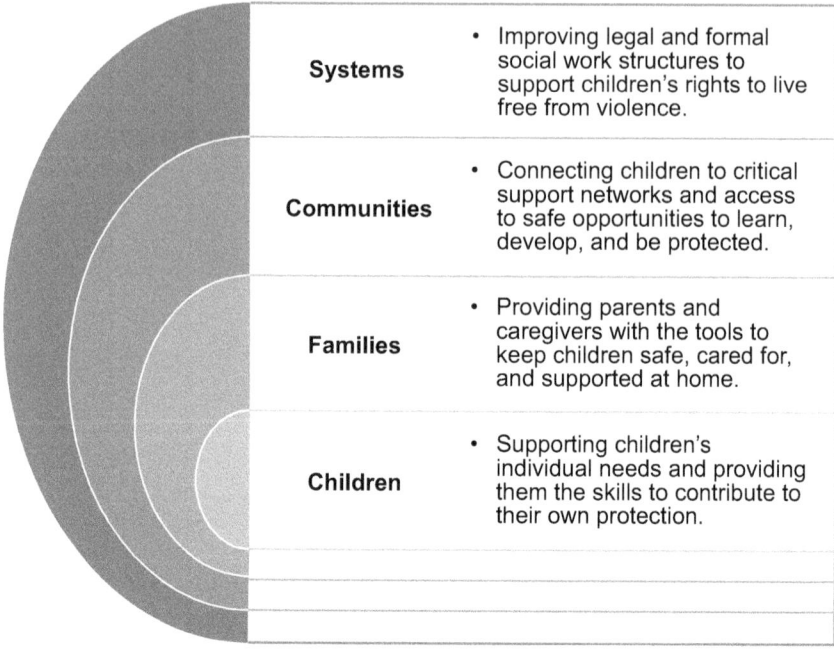

Figure 7.1 Levels of child protection interventions

their protection and wellbeing. Integrating CP and WASH interventions requires ensuring that WASH activities include children and their needs in the design, implementation, and monitoring of programmes. It also includes specific programmes for children, and appropriate referrals for children and families in need of specialized CP support.

Key actions for integrated CP and WASH

The *Minimum Standards for Child Protection in Humanitarian Action* (2019) is the most comprehensive guide for integrated WASH and CP programming. While not all actions are relevant to all settings, many of these best practices are directly applicable to development and nexus settings. Standard 26 addresses WASH and CP and requires:

> All children have access to appropriate water, sanitation and hygiene services that support their dignity and minimize risks of physical and sexual violence and exploitation (The Alliance for Child Protection in Humanitarian Action, 2019).

It also notes that Standard 7: Dangers and injuries, Standard 15: Group activities for child well-being, Standard 23: Education and child protection, and Standard 24: Health and child protection, should be read in conjunction with Standard 26 in order to fully integrate WASH and CP.

There are three suggested areas of collaboration for WASH and CP, in addition to the more specific key actions listed below. These suggested areas of collaboration include:

1. Providing WASH services in child protection interventions;
2. Adapting WASH facilities so that they are accessible and child-friendly and minimize potential risks to children; and
3. Implementing adequate and safe menstrual hygiene management (MHM) interventions for girls (The Alliance for Child Protection in Humanitarian Action, 2019).

The following key actions are taken directly from Standard 26 and are divided into actions for CP and WASH personnel to conduct together and independently (The Alliance for Child Protection in Humanitarian Action, 2019).

Key actions for child protection and water, sanitation, and hygiene actors to implement together

1. Adapt existing assessment and monitoring tools, methodologies and indicators for joint identification, analysis, monitoring and response to households at risk of WASH-related disease or infection and/or child protection concerns by: Including children's own perceptions in all monitoring and assessments; and Building on the WASH sector's minimum commitments to the safety and dignity of affected people.
2. Collect baseline data on children's WASH and protection status.
3. Assess whether child protection concerns are improving or worsening the WASH status of communities, including children.
4. Agree upon the most effective mechanism for coordinating and sharing information generated by assessments, evaluations and analysis.
5. Identify common areas of concern to WASH and child protection through consultation with communities, including children.
6. Establish joint prioritisation criteria for targeting children and households at risk.
7. Support households at risk of WASH-related disease or infection and/or child protection concerns throughout all phases of the programme cycle.
8. Ensure an adequate representation of children in decision-making processes and community-based participation structures relating to WASH.
9. Ensure all interventions: 1) Are safe, accessible, inclusive and protective to all children, including the most at risk; and 2) Address children's genders; ages; disabilities; developmental stages; water, sanitation and hygiene needs; and household and care settings.
10. Train WASH staff on child protection concerns, principles and approaches, including child-friendly communication.
11. Develop, implement and train staff on child-friendly, multisectoral child protection referral mechanisms.

12. Establish joint data protection protocols and confidential referral mechanisms for child survivors, children at risk and their families.
13. Prepare joint messages for children and their families that provide children with life-saving, disability- and gender-specific messages on: 1) The importance of good hygiene; and 2) Child protection risks and prevention strategies.
14. Collaborate with children and other stakeholders to design, establish, implement and monitor joint, child-friendly, accessible and confidential feedback and reporting mechanisms.
15. Ensure that all WASH workers (including subcontractors' staff) and child protection staff are trained on and sign safeguarding policies and procedures.
16. Document and address any unintended negative consequences and reproduce promising practices in relation to the impact of: 1) Water, sanitation and hygiene interventions on children's safety and well-being; and 2) Child protection interventions on households' risk of WASH related disease or infection.
17. Review at regular intervals the links and collaboration between child protection and water, sanitation and hygiene. Track progress in line with WASH Minimum Commitment 4.

Key actions for child protection actors

18. Assess the level of access that children in a range of care or household structures (such as residential care, child-headed households, children living or working on the street, etc.) have to safe water, sanitation and hygiene items.
19. Budget for necessary water, sanitation and hygiene interventions in child protection activities.
20. Require all WASH interventions to conduct comprehensive consultations with diverse children, especially those most at risk. Consultations should include: 1) Girls' safety around WASH facilities; 2) Girls' menstrual hygiene management and supply needs, particularly for girls with disabilities [note: menstruation may start at the age of 8]; 3) Children with disabilities' needs regarding hygiene management and supplies; and 4) The needs of children with incontinence.
21. Prioritise, develop and distribute accessible information for children and families about WASH interventions and issues.
22. Share with WASH actors information or guidance on: 1) The location of all child-targeted services; and 2) How to tailor WASH interventions so they are safe and accessible to all children.

Key actions for WASH actors

23. Conduct a risk analysis during programme design that: 1) Provides baseline data on children's WASH and protection status; 2) Assesses the

physical safety risks involved in accessing WASH facilities, particularly for women and girls; 3) Identifies requirements for recipients, such as literacy or identification; 4) Assesses the best timing and location for facilities and interventions; and 5) Determines the needs of specific groups, such as those caring for young children.
24. Involve child protection, gender and disability experts in designing, implementing and monitoring WASH interventions.
25. Prioritise children's safety and well-being when constructing WASH facilities.
26. Support parents and communities to encourage safe water collection by children that is adapted to individual gender, age, disability, size and development.
27. Promote the hiring of female staff.
28. Provide contextually appropriate hygiene, dignity and menstrual products to (a) girls from 8 years of age (if culturally appropriate) up to 18 years and (b) children with disabilities. These interventions should be designed and monitored with affected children's feedback.
29. Provide inclusive, child-friendly guidance and educational activities when distributing WASH kits, cash and voucher assistance.
30. Ensure assistance reaches all members of the affected population by using assessment data to identify: 1) Children who may have difficulty accessing WASH facilities and supplies; 2) Children at risk of abuse, neglect, exploitation or violence; 3) Barriers to access for specific groups; and 4) Strategies to implement to overcome barriers.
31. Provide WASH facilities that are: 1) Safe (well-lit, lockable, separated by sex); 2) Durable; 3) Accessible and appropriate for all children, including children with disabilities; 4) Aligned with principles of universal design; 5) Located where child-centred services are provided; and 6) Culturally appropriate.

Suggested indicators for measuring integrated WASH and CP include: 1. the percentage of WASH projects where child safety and wellbeing are reflected in the initial risk analysis, design, and monitoring and evaluation framework and 2. the percentage of surveyed WASH staff who can provide the name of at least one place where they can refer a child at risk to support services. The intended target measurements for these are 100 per cent and 90 per cent, respectively (The Alliance for Child Protection in Humanitarian Action, 2019).

WASH and CP in schools

This chapter will also highlight WASH and CP in schools because keeping children in schools is key to their protection. In-school children are less likely to participate in child labour, experience child, early- and forced marriages and pregnancies, as well as other forms of GBV and abuse (The Alliance for Child Protection in Humanitarian Action, 2018). Schools also serve as an important point of identification and referral of at-risk children to CP services. In-school children at risk of, or experiencing, these harms are more likely to be identified for CP support than out-of-school children because of their interactions with teachers and other school staff.

Adequate WASH facilities in schools are key to facilitating a protective educational environment. UNICEF (n.d.) estimates that '[n]early half of all schools do not have basic hygiene services, with 1 in 3 lacking basic sanitation and water. Children who cannot wash their hands face a greater risk of infection and diarrheal disease ... putting them at risk of missing more school days.' Safe drinking water, gender-segregated toilets, soaps, handwashing stations, and MHM supplies are crucial to keep children safe and learning in schools.

Linkages to conflict, climate change, and COVID-19

Integrating WASH and CP programmes is increasingly important to meet children's needs caused or exacerbated by complex crises. This section discusses the multisectoral needs of children who experience conflict, the effects of climate change, and the COVID-19 pandemic, and how integrated WASH and CP activities can help meet these needs. It suggests ways to contextualize the key actions above in these complex crises.

Firstly, it is important to understand that conflict, COVID-19, and climate change (the 3Cs) do not act independently; in fact, they often mutually reinforce each other and further marginalize the most vulnerable children. The below graphic introduces the intersections between these types of crises.

The sections below discuss the integrated CP and WASH risks and mitigating factors in the selected crisis. They are divided using the socio-ecological model into child-level, family-level, and community-level discussions.

Each section also includes a 'Spotlight on schools' because of the key role of education in the intersection between WASH and CP. According to the Alliance for Child Protection in Humanitarian Action (2018),

> *Integrating child protection and education creates a mutually reinforcing cycle that can reduce children's vulnerability in emergencies. A quality education increases children and families' resilience in adversity, empowers children and promotes a protective environment. An environment free from unchecked child abuse, neglect, violence, or exploitation fosters quality education. Integrating child protection and education programmes, policies and minimum standards maximizes available resources to better address the multifaceted challenges and risks children face in humanitarian settings.*

Integrated WASH and CP in areas affected by conflict

Conflict and humanitarian crisis exacerbate existing CP concerns and cause additional risks to children's safety and wellbeing. They can also damage or destroy existing WASH infrastructure and increase WASH needs associated with displacement. UNICEF (2019) estimates that, '[g]lobally, an estimated

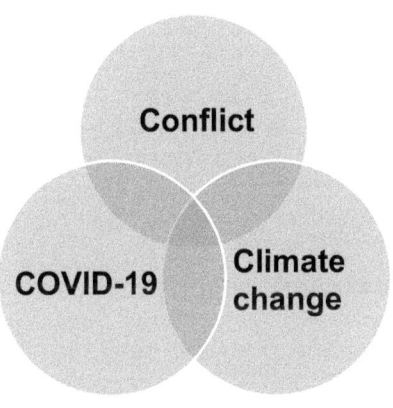

Conflict x COVID-19:

Conflict-affected areas are least likely to have access to COVID-19 vaccination and treatment due to conflict-weakened health systems. Displaced populations are more likely to live in congregate settings, including refugee and internally displaced persons (IDP) settlements, where preventative measures, such as social distancing and handwashing, are unrealistic.

COVID-19 x climate change:

Climate change brings humans into closer contact with animal reservoirs of disease, causing animal to human spillover of viruses that can make pandemics more likely.

Conflict x climate change:

Climate change can cause or exacerbate conflict due to migration and/or competition for diminishing water, food, and land resources. Climate-change related disaster-risk reduction policies and practices are often interrupted, delayed, or never started during conflict due to lack of resources, government attention, and civil society support.

Figure 7.2 Intersection between conflict, COVID-19, and climate change

800 million children live in fragile and conflict-affected areas and 1 in 10 live in extremely fragile contexts'. These children require multisectoral integrated responses to meet their complex needs along the entire humanitarian development nexus.

Influences of conflict on WASH and CP at the child level

Unsafe water and disease: conflict decreases children's access to safe drinking water and sanitation, and damages infrastructure, including wells and pipes (UNICEF, 2019). This includes significant increases in open defecation (threefold), decreases in access to basic sanitation (fourfold) and decreases in access to basic drinking water (eightfold). UNICEF estimates that in conflict settings, children under 15 are 'nearly three times more likely to die from diseases linked to unsafe water and sanitation than from direct violence' (UNICEF, 2019), and this discrepancy increases to 20 times for children under five years old. Common waterborne diseases spread in conflict settings due to lack of WASH infrastructure include cholera and diarrhoea. The destruction of hospital water infrastructure also limits the ability to adequately treat patients with these and other diseases, and keep facilities clean (UNICEF, 2021d).

Water collection and violence: water collection in any context is a dangerous task that puts children, especially girls, at risk of violence on their walks alone through deserted areas. Conflict increases water scarcity, increasing the number of children sent to collect water and the distance they may have to travel to find water. It also increases the risks children face on their routes, including sexual violence, injury, death, trafficking, kidnapping, and recruitment into armed forces or groups (UNICEF, 2019; UNICEF, 2021d).

Increased vulnerability: conflict increases children's vulnerability, placing them at risk of becoming associated with armed groups, being unaccompanied and separated from their caregivers, and experiencing violence and abuse. These children require additional CP support, including comprehensive case management, mental health and psychosocial support, and family tracing and reunification. They may also face additional barriers to inclusion in WASH activity design and implementation; specifically, CAAFAG often face community-wide inclusion issues when reintegrating and may be intentionally excluded because of their former role in the conflict. UASC may be less visible to programme staff because they are child-headed households. The key actions from the CPMS discuss access to WASH for all children, including the most at risk (Action #9) and that WASH staff should be trained to identify and refer cases that they encounter through their work (Action #11).

MHM needs: conflict, especially displacement, disrupts the menstrual hygiene routine for many women, girls, and other people who menstruate. Menstrual supplies and dignity kits (Action #20) should be prioritized to meet the joint WASH and protection needs associated with menstruation.

Influences of conflict on WASH and CP at the family level
Displacement: reductions in WASH and CP services due to conflict and increased risks to families can force displacement to safer areas with more stable WASH and protection infrastructure. Decreased household and community prosperity from the conflict can also cause families to flee (UNICEF, 2021d). As mentioned above, displacement can increase family separation and risks to children. It also increases the likelihoods of living in congregate settings and settlements, the risks of which are discussed below in the community-level section. Children are particularly affected, with UNICEF estimating that 'children make up less than one third of the global population, but almost half among the world's refugees in 2020' (UNICEF and WHO 2020).

Household water rationing: destruction or impediment of WASH infrastructure in conflict leads households rationing water usage. Rationing water both encourages the consumption of less (and sometimes significantly less) drinking water and limits hygiene activities, like bathing and handwashing (UNICEF, 2021d). The effects of both of these limitations of water uses, which include increased skin diseases and faecal-orally transmitted diseases, have disproportionate effects on women and children (UNICEF, 2021d).

Influences of conflict on WASH and CP at the community level
Congregate settings and settlements: conflict-related displacement can also lead children and families to refugee or IDP settlements. This makes Action #31 (safe WASH facilities) even more important to reduce risks, including GBV, in camp settings. Community mapping should be used with children to ensure the WASH infrastructure is built where they feel safe. For example, children should not have to walk through areas reserved for single men in order to access WASH services.

Social, political, and economic exclusion: it is well known that exclusion – social, political, economic, among others – can cause or fuel conflicts. Water insecurity has increasingly become a point of instability, which 'threatens the survival, health and development of children and their communities, as well as peace and development at all levels' (UNICEF, 2019). Exclusion from WASH services, and especially when interacting with other forms of exclusion, can cause or exacerbate conflict (UNICEF, 2019). It is necessary for WASH interventions to be both conflict- and child-sensitive to ensure inclusion and prevent, mitigate, and respond to conflict (UNICEF, 2019).

Reduction in community services: both CP and WASH services often struggle to function in conflict, whether because of direct attacks, limited or damaged infrastructure, reduced personnel due to displacement, minimized supplies and funds from the government, or increased demand for treatment for diseases and conflict injuries. This limits children's access to key services that help them survive and thrive in a protective environment (UNICEF, 2021d).

Spotlight on schools
Conflict causes significant disruptions to children's schooling, removing them from a crucial educational and protective environment for significant periods of time. Schools close or are unlawfully targeted by armed actors, or children are displaced or on the move and unable to register in a new school or be in a consistent environment for attendance (UNICEF, 2021d).

Conflict can also reduce children's access to education if WASH services are destroyed at the school, or at home. Lack of services at school mean that children cannot expect to use toilets or handwashing stations, which in turn leads to increased risks of violence, exclusion of menstruating children, and disease outbreaks (UNICEF, 2021d). Lack of household WASH services increases the likelihood that children are pulled out of school in order to collect water from elsewhere (UNICEF, 2021d).

Integrated WASH and CP in a changing climate

Climate change already has significant effects on children, which are expected to worsen as the average temperature rises and to particularly affect the most vulnerable children in low- and middle-income countries (Ryan, 2021). According to a Save the Children study (Ryan, 2021), children born in 2020 are twice as likely to experience wildfire, 2.8 times more likely to experience crop failures, 2.6 times more likely to experience drought, 2.8 times more likely to experience river floods, and 6.8 times more likely to experience heatwaves than children born in 1960. UNICEF estimates that 25 per cent of children (an estimated 600 million) will be 'living in areas of extremely high water stress by 2040' (Plush and Nyamadzawo, 2021). Despite children experiencing a significant portion of the effects of climate change, they have the least ability and agency to prevent, mitigate, and respond (Ryan, 2021).

Influences of climate change on WASH and CP at the child level

Drought and demand for water: as droughts and heat waves become more frequent, longer, and more intense, demand for water, crop failures, and environmental risks increase (Dooley and UNICEF, 2017). These events have significant impacts on children, impacting on their food security and leading to malnutrition, disease outbreaks, and family instability and displacement (Dooley and UNICEF, 2017). Water scarcity also increases the likelihood of children collecting water on longer and more dangerous routes (Habib, 2020; Nnah-Ogbonda and Jennings, 2021). Accessible and safe water access points, as well as food security programmes, are crucial to mitigate these risks to children.

Sexual harassment and gender-based violence (SGBV): drought and other effects of climate change have been shown to increase SGBV against children. A Save the Children study in Somalia found that rape and molestation of children increased after a drought, with 30 per cent of respondents noting a higher risk of SGBV compared to before the drought (Save the Children, 2017). Additional links between violence against children and drought include '[s]exual abuse, rape and molestation, child marriage, inability of parents providing for children's basic needs, harmful agricultural labor, intimate partner violence, more aggression, migration, abandonment, child trafficking, increased conflict, psychological distress, aggressive behavior' (Nnah-Ogbonda and Jennings, 2021). After disasters, displaced adolescent girls in shelters are also more likely to experience sexual harassment and abuse (Khan, 2015; Nnah-Ogbonda and Jennings, 2021).

MHM needs: the above shelter-based harassment is largely attributed to lack of privacy, a key mitigation area for WASH actors to ensure safe latrine and MHM locations (Khan, 2015; Nnah-Ogbonda and Jennings, 2021). Given that up to 80 per cent of people displaced due to climate change are female, it is crucial to meet MHM needs, include safe and socially appropriate places to use, store, and clean menstrual hygiene products (Rees and UNICEF, 2021).

Mental health: climate change has significant mental health effects on children and their families. Save the Children found 'high levels of psychological distress faced by children who are exhibiting unusual symptoms like bouts of crying and screaming ... [in] communities since the drought' (Save the Children, 2017). One hundred percent of respondents reported worsened distress in children, and many also reported concerns about rising violence against both children and adults (Save the Children, 2017).

Influences of climate change on WASH and CP at the family level
Increased food insecurity and household violence: food insecurity stems from a wide variety of climate change effects on crop production and animal husbandry, including drought, flooding, and heat waves. Food insecurity and poverty increase household stress, which increases levels of domestic violence, including family violence against children (Epstein et al, 2020; Nnah-Ogbonda and Jennings, 2021). Mitigating the effects of climate change via WASH activities and responding to protection concerns are crucial to protect children within their homes.

Family separation and migration: climate change can cause mass migration, particularly of families in search of safe conditions that can support livelihoods. While some families migrate as a unit, others are separated when just parents or adolescents migrate. When young children are left behind, their risks of participating in child labour and forming child-headed households, among other CP risks, rise significantly (Sevekari, 2016). Migrating adolescents are also at risk of child labour and sexual violence, including intimate partner violence, while traveling to, and once arrived at, their destinations (Epstein et al, 2020; Sevekari, 2016).

Influences of climate change on WASH and CP at the community level
Displacement and community protection: the displacement that follows climate disaster also reduces community protections around children, leading to increases in UASC, GBV, and child labour because the protective measure to prevent, mitigate, and respond are disrupted as communities separate. As climate change effects are likely to be permanent and to worsen, many people from displaced communities are unlikely to be able to return to their the original homes and community groups (Levy et al, 2017; Nnah-Ogbonda and Jennings, 2021).

Destruction of community infrastructure: destruction of community infrastructure can both cause migration and make life difficult for those who remain. Communities that remain in severely climate-affected areas require resilient systems to prevent and mitigate disasters. According to UNICEF, 'Safe water, sanitation and hygiene (WASH), including potable water supplies, effective drainage systems and working latrines can mean all the difference in the ability to cope with the impacts of climate change' (Rees and UNICEF, 2021). There is additional evidence that girls are more vulnerable to climate-related WASH risks because of existing gender inequality, and that poor children in dense urban areas are more vulnerable because fewer coping mechanisms are available to them. (Rees and UNICEF, 2021).

Spotlight on schools
Extreme weather caused by climate change has, and will continue to, limit children's access to education. Around half of the 75 million children whose education is interrupted in a given year are prevented from attending school because of extreme events like droughts and floods (Cowley, 2021). In countries where access to education is already vulnerable, children are at the highest

risk of losing access to schooling because of climate-related weather events (Cowley, 2021).

As already discussed, water scarcity results in more children spending more time collecting water, often resulting in them not attending school or being too exhausted to learn when they can attend (Dooley and UNICEF, 2017). Water collection is also very gendered, with the responsibility falling much more heavily on girls than boys. UNICEF estimates that, 'in Ethiopia, approximately 20 per cent of girls miss school to assist with water fetching, in comparison to just 5 per cent of boys. As climate change places increased strain on water resources, a young girl's WASH responsibilities will only become more difficult to achieve' (Rees and UNICEF, 2021).

Additionally, children with less schooling become more vulnerable to climate-related issues in the future (Rees and UNICEF, 2021):

> *When confronted by climate shocks, educated children, families and communities are often more empowered and adaptive in their disaster preparedness, response and recovery. By contrast, in families with lower levels of education, children are more likely to be removed from school in order to work when disaster strikes. The least educated children are also more likely to be displaced.*

Age-appropriate disaster preparedness activities for children can have positive effects on their future protection, including fulfilling WASH needs. These types of activity teach children 'the skills necessary to manage risks whether they be climate, or economic or even conflict-related' (Rees and UNICEF, 2021).

Integrated WASH and CP during the COVID-19 pandemic response

The COVID-19 pandemic has had significant impacts on children throughout the world – from direct effects of infection on themselves or their families, to secondary effects from lockdowns and school closures. Children have experienced more risk, with fewer prevention and response services available to meet their needs (Edwards, 2020). Already vulnerable children, those whose protection and WASH needs were already unmet or only partially met, have been even more severely impacted (Edwards, 2020).

Influences of the COVID-19 pandemic on WASH and CP at the child level
Risk of infection: while not the demographic group most severely affected by COVID-19 infection, children and adolescents under 20 years old still make up 20 per cent of reported COVID-19 cases (UNICEF, 2021b; Fore, 2020). It should be noted that, due to data collection issues, all estimates of COVID-19 cases and deaths, particularly in developing contexts, are assumed to be undercounted (UNICEF, 2021b).

Mental health and pandemic messaging: the mental health of children has been severely impacted by COVID-19-related lockdowns, school closures, and the grief associated with loss of loved ones, including parents (Edwards, 2020). COVID also highlighted the importance of child-friendly WASH messaging for disease prevention and control. Child-friendly, age-appropriate materials are needed to explain disease prevention, handwashing, and other WASH topics without being frightening (Save the Children, 2020; Save the Children, 2021).

Influences of the COVID-19 pandemic on WASH and CP at the family level
Caregiver death and family separation: the COVID-19 pandemic has led to extreme levels of loss for children, including the loss of one or both parents or primary caregivers, as well as losses of secondary caregivers and older relatives, such as grandparents. It is estimated that over one million children experienced the death of a primary caregiver and over one and a half million children experienced the death of at least one primary or secondary caregiver (Hillis et al, 2021). The loss of caregivers increases risks to children's mental health, wellbeing, and overall protection. These risks are further heightened when children are left without adequate care and form child-headed households when unaccompanied.

Lockdowns and family violence: COVID and the associated lockdowns have led to increased risks to children, especially girls, because of more time spent at home with abusers and fewer potential interveners, such as teachers and other community members, and active protection services. This has increased incidences of domestic violence and femicide (Edwards, 2020; Williams and Pontalti, 2020). A survey by Save the Children found that '[n]early one third (32 per cent) of households had a child, parent or caregiver who said that there had been physical or emotional violence in their home since the start of the pandemic' (Edwards, 2020).

Because the global COVID-19 response has increased funding for and implementation of WASH programming, WASH implementers may be the most likely to access at-risk children in their homes. They should be trained to identify at-risk children and refer them to CP partners for follow-up. Particularly vulnerable children, such as pregnant girls, children without caregivers, and out-of-school children may have additional WASH needs associated with COVID-19.

Influences of the COVID-19 pandemic on WASH and CP at the community level
WASH and CP service disruption: both prevention and treatment services for all sectors, including WASH, protection, and health, have often been limited or disrupted during the pandemic. Some services, like health and even protection services, have shifted to exclusively serve COVID patients (Fore, 2020; United Nations, 2020a, 2020b). Additionally, transportation, staffing, and PPE gaps have prevented children from accessing care. A Save the Children study found that '89% of respondents to the survey reported that COVID-19 has impacted their access to healthcare, medicine and medical supplies' (Edwards, 2020). In some cases, fear of COVID infection has prevented children and families from seeking essential CP services (UNICEF, 2021c). At the beginning of the pandemic, child-friendly information was lacking, and with GBV cases rising, there was increased need for services. (Williams and Pontalti, 2020).

Spotlight on schools
The pandemic has led over 1.5 billion children (90 per cent of students worldwide) to be affected by school closures (Edwards, 2020; UNICEF and WHO 2020). This removes children from a protective and educational environment and raises their risks of violence and early pregnancy. (UNICEF and WHO 2020) highlighted

> 'the need to accelerate progress on WASH in schools. Global school closures in response to the COVID-19 pandemic present an unprecedented risk to children's education and wellbeing. Prolonged closures will have negative impacts on learning outcomes and disrupt school-based services essential for the nutrition, health, welfare and protection of vulnerable children'.

A Save the Children study found that reported violence at home doubled when schools were closed (17 per cent) compared to when they were open for in-person instruction (8 per cent) (Edwards, 2020). The WASH sector had, and continues to have, an important role to play in reopening schools and keeping them open, as well as contributing to children's protection. The global framework for reopening schools contains requirements for safe operations including hygiene, PPE use, and cleaning protocols, as wells as access to water for handwashing, toilets, and MHM (UNICEF and WHO 2020). With schools reopening and the world dealing with multiple variant strains of COVID, there are opportunities to teach WASH COVID-prevention messages, including PPE use and handwashing. These help to protect children from infection and empowers them to protect others by sharing the information with their families and communities.

Box 7.1 Case study 1: COVID-19 response in Syria

Case studies, both of successful and unsuccessful WASH and CP programming, offer useful learning and information to improve integrated responses. This section includes two case studies, one from Save the Children's COVID-19-related hygiene promotion activity in Northwest Syria, and the second from a large INGO's latrine-building intervention in Dadaab Refugee Complex, Kenya. The first discusses the successes and challenges of hygiene promotion programming, and the second outlines a programme that did not accomplish its objectives for increased latrine access. This INGO will remain unnamed to promote the free sharing of information about the less successful programming for the benefit of future programmes.

This case study was shared by Abraham Varampath, Senior WASH Advisor at Save the Children UK. It is based on his experience working on a COVID-19 response hygiene promotion project in Northwest Syria in 2020 (Varampath, 2020).

What was the project? The project, the 'COVID-19 Hygiene Promotion Initiative' in Northwest Syria, was planned in advance of the arrival of COVID-19 in the region due to its remote location. This allowed time for the programme staff, community members, and children to plan activities and operationalize them within ten days of the first COVID-19 case being detected in Northwest Syria. COVID-19 prevention information was contextualized for Syria and distilled into five key messages to ensure the population would remember and implement the most important actions. The messages, originally intended for in-person distribution, had to be adapted to remote modalities, including radio sessions and information leaflets on bread bundles. They were designed for both basic hygiene

(Continued)

Box 7.1 Continued

generally, with specific COVID-19 prevention added. These were: handwashing, drinking safe water, using and maintaining the latrine, social distancing, and using a mask or avoiding touching faces (Varampath, 2020).

How was it children-centred? Children added valuable inputs to both the design and implementation of the programme. They provided ideas for developing the radio sessions and even selected the name of the radio programme overall. Children's input was crucial in making the hygiene promotion language accessible and fun for their peers. Seeing their ideas and opinions taken seriously and put into action by adults resulted in improved psychosocial behaviours, including increased self-confidence and self-expression. The children, along with the adults on the project, continued to share their ideas with other community members in the settlements after the programme had ended. (Varampath, 2020)

What were the challenges? The project faced safety, security, and operational challenges in implementation. COVID-19 itself forced the project to end face-to-face activities and adapt to different modalities; new remote and hybrid sessions included informational materials on bread bundles, a COVID prevention song, smaller group sessions, and radio programming. This was the first project with the local partner that deliberately involved children in the design and implementation, so additional training time was required to strengthen the partner organization's capacity for working with children. Additionally, the COVID song had to be adapted to ensure no conflicts with local Islamic or cultural norms (Varampath, 2020).

What are the key takeaways? Collaborate with children early and throughout the design and implementation of programmes to ensure information is easily accessible and non-intimidating (and even fun) for children. It is important to have flexible programming to be able to adapt for changing environments, allowing for in-person, remote, and hybrid engagement.

Case study 2: integrating CP and WASH in Dadaab Refugee Complex

This case study was shared by Jean Syanda, humanitarian child protection advisor at Save the Children US. It reflects her experience of working on integrated CP and WASH with a large INGO in the Dadaab Refugee Complex in Kenya from 2011 to 2013.

What was the project? The project was a pilot programme for CP mainstreaming with the health sector. The key WASH-protection intervention was the construction of disability-friendly, accessible toilets. Because there was no in-house disability and inclusion team, the protection staff conducted their own research into an appropriate design for accessible toilets, with particular focus on accessibility for people who use wheelchairs. People with disabilities were consulted in the design phase. They shared very useful feedback and ideas that were incorporated into the design.

However, in the end, wheelchair users struggled to use the toilets and people without mobility issues were almost exclusively the users of these facilities. Some people with limited mobility issues (including the use of crutches) also used the toilets out of necessity, though not with ease. This left the groups most impacted by mobility issues, including wheelchair users, without access to the toilets intended for them.

Why did this not work? Jean shared that, while people with disabilities were consulted on the design, the contractors hired to implement the design were not well trained on disability and inclusion, and did not have an adequate understanding of the unique needs of the intended users. For example, ramps were too high or steep, and doors too narrow for wheelchair use. There was also an issue related to the ability to clean the toilets from a seated position. When reflecting on the project, the implementing team realized that the lack of a formal needs assessment (which had been replaced with a brainstorming session by the protection team) meant that they could not even been certain that mobility issues were the most common or severe disability restricting standard toilet use.

(Continued)

> **Box 7.1** Continued
>
> **What could have improved it?** Jean mentioned many ideas that could have improved the programme, and she has brought this expertise to her later WASH and CP integrated projects. First, either an in-office disability team or partnership with a disability-focused NGO would have provided important insights into needs assessments, programme design, and implementation.
>
> The team should have also facilitated meetings between people with disabilities and the contractors, so that the intended users could share their needs directly and answer questions from the contractors. This focus group of people with disabilities should have also toured the facilities after they were framed out to allow for identification and mitigation of any issues before construction was completed.
>
> Additionally, consultations specifically with children with disabilities and their caregivers would have provided information about their unique needs. For example, because children with disabilities are often aided by a caregiver when using toilets, they may need additional space for an aide to manoeuvre around the wheelchair. Older children and adolescents could have been consulted directly about their needs, while the caregivers would have provided more relevant feedback about young children's needs.

Child safeguarding

While activities in the CP sector focus on preventing, mitigating, and responding to risks to children in their communities, all sectors must commit to child safeguarding.

Child safeguarding ensures that programmes and activities in any sector are safe for children and that participation does not increase their risk of harm. There are some key considerations for child safeguarding for integrated CP and WASH programmes.

The following recommendations are taken directly from Save the Children's 'Safeguarding children in WASH' guidance note (Carter, 2019).

Key considerations for safeguarding children in integrated WASH and CP programming

1. Staff, volunteers, partners (or any representatives) should never be alone with a child with whom they are working.
2. Building sites are always dangerous for children – make sure that children are prevented [from entering] building sites, and that all excavations are well secured 24/7 so children cannot fall in; and that all machinery and equipment are also secured safely 24/7.
3. Any drivers, suppliers, or volunteers with direct access to our beneficiaries (e.g. water truck drivers) must be trained on, and adhere to, [the] Child Safeguarding Policy.
4. Regular training on child safeguarding, especially safer programming, helps staff, volunteers, and contractors to think through a 'child-lens' and avoid risks.
5. Power dynamics will have an impact on [programmes] – think about gender inequalities, power dynamics between NGO workers and community members and address [them].

6. Risk management is an active, ongoing process that never stops! Don't be afraid to challenge each other to ensure children are safeguarded.

WASH activities that involve construction and large water tanks or latrines present dangers to children, such as drowning and injury (Carter, 2019). Mitigation measures, such as fences, may be removed by community members with needs for the materials, so both permanent fixtures and community engagement is needed to ensure children's safety (Carter, 2019). Safety messaging should be written clearly in the appropriate languages and with pictures, as well as repeated verbally by a variety of community members (Carter, 2019). Additional activities to ensure safe access to completed WASH facilities and services were already discussed above. Child safeguarding advisors should be consulted for programme-specific risk identification and mitigation (Carter, 2019).

Suggestions and a way forward for integrated CP and WASH

There is clear evidence that integrated WASH and CP programming is necessary to meet the needs of children, families, and communities. Integrated programming is especially important to respond to the complex emergencies of the 3Cs. The following are thematic suggestions for the future of integrated CP and WASH.

Start early: it is much easier to start with activities that involve children, including the most vulnerable (UASC, CAFAAG, children with disabilities), at the earliest stages of the design, when they can have the most influence over the design and implementation of activities. It is also much easier to start an equal partnership when not just seeking basic approval, but a true partnership. Meeting with stakeholders can ensure interventions are relevant to the population and save time and resources by preventing implementation issues before they occur.

Engage children and youth: children and youth are the experts of their own experiences and protection needs. While it is ultimately the responsibility of adults and government to ensure that children's needs are met and they fully realize their rights, children and youth have important insight and deserve to be heard. Climate-related WASH and CP programmes are improved when 'they consider children and young people as rights holders; are holistic and multisectoral; [and] address the specific risks and vulnerabilities of children and young people' (Plush and Nyamadzawo, 2021). Currently, children are not fully included in climate-related commitments. For example, '[w]hile 86% of the NDCs[National Determined Contributions, or countries' climate action plans] have water commitments, indicators or targets, only 28% include a child-sensitive approach' (Plush and Nyamadzawo, 2021). Technology-assisted interviews for input have been successfully implemented for latrine design and use in a Save the Children programme in Bangladesh (Elrha, 2019).

Consider intersectionality: intersectionality is 'a lens, a prism, for seeing the way in which various forms of inequality often operate together and exacerbate each other' (Steinmetz, 2020). Various forms of oppression based on gender, race, ethnicity, (dis)ability, socio-economic status, religion, literacy, and community position, among others, mean that not all groups are able to access, participate in, and benefit from WASH and CP programmes in the same ways. Programmes should be designed and implemented with careful analysis for inclusion and belonging of all groups, especially the most vulnerable ones.

Cross-training and relationships: as stated above, there are actions that need to be taken by WASH and CP actors both individually and together. This requires elements of cross-training on the other sector, as well as strong relationships to work together in the design, implementation, monitoring, and evaluation of integrated programming.

WASH infrastructure and education in schools: further expansion of CP and WASH integration in and around schools is necessary to meet children's needs. This includes developed WASH infrastructure to ensure children can stay at school and learn safely. It also includes WASH education in the classroom, including WASH clubs that can be created to provide age-appropriate education on handwashing and safe maintenance of toilets.

Support preparedness and anticipatory action: preparedness and anticipatory actions should be enacted to prepare CP and WASH activities to respond quickly to new threats.,Planning should include how to strengthen CP systems, including referrals and monitoring, WASH infrastructure and programming, and education systems against shocks such as conflict, climate-change, and COVID-19 (Cowley, 2021). Linking WASH committees with CP committees can allow for both groups to more effectively prepare for future implementation, including CP staff participation in WASH awareness-raising activities and WASH staff identification and referral of CP concerns.

Investments: increased investment is needed to implement key integrated actions and make integrated systems both higher quality and more resilient to shocks such as the 3Cs. For example, according to UNICEF, '[i nvestments that improve access to resilient water, sanitation and hygiene (WASH) services can considerably reduce overall climate risk for 415 million children ... Investments that improve access to social protection and reducing poverty can considerably reduce overall climate risk for 310 million children.' (Rees and UNICEF, 2021)

These are just some examples of the important work for integrated WASH and CP in development, nexus, and humanitarian settings. Children's needs, voices, and protection must be considered and prioritized in all interventions.

Acknowledgements

The author thanks her Save the Children US colleagues Phoebe Marabi, humanitarian child protection senior advisor, and Emily Varni, education in emergencies advisor, for their technical review of this chapter. She also thanks

Jean Syanda, humanitarian child protection advisor at Save the Children US and Abraham Varampath, senior WASH advisor at Save the Children UK, for sharing their experiences for the case studies. Additionally, the author thanks Peter Della-Rocca for his assistance copy-editing this chapter.

References

Carter, C. 2019. 'Safeguarding children in WASH'. Save the Children. <https://resourcecentre.savethechildren.net/pdf/sc_child_safeguarding_wash_2019.pdf>

Cowley, A. 2021. 'Build forward better: how the global community can protect education from the climate crisis'. Save the Children. <https://resourcecentre.savethechildren.net/pdf/Build-Forward-Better_How-to-protect-education-from-the-climate-crisis_FINAL.pdf>

Dooley, T. and UNICEF. 2017. 'Thirsting for a future: water and children in a changing climate'. <https://www.unicef.org/media/49621/file/UNICEF_Thirsting_for_a_Future_ENG.pdf>

Edwards, J. 2020. 'Protect a generation: the impact of COVID-19 on children's lives'. Save the Children. <https://resourcecentre.savethechildren.net/pdf/vr59-01_protect_a_generation_report_en_0.pdf>

Elrha. 2019. 'Latrine design process becomes child's play'. <https://www.elrha.org/project-blog/latrine-design-process-becomes-childs-play>

Epstein, A. and E. Bendavid, D. Nash, E.D. Charlebois, S.D. Weiser. 2020. 'Drought and intimate partner violence towards women in 19 countries in sub-Saharan Africa during 2011–2018: a population-based study'. *Plos Medicine* 17(3): e1003064. <https://doi.org/10.1371/journal.pmed.1003064>

Fore, H.H. 2020. 'A wake-up call: COVID-19 and its impact on children's health and wellbeing'. *The Lancet*. <https://doi.org/10.1016/S2214-109X(20)30238-2>

Habib, M. 2020. 'COVID-19 exacerbates the effects of water shortages on women in Yemen'. [blog post]. Wilson Center. 20 August. <https://www.wilsoncenter.org/blog-post/covid-19-exacerbates-effects-water-shortages-women-yemen

Hillis, S.D. and H.J.T. Unwin, Y. Chen, L. Cluver, L. Sherr, P.S. Goldman, O. Ratmann, et al. 2021. 'Global minimum estimates of children affected by COVID-19-associated orphanhood and deaths of caregivers: a modelling study'. *The Lancet* 398(10298): 391–402. <https://doi.org/10.1016/S0140-6736(21)01253-8>

Khan, N. 2015. 'Scoping study: women's sexual & reproductive health and rights (SRHR) and climate change: what is the connection?' Khan Foundation and ARROW. <https://arrow.org.my/wp-content/uploads/2016/05/Climate-Change-and-SRHR-Scoping-Study_Bangladesh.pdf>

Levy, B.S. and V.W. Sidel, J.A. Patz. 2017. 'Climate change and collective violence'. *Annual Review of Public Health* 38: 241–257. <https://doi.org/10.1146/annurev-publhealth-031816-044232>

Nnah-Ogbonda, E. and S. Jennings. 2021. 'Exploring the link between climate change and violence against children'. Save the Children. <https://resourcecentre.savethechildren.net/pdf/Investigating-climate-change-and-violence-against-children.pdf>

Plush, T. and L. Nyamadzawo. 2021. 'Making climate and environment policies for & with children and young people'. UNICEF. <https://www.unicef.org/media/109701/file/Making-Climate-Policies-for-and-with-Children-and-Young-People.pdf>

Rees, N. and UNICEF. 2021. 'The climate crisis is a child rights crisis: introducing the children's climate risk index'. <https://www.unicef.org/reports/climate-crisis-child-rights-crisis>

Ryan, E. 2021. 'Born into the climate crisis: why we must act now to secure children's rights'. Save the Children. <https://resourcecentre.savethechildren.net/pdf/born-into-the-climate-crisis.pdf>

Save the Children. 2021. 'Plan familia para prevenir el COVID-19'. <https://resourcecentre.savethechildren.net/pdf/Plan Familia para prevenir el Covid19.pdf

———. 2020. 'Stress busters'. <https://resourcecentre.savethechildren.net/pdf/ch1426389.pdf>

———. 2017. 'Children face increased violence and exploitation as famine looms in drought-stricken Somalia'. [press release]. April 27. <https://www.savethechildren.org/us/about-us/media-and-news/2017-press-releases/children-face-increased-violence-and-exploitation-as-famine-loom>

———. 2007. 'Save the Children's definition of child protection'. <https://resourcecentre.savethechildren.net/document/save-childrens-definition-child-protection>

Sevekari, P.B. 2016. 'When coping crumbles: drought in India 2015-16'. UNICEF India. <https://reliefweb.int/sites/reliefweb.int/files/resources/pub_doc117.pdf>

Steinmetz, K. 2020. 'She coined the term "intersectionality" over 30 years ago. here's what it means to her today'. *Time*. 20 February. <https://time.com/5786710/kimberle-crenshaw-intersectionality>

The Alliance for Child Protection in Humanitarian Action. 019. *Minimum Standards for Child Protection in Humanitarian Action*. <https://alliancecpha.org/en/CPMS_home>

———. 2018. 'Advocacy brief: integrating child protection and education in emergencies'. <https://alliancecpha.org/en/child-protection-online-library/advocacy-brief-integrating-child-protection-and-education>

UNICEF. 2021a. 'Child displacement and refugees'. UNICEF DATA. <https://data.unicef.org/topic/child-migration-and-displacement/displacement>

———. 2021b. 'COVID-19 confirmed cases and deaths'. UNICEF DATA. <https://data.unicef.org/resources/covid-19-confirmed-cases-and-deaths-dashboard>

———. 2021c. 'Tracking the situation of children during COVID-19'. UNICEF DATA. <https://data.unicef.org/resources/rapid-situation-tracking-covid-19-socioeconomic-impacts-data-viz>

———. 2021d. 'Water under fire: attacks on water and sanitation services in armed conflict and the impacts on children'. <https://www.unicef.org/media/98976/file/Water%20Under%20Fire%20%20%20Volume3.pdf>

———. 2019. 'UNICEF Fast Facts: WASH in conflict'. <https://www.unicef.org/stories/fast-facts-water-sanitation-hygiene-conflict>

UNICEF. 2019. 'Water under fire: emergencies, development and peace in fragile and conflict-affected contexts'. <https://www.unicef.org/reports/emergencies-development-peace-in-fragile-and-conflict-affected-contexts-2019>

UNICEF and WHO. 2020. 'Progress on drinking water, sanitation and hygiene in schools: special focus on COVID19'. <https://data.unicef.org/resources/progress-on-drinking-water-sanitation-and-hygiene-in-schools-special-focus-on-covid-19>

United Nations. 2020a. 'Policy brief: the impact of COVID-19 on women'. <https://www.unwomen.org/sites/default/files/Headquarters/Attachments/Sections/Library/Publications/2020/Policy-brief-The-impact-of-COVID-19-on-women-en.pdf>

United Nations. 2020b. 'Policy brief: the impact of COVID-19 on children'. <https://unsdg.un.org/sites/default/files/2020-04/160420_Covid_Children_Policy_Brief.pdf>

Varampath, A. 2020. 'COVID-19 hygiene promotion initiatives – Save the Children in North West Syria' [unpublished].

Williams, T.P. and K. Pontalti. 2020. 'Responding to the shadow pandemic: taking stock of gender-based violence risks and responses during COVID-19'. *Child Protection Learning Brief #1*. UNICEF. <https://www.unicef.org/ukraine/media/8301/file/Gender-Based-Violence-in-Emergencies-CP-Learning-Brief-Aug-2020.pdf>

CHAPTER 8

Focusing on the future: integration of WASH around conflict, COVID-19, and climate change

Mariëlle Snel[1] and Nikolas Sorensen

Introduction

Humanitarian crises are increasingly complicated, as responders must negotiate the consequences of the 3Cs – conflict, COVID, and climate change.[2] When we conceptualized this publication, the COVID-19 pandemic dominated humanitarian conversations, as the outbreak exacerbated the needs of those living in humanitarian settings. Now, as we bring this work to a close, we are watching another major conflict in Ukraine bring a flood of refugees into eastern Europe. The conflict in Ukraine has captured the attention of the media, funders, and humanitarian organizations. There is growing concern that this conflict in eastern Europe will significantly impact already underfunded crises in places like Afghanistan, Bangladesh, Ethiopia, Horn of Africa, Myanmar, The Sahel, Syria, and Yemen, as the west focuses on this new conflict that is 'closer to home' (Egeland, 2022; Anyadike et al, 2022; Høvring, 2022). This is highlighted, for example, with the current drought and famine crisis in the Horn of Africa, which is facing once of the worst droughts in at least 40 years, missing a fourth harvest season in a row (OCHA, 2022c). In 2021 the number of people in need of humanitarian assistance and protection increased by some 39 million, from 235 million to 274 million – a nearly 15 per cent increase, the highest figure in decades (OCHA 2022a; 2022b). The number of those requiring humanitarian assistance is likely to continue to rise as the full impact of the conflict in Ukraine and other ongoing crises found throughout the world becomes clear.[3]

The UN reports that a quarter of the world's population, or about 2 billion people, currently live without access to safe water in their homes, and nearly half of the world's population lives without adequate sanitation (WHO and UNICEF, 2021). These conditions had staggering implications with the onset of the COVID-19 pandemic. UNICEF reported that '3 in 10 people worldwide could not wash their hands with soap and water within their homes' (UNICEF, 2021).

WASH is an ideal entry point for multisectoral integration, as it is a critical precursor to effective health, nutrition, shelter, education, and child protection response and is vital in order to reach the desired impact as outlined in many of the sustainable development goals (SDGs) by 2030.

In many organizations, specifically INGOs, there is a growing focus on integrating WASH with different subsectors, such as health, nutrition, shelter, education, and child protection programming, with the aim of improving the reach and impact of WASH services. Implicitly, integrated programming intends to allow more people within and across communities, nations, and regions to access improved WASH services. However, there remain critical gaps in coordination and integration between various actors within the humanitarian and the development WASH subsectors, which represent opportunities for further growth and improved programme outcomes.

Integrated WASH, as stated in the introduction, refers to innovative, multisectoral programming in both humanitarian and development settings that can not only bridge the humanitarian and development divide, but also subsector silos. This requires systematic alignment between multisector organizations and intersectoral ministries, all working towards a shared vision for emergency response, recovery, development, and future resilience. External factors from climate change to food insecurities, pandemics such as COVID, and global conflicts will continue to force WASH professionals to move more rapidly, with scarcer resources and divided attention, as they face the ever-growing and prolonged nature of today's emergencies. Beyond this, practitioners must also balance humanitarian response with the consequences of crucial external factors, such as fragile states, socio-economic and political tensions, water scarcity due to climate change, and food insecurity, as they seek to connect emergency response to long-term WASH programming. Hence, the integrated role of WASH with other subthemes will be far more visible in the coming years (Bill and Melinda Gates Foundation, n.d.). Non-household settings and integrated programming will also play a further vital role in future WASH developments, including how we develop and structure ongoing responses.

One strong example of sectors working together to meet the needs of those living in humanitarian settings is the joint operational framework (JOF) leveraging the humanitarian response to cholera between the Global Health Cluster and the Global WASH Cluster (GHC and GWC, 2020). This framework is a good example of the intersectoral nature of WASH. It highlights the value that can be achieved by different humanitarian sectors integrating their programming to meet humanitarian challenges. This framework can be used as a template to integrate humanitarian WASH with other sectors like those discussed in this book, including health, nutrition, shelter, education, and child protection, as well as other critical sectors, like food security and safety. Furthermore, this framework is a crucial development in the ongoing discussion on integrated WASH programming and is a vital tool for aiding the humanitarian sector's ability to bridge the humanitarian–development–peace nexus.

Building frameworks for integrated WASH programming with other vital sectors is crucial. This type of integration requires reimagining how humanitarian sectors and development organizations work together. Among other changes, as we have argued in the past, this requires rethinking how data is created and shared, and how organizations can more effectively collaborate to meet challenges during the humanitarian response (Snel and Sorensen, 2021). Developing reliable data, be it financial, environmental, institutional, technical, and/or social, based on research in humanitarian settings will be critical for moving the WASH sector forward. This also necessitates developing more evidence of success and a more significant commitment by humanitarian as well as development organizations and responders to conduct and produce research beyond the general aid reports that focus primarily on what happened and what was delivered (Deola et al, 2021). This will require a synthesis of evidence and linking of case studies that not only bridge the humanitarian–development divide but, vitally, cross organizational lines, linking impact and learning from many different responders and allowing for a deeper understanding of the breadth of response during a crisis.

In chapter 2, Grieve highlights six key drivers for increasing better cooperation and integration in the humanitarian–development WASH sector:

1. an increasing number of protracted, overlapping, and recurrent crises;
2. water insecurity and degradation of water systems;
3. a severe lack of access to WASH services and unsafe community WASH behaviour, particularly in these contexts;
4. an exposure and vulnerability to shocks and stresses exacerbate the severe lack of WASH services;
5. an inability to effectively finance resilient WASH systems; and
6. the ineffectiveness of the siloed approach.

It is primarily the last point that the silo approach is no longer working that needs to be emphasized. Grieve argues that,

> *Significant structural barriers must be overcome to break down the silos between the humanitarian, development, and peace pillars. Different mandates, priorities, planning horizons, funding cycles, and modes of operation have led to norms, culture, and language specific to each pillar, consequently creating disincentives to collaborate (Mason and Mosello, 2016). For example, with respect to funding, humanitarians are often bound by short-term funding cycles, while many development actors lack the capacity to operate in insecure environments over the long term (Tuchel, 2020).*

Remedies to these problems are not simple, often requiring a new and more profound rethinking of systems as they stand. Yet, it is from this engagement that innovation focused on a holistic picture of the lives of those we serve emerges, and new avenues to meaningful impact appear. It is in this line of thinking that the notable central theme throughout the previous chapters has been focused on conflict, COVID-19, and climate change. The tremendous impact of these 3Cs on the livelihoods and prosperity of those living in poverty is devastating, and disproportionally affects the most marginalized populations. Until now, there has not been any specific WASH publication of this kind that reflects on these fundamental external factors that inevitably will play a vital role in the delivery of WASH services over the humanitarian–development divide within the context of fundamental subsectors. In this publication, we have sought, with the help of our contributors, to fill this vital knowledge gap by addressing the 3Cs from the perspective of multiple sectors.

Conflict has long been the most visible and devastating source of forced displacement, yet the effect of climate change on global displacement is growing in impact. Access to safe water and sanitation facilities, and adopting effective hygiene practices are fundamental to reducing maternal and child morbidity and mortality globally, especially in conflict. In armed conflict settings, inadequate WASH infrastructure poses significant health risks to all, especially women and children. UNHCR cites that in mid-2021, for the first time in recorded history, the number of people forcibly displaced was 89.3 million, with over 27.1 million refugees (UNHCR, 2021). These displacement numbers are due to conflict, geopolitical instability, economic challenges, and climate change factors (Marshall, 2015). Climate change is, and will continue to be, one of the most significant contributors to forced displacement globally. As Dehghan (2021) states, 'intense storms and flooding triggered three times more displacements than violent conflicts did last year, as the number of people internally displaced worldwide hit the highest level on record'. Climate-related displacement amplifies conflicts between people and nations as resources, particularly water, become harder to secure.

Climate changes can severely affect countries worldwide, impacting infrastructure, moving, or reducing water supply. They can also lead to contamination, as sewage and human waste requirements and capabilities change. UNECE (2022) notes that, 'globally, each 1°C of temperature increase caused by global warming is projected to result in a 20% reduction in renewable water resources and to affect an additional 7% of the population'. As temperatures rise, these problems will continue to compound and will have the greatest impact on poor, marginalized populations who are already at higher risk of conflict and forced migration that come from increased water insecurity.

The COVID-19 pandemic, in contrast to conflict and climate change, thus far, has not had a direct influence on displacement but instead has had an amplification impact on the conditions of those living in displacement. Desye (2021) showed the direct link between effective COVID-19 response, WASH services, and public health, noting how 'strengthening and ensuring access to WASH services are important for preventing COVID-19 and realizing human rights'. This systematical review from 2021 identified the impacts and challenges of COVID-19 in the provision of WASH services. The results implied that COVID-19 has significant implications on WASH services that can affect the health of individuals, families, and communities. Community engagement can also be used to support the prevention and management of COVID-19. Countries need to expand their investment in WASH services as an essential mechanism for mitigating COVID-19. Additionally, there is a tremendous need for national governments and international organizations to increase funding assistance to aid communities in improving WASH infrastructure and services. To protect public health during the outbreaks of infectious diseases, including the COVID-19 pandemic, the provision of WASH services is vitally important. The challenges of inaccessible WASH services, along with the pandemic of COVID-19 in low-income countries, can lead to devastating problems (Desye, 2021).

Synthesis of each chapter

As we have stated several times, integration is complex and requires a change in the way we think and organize humanitarian and development responses. There is a delicate balance between increasing coordination and integration across sectors and silos, and over-integration, which may lead to confusion, unneeded complexity, and disengagement. However, finding this balance requires agreement on the need and value of coordination. All the authors here agree that integration, though not a silver-bullet solution, brings the potential for added value and impact to the lives of those served. Gibbons, Mena-Lander, and Khan in chapter 1 state that 'there is arguably no longer as much of a need to prove the causal connection between WASH and the prevention of these larger public health issues to justify the resources and commitment needed to ensure successful [intersectoral collaboration] between it and other sectors.' However, it is much easier to say integration is needed than it is to pull it off successfully.

This is where Grieve's JOF, in chapter 2, significantly contributes to the ongoing discussion around integrated WASH programming. Grieve argues that,

> *The purpose of the JOF is to assist policymakers, directors, coordinators, and practitioners within government, civil society, private sector, UN agencies, banks, donors, and academia at the regional, transboundary, national, and subnational level to integrate (where feasible) resilience, conflict sensitivity, and peacebuilding capacities into existing and new WASH programmes by leveraging the nexus approach.*

> *Leveraging the nexus approach means encouraging collaboration and programming coherence and coordination across humanitarian, development, and peace pillars within the WASH sector, while respecting organizational mandates and acknowledging that solutions are context-specific and locally driven.*

Gibbons, Mena-Lander, and Khan agree with Grieve's push for more coordination and the need for an overall 'coherence' between WASH programme designers and responders across the humanitarian, development, and peace sectors. Grieve argues that the process to achieve this requires actors to:

- Mainstream the nexus approach in WASH programmes at the national and sub-national level, especially in protracted and recurrent crisis contexts.
- Adopt flexible and sustainable financing strategies into protracted and recurrent crisis contexts, and leverage financing to achieve the SDGs.
- Advocate for predictable, un-earmarked and flexible multiyear funding, and the development of innovative financing and forecasting models.
- Continue to build key evidence, learning and capacity.

One of the strongest recommendations found across all the chapters in this volume is the call for shared analysis and planning. This discussion often centred on the early analysis and planning at the beginning of a crisis and during all phases of monitoring, evaluation, and learning. Dodos and Riems, along with Webb, argue for the need to conduct joint, multisectoral assessments between WASH and the subsectors of nutrition and shelter. Dodos and Riems in chapter 4 suggest further that joint assessments are 'more likely to foster a comprehensive understanding of the situation and context-specific needs and encourage an integrated response'. All the authors from our five subsector chapters discuss the importance of shared monitoring, evaluation, and learning and the benefits of united analysis and understanding of programme impacts as well as coordinated learning and response around new gaps. However, indicators across the WASH humanitarian and development silos, as they stand now, often focus on access to WASH services, too often honing in on the quantitative number of hardware constructed and forgetting measures of impact on health outcomes. In a previous publication, we discussed WASH indicators as they transition from humanitarian to development contexts (Snel and Sorensen, 2021); however, there is still significant room for improvement, especially in humanitarian contexts, as we look for ways to connect access to services to decreases in health risk. Furthering this point in chapter 6, Corwith and E. Sorensen note that, 'while access is necessary, the short-term focus on access does not adequately address longer-term needs to ensure the sustainability and resilience of WASH services'. All the contributors in this publication note the need for changes in the way we measure, share, and learn from WASH services in various contexts, to meet the unique perspectives that integration demands. As such, the humanitarian and development WASH indicators, when aligned with integrated programming, may not suffice. Showing impact is key to solving funding gaps and increasing coordination and integration of WASH services with other sectors (Ramesh et al, 2015; Esteves and Cumming, 2016).

As discussed earlier, Grieve suggests that one of the critical reasons for integration is that siloed responses to emergencies are no longer working. In chapter 5, Webb makes a similar argument, suggesting that siloed programme design, particularly in urban areas, is no longer ideal. Webb suggests further that,

> [a] renewed focus on environmental health and an operational approach which brings together normally siloed sectors in order to achieve wellbeing outcomes aligns with humanitarian mandates and development goals. Both Shelter and WASH have important roles to play: the positive impacts of healthier homes will contribute to recovery and therefore bridge the humanitarian–development nexus. A new coordinated approach to displaced people's shelter and WASH needs, guided by environmental health, will prompt better long-term outcomes and contribute to the achievement of the Sustainable Development Goals.

Webb's discussion goes well beyond the connections between WASH and shelter, but is critically true for connections between WASH and health, nutrition, shelter, education, child protection, and beyond. Bridging between silos has a compounding impact on people's lives and livelihoods, and can lead to more substantial long-term outcomes.

Each of our contributors discusses community-led programming and the need for local, ground-up input in integrated WASH programme design and implementation. It cannot be overstated how true this is everywhere. However, it is particularly true when it comes to children. Child, family, and community inputs are required at every stage of programme implementation, particularly in the early stages of humanitarian response, when the foundations of WASH design are being made. Jeffery, in chapter 8 argues that,

> *Integrating child protection and WASH interventions requires ensuring that WASH activities include children and their needs in the design, implementation, and monitoring of programmes. It also includes specific programmes for children, and appropriate referrals for children and families in need of specialized child protection support.*

This is equally discussed in Corwith and E. Sorensen's chapter 6 analysis of integrated WASH with education. The ways we consider, discuss, and plan for children's physical, social, and cultural needs are vital to their nutrition, health, education, and overall safety. Integration across various subsectors, and the humanitarian and development divide, allows for these essential considerations to be made early in the planning cycle and leads to more robust, safer programming.

However, we must be realistic about how organizations navigate integration across the different humanitarian and development response phases. Webb, in chapter 5, argues that we must also be pragmatic and allow local context and circumstances to dictate what is appropriate and feasible. Webb continues, 'the humanitarian system has many demands for the integration of cross-cutting issues. Asking individuals, agencies, and clusters to consider further integration and operational change can be unwelcome'. Hence there is a need to balance calls for integration with a realistic view of local context and organization capability, which dictates to what extent integration across subsectors is possible. However, we must be careful to avoid arguments around the difficulty of integration from preventing or avoiding the value that comes from further coordination and bridging efforts.

In chapter 1, Gibbons, Mena-Lander, and Khan highlight additional barriers to integration, noting significant ambiguity around organizations' roles, and how resources are designed and utilized. Furthermore, real challenges and disagreements exist on when, where, and how information measurement and sharing should and can take place. These concerns are not easily overcome and require context-specific considerations that prevent simple silver-bullet solutions. Arguments for integration inherently require practitioners to retrain their focus. It is not about connecting any given subsector with others but about seeing the marginalized individuals we aim to serve, and to address the sum of their needs and aspirations. Gibbons, Mena-Lander, and Khan argue further that the humanitarian sector spends too much time focused on 'saving lives as usual' and too little time on emergency's social and economic causes in the first place. Integration across the humanitarian–development–peace nexus requires us to consider solutions that address not only the situation marginalized groups are in, but how they got there, where they want to go, and what they want to become.

What do these drivers of action mean for the future?

In a previous publication, we discussed the next generation of humanitarian and development practitioners and the skills they will need in the future. We stated that,

> Predictions made by various professionals state that, over the next 10 years, the humanitarian and development field will face significant changes as new skills, expanded technologies, shifting funding streams, and growing complexity all collide within the sector. This will require professionals to be even more open-minded, proactive, and innovative to remain successful. Additionally, this will require teams, especially in multi-mandated organizations, to reimagine their systems, organizational structures, implementing principles, and expectations in ways that promote 'collaborative co-production' between teams and lead to new shared outcomes. (Snel and Sorensen, 2021).

We see a future in which the humanitarian WASH practitioner's primary focus will still be on saving lives. But, by necessity, they will be required to save lives while strengthening the resilience of the WASH sector to ensure predictable emergency responses and protect gains towards the SDGs. This will require synergies to be built between acute humanitarian situations, protracted contexts, and the development sector, especially around ongoing external factors that will continue to exasperate around conflict, COVID-19/

pandemics, and climate change. This is done by focusing on humanitarian WASH programme designs that emphasize long-term programming and perspectives from the beginning, including building community preparedness, coordinated transitions, and stronger resilience at each stage of the humanitarian, transitional, and development spectrum.

We continue here the argument we made previously, only now with an added emphasis on the 3Cs linked to a multisectoral integrated approach. Successful WASH practitioners will realize that the sustainable management and use of conflict, COVID-19/pandemic, and climate change-resilient water and sanitation services will further enhance WASH efforts linked to human rights that are respected at all times, including during and after natural and human-made disasters. This, we argue, will require a further reflection on integrated WASH systems based on a systems approach that builds a holistic understanding of WASH systems, especially in humanitarian settings, and identifies and works around barriers that block the realization of inclusive, sustainable, and universal access to WASH services.

Notes

1. Marïelle Snel is the Senior Global Humanitarian WASH advisor for Save the Children International, however the opinions addressed in this chapter are expressly her own and do not represent Save the Children in any way.
2. The United Nations reports that a quarter of the world's population, or about 2 billion people, currently live without access to safe water in their homes (WHO and UNICEF 2021). This same report indicated that nearly half of the world's population lives without adequate sanitation (WHO and UNICEF 2021). These conditions have staggering implications with the onset of the COVID-19 pandemic: '3 in 10 people worldwide could not wash their hands with soap and water within their homes' (UNICEF 2021). Water, hygiene, and sanitation (WASH) is an ideal entry point for multisectoral integration, as it is a critical precursor to effective health, nutrition, shelter, education, and child protection response.
3. At the time of this publication other key conflicts include: Haiti, Ukraine, Ethiopia, Yemen, Afghanistan, Myanmar, Taiwan, and Iran (International Crisis Group 2021).

References

Anyadike, O., and P. Kleinfeld, I. Loy, A. Slemrod, P. Dodds, E. Reidy. 2022. 'Beyond Ukraine: eight more humanitarian disasters that demand your attention.' *The New Humanitarian*. 7 March. <https://www.thenewhumanitarian.org/news/2022/03/07/beyond-ukraine-eight-other-humanitarian-crises-raging-around-globe>

Bill and Melinda Gates Foundation. n.d. 'Integrated development'. [web page] <https://www.gatesfoundation.org/our-work/programs/global-health/integrated-development>

Deola, C. and S.Y.A. Khan, A. Torres, E. Kearney, and R. Schweitzer. 2021. 'Breaking down silos: integrating WASH into displacement crisis response'. *Forced Migration Review* 67 (August): 4–7.

Dehghan, S.K. 2021. 'Climate disasters "caused more internal displacement than war" in 2020'. *The Guardian*. 20 May. <https://www.theguardian.com/global-development/2021/may/20/climate-disasters-caused-more-internal-displacement-than-war-in-2020>

Desye, B. 2021. 'COVID-19 pandemic and water, sanitation, and hygiene: impacts, challenges, and mitigation strategies'. *Environmental Health Insights* 15 (January): 11786302211029448. <https://doi.org/10.1177/11786302211029447>

Egeland, J. 2022. 'The "Ukraine effect" on the world's poorest and most vulnerable'. 5 April. <https://www.aljazeera.com/opinions/2022/4/5/the-ukraine-effect-on-the-worlds-poorest-and-most-vulnerable>

Esteves, J. and O. Cumming. 2016. 'The Impact of water, sanitation and hygiene on key health and social outcomes: review of evidence'. UNICEF. <https://www.lshtm.ac.uk/sites/default/files/2017-07/WASHEvidencePaper_HighRes_01.23.17_0.pdf>

GHC and GWC. 2020. 'Joint operational framework: improving coordinated and integrated multi-sector cholera preparedness and response within humanitarian crises'. <https://healthcluster.who.int/publications/m/item/joint-operational-framework-improving-coordinated-and-integrated-multi-sector-cholera-preparedness-and-response-within-humanitarian-crises>

Høvring, R. 2022. 'The war in Ukraine is bad news for the world's refugees'. *NRC*. 25 March. <https://www.nrc.no/perspectives/the-war-in-ukraine-is-bad-news-for-the-worlds-refugees>

International Crisis Group. 2021. 'Ten conflicts to watch in 2022'. 9 December. <https://conflicts2022.crisisgroup.org>

Marshall, T. 2015. *Prisoners of Geography: Ten Maps That Explain Everything About the World*. London, England: Elliott & Thompson.

Mason, N. and B. Mosello. 2016. 'Making humanitarian and development WASH work better together'. Overseas Development Institute. <https://odi.org/en/publications/making-humanitarian-and-development-wash-work-better-together>

OCHA. 2022a. 'Appeals and response plans 2022 | Financial tracking service'. <https://fts.unocha.org/appeals/overview/2022>

———. 2022b. 'Global humanitarian overview 2022'. <https://www.unocha.org/2022gho>

———. 2022c. 'Horn of Africa drought: humanitarian update'. [press release] 10 June. <https://reliefweb.int/report/ethiopia/horn-africa-drought-humanitarian-update-10-june-2022#:~:text=Communities%20in%20the%20Horn%20of,meteorological%20agencies%20and%20humanitarian%20organizations>

Ramesh, A. and K. Blanchet, J.H.J. Ensink, B. Roberts. 2015. 'Evidence on the effectiveness of water, sanitation, and hygiene (WASH) interventions on health outcomes in humanitarian crises: a systematic review'. *PloS One* 10 (9): e0124688. <https://doi.org/10.1371/journal.pone.0124688>

Snel, M. and N. Sorensen. 2021. *Bridging the WASH Humanitarian–Development Divide: Building a Sustainable Reality*. Rugby, UK: Practical

Action Publishing. <https://practicalactionpublishing.com/book/2577/bridging-the-wash-humanitariandevelopment-divide>
Tuchel, L. 2022. 'Multi-year humanitarian funding: global baselines and trends'. Development Initiatives. <https://devinit.org/documents/706/Multi-year_humanitarian_funding_Global_baselines_and_trends.pdf>
UNECE. 2022. 'Climate change threatens access to water and sanitation, warn UNECE & WHO/Europe, urging reinforced measures under protocol to boost resilience'. [press release]. 20 May. <https://unece.org/climate-change/press/climate-change-threatens-access-water-and-sanitation-warn-unece-whoeurope>
UNHCR. 2021. 'UNHCR – refugee statistics'. <https://www.unhcr.org/refugee-statistics/#:~:text=At%20the%20end%20of%202021,below%2018%20years%20of%20age.&text=Between%202018%20and%202021%2C%20an,a%20refugee%20life%20per%20year>
UNICEF. 2021. 'Billions of people will lack access to safe water, sanitation and hygiene in 2030 unless progress quadruples – warn WHO, UNICEF'. [press release]. 1 July. <https://www.unicef.org/press-releases/billions-people-will-lack-access-safe-water-sanitation-and-hygiene-2030-unless>
WHO and UNICEF. 2021. 'Progress on household drinking water, sanitation and hygiene 2000-2020: five years into the SDGs'. Geneva: WHO and UNICEF. <https://www.who.int/publications/i/item/9789240030848>

Index

Accountability 4–5, 11, 25, 37–38, 40, 46, 48, 59, 78, 100, 113, 123, 145
Advocacy 48, 60, 69, 79, 116–117, 120, 127–128, 131
Agriculture 6–8, 11–14, 17–18, 91, 94–95, 110, 123, 162
AIDS 12–13, 71 (also see HIV)

BabyWASH 89, 98–99
Behaviour Change 9, 15, 20, 67, 76, 89, 101

Camp settings 75–76, 120–121, 161
Caregivers 74, 90, 97–98, 100, 153–154, 160, 165, 168
Cash and Vouchers 48, 121
Center of Disease Control (CDC) 67
child nutrition xii, 92
child protection x, xiii, 110, 126, 153–158, 167, 170–171, 176, 181, 183
child safeguarding xiii, 153, 168–169
Cholera 6, 8, 17–19, 67, 69, 74, 92–93, 112, 159, 176
clean clinic approach 20, 26–27
Clean Water 16, 24, 67, 98, 112, 122, 135, 139, 143
Clusters 1, 3, 6, 8, 11, 14, 16–17, 20, 28, 109–110, 113, 118, 127, 129, 131, 181
Collaboration xii, 1, 3–4, 13, 16, 19–20, 22, 27, 34–35, 37–40, 46–47, 50–51, 53–55, 57–58, 61, 74–76, 79–80, 109, 128–129, 138, 141, 155–156, 179
Collective Outcomes 9, 21–22, 39, 41–44, 46, 50–52, 55–57
Community
  Engagement 8, 40, 48, 117, 146, 169, 179
  Level 19–20, 46, 100, 114, 117, 129, 158, 161, 163, 165
  management of acute malnutrition (CMAM) 88
  mobilization 117
Community-led total sanitation (CLTS) x, 28, 88, 98
Comparative Advantage 53–54
Conflict-sensitive 42, 44, 140–141
Coordination 1–11, 13, 16, 18–22, 25–27, 34–35, 37–41, 43, 47–54, 57–61, 69, 72, 75–76, 78–79, 81, 101, 109, 114, 118–119, 129–131, 142, 176, 179–180, 182
cross-sectoral 10, 13, 19, 25
Cultural 70, 90, 111, 114, 157, 167, 181

Development nexus *see* nexus
Diarrhea 67, 79, 87–89, 92, 98, 139, 158
Dignity Kits 160
Disease Outbreaks ix, 18, 44, 77, 99, 119, 161–162
do no harm 38–39, 42, 140

economic 15, 18, 21, 23–24, 34, 41, 67–72, 81, 85–86, 93, 95–96, 140, 145, 161, 164, 178, 182
Emergency Response xii, 1, 5–6, 10, 13, 15, 17, 20, 40, 45, 49, 59, 111–112, 114, 138, 176, 182
Environmental x–xi, 4, 14, 17–18, 24, 37
environmental Health 99, 110–112, 125, 128–130, 181
evaluation xiii, 6–10, 12, 21, 26–27, 48, 60, 69, 78–80, 98, 100, 120, 123, 127, 141–142, 155, 157, 170, 180

Faecal-oral diseases 89–90, 160
Financial x, 14–16, 48, 58, 94, 122, 145, 177
Food security 1, 17, 24, 41, 55, 93, 95, 110, 162, 176
Food shortages 91
Fragile contexts 33, 37, 58, 61, 95, 159

Gender 28, 37–38, 71, 99, 109, 112, 115, 119, 122, 124, 129, 135–136, 143, 147, 153, 155–158, 162–164, 168, 170
Gender-based violence 37, 71, 115, 119, 122, 124, 153, 162
Geographical 100
Global Health Cluster (GHC) 6, 109, 176
Global WASH Cluster (GWC) 1, 4–6, 8, 10, 23, 33, 109
Government
  Local 19, 53–54, 56, 74, 98, 114
  policies 25
Grand Bargain 34, 37
Groundwater 39, 95

Handwashing 21, 68, 73, 76–77, 89–90, 93, 97–99, 125, 135–136, 138, 143, 158–159, 161, 165–167, 170
health care facilities xii, 20, 27, 67–68, 70–73, 75, 79–80, 92, 97
HIV 12–13, 71, 87 (also see AIDS)
Housing xii, 76, 109–111, 117–119, 121, 125, 130
Human Rights 38, 42, 109, 178, 183
Humanitarian
  Actors 3, 21–22, 40–41, 53, 56, 59, 78, 110, 113, 124, 129
  Assistance 7, 16, 36, 43, 72, 111, 131, 135, 175
  Crisis 2, 130, 137, 139, 158
  nexus: *see* nexus
  response ix, xii, 1–6, 12, 16, 21, 28, 52, 56, 62, 78, 129, 135, 141, 148, 176–177, 181

infection prevention and control (IPC) 2, 15–16, 20–21, 27, 97
Infections 14, 23, 71, 85–90, 99, 112, 137

Insecurity (*also see* security) 1, 36–37, 86, 90–91, 94, 96, 140, 161, 163, 176–178
Institutional x, 15, 20, 25–27, 78, 115, 177
Inter-Agency Standing Committee (IASC) 2, 5–6, 11, 21, 53, 131
Internally Displaced Persons (IDPs) xii, 53, 67–68, 74–77, 122, 159, 161

joint operational framework xii, 6, 33, 176

Latrines 4, 17, 20, 72, 74–75, 90, 97, 110, 113–114, 117–120, 122, 125, 131, 142–143, 148, 163, 169
Learning x, 33, 40, 50, 54, 58–59, 61, 67, 70–71, 77–80, 100, 109, 123, 128, 135–137, 141–142, 144, 147–148, 158, 166, 177, 180
Livelihoods xi, 36–37, 75, 91, 110, 124–125, 163, 178, 181
Local Funding 145
Localization 2, 4, 21, 38–39, 51, 74, 145
long term indicators xiii, 143

Mainstream 60, 70, 109, 153, 167, 180
Malaria 23, 74, 86–87, 93, 99, 112
Malnutrition 1, 10, 12, 14–15, 17, 26, 74, 85, 88–95, 97–99, 162
Marginalized 68–71, 75, 77, 144, 178, 182
Menstrual Hygiene 12, 70, 113, 136, 141, 155–157, 160, 162
Menstrual Hygiene management (MHM) 10–11, 13, 113, 136, 143, 155, 158, 160, 162, 166
Mental Health 24, 111–113, 115, 123–125, 128, 153, 160, 162, 164–165
Migration 1, 18, 26, 69, 72, 75, 77, 81, 94, 114, 138, 159, 162–163, 178
Millennium Development Goals 113
Mobile Clinics 17, 71

Monitoring and Evaluation 9, 27, 120, 127, 141–142, 157, 170
Monitoring, Evaluation, Accountability and Learning (MEAL) 100, 123, 127
Morbidity 92, 178
Mortality 23, 77, 88, 90, 92, 95, 178
Multisectoral ix–x, xii, 5, 7, 9, 11, 16, 25, 67, 99–100, 109, 114–115, 118, 126–127, 139, 145, 155, 158–159, 169, 176, 180, 183
multisectoral preparedness coordination framework, 5, 11
Municipalities 120

Natural disasters 1, 3, 138–139
Neglected Tropical Diseases (NTDs) 8–9, 14–15
New Way of Working (NWOW) 9, 34–35, 43
nexus: (referred to as the 'Humanitarian and development nexus,' 'peace nexus,' 'triple nexus' or 'nexus') ix–x, xii, 2, 21–22, 33–36, 39–42, 46, 49–50, 55, 59–61, 109–111, 130, 136–138, 140–141, 143–144, 148–149, 154, 159, 170, 176, 179–182
non-household settings xii, 67, 70, 176

Organization for Migration (IOM) 52, 114, 130
Overcrowding 77, 112, 115, 122–124

Paris Agreement 35
Participatory 12, 18–19, 24, 28, 60, 70, 87, 129, 145
Peace Nexus: *see* Nexus
Policymakers 33, 35, 47–50, 95, 110, 179
Pollution 36, 68–69, 94, 112
Poverty ix, xi, 36, 86, 91, 96, 99, 118, 135, 144, 163, 170, 178
psychosocial 70–72, 111, 124, 128, 136–137, 140, 147, 160, 167

Refugee Settlements 92
Refugees 18, 45, 73, 76, 78, 124, 141, 144, 160, 175, 178

Regional 11, 13, 33, 35, 49, 51, 52, 54, 100, 116, 179
Roadmap 125

Safe Schools Declaration 140
Sanitation and Water for All (SWA) x, 33, 46
Sustainable Development Goals (SDGs) xi, 2–3, 15, 22–23, 26, 35, 37, 55, 60, 68, 112–113, 120, 130, 135–136, 140, 148, 176, 180, 182
Security (*also see* insecurity) 1, 15, 17, 24–25, 28, 34–35, 39–42, 45, 55, 69, 71, 91, 93, 95, 110–112, 135, 141–142, 162, 167, 176
Sendai Framework 35
Sexual harassment 162
Social x–xi, 4, 15, 21, 23–24, 28, 36, 42, 44, 48, 61–62, 67–68, 70, 75–76, 79, 86, 92, 96–97, 112, 125, 140, 143–144, 154, 159, 161–162, 167, 170, 177, 181–182
socio-economic ix, xi, 4, 28, 37, 86–87, 90, 170, 176
SPHERE 2, 120, 135, 148
Sustainable WASH Model x
Sustainability 40–41, 51, 136, 139, 142–145, 147, 149, 180
Sustaining Peace Agenda 35

Technical x, 12, 17, 22–23, 33, 49, 52, 100, 110–111, 113, 115–117, 120, 126–127, 139, 143, 170, 177
Technical and vocational training (TVET) 143–144, 149
Temperature extremes 112
The World Bank 90
Total Sanitation Campaign (TSC) 88
Trafficking 160, 162
Training xiii, 7, 11–13, 16–17, 69, 78, 111, 113, 117–118, 120, 127, 131, 136, 141–145, 148–149, 153, 167–168, 170
Transboundary 35–36, 41, 49, 51–51, 54, 56, 179
Transmission pathway 89–90, 97, 99

Triple nexus: *see* Nexus
Typhoid 67, 93

Unaccompanied and separated children (UASC) 153, 160, 163, 169
Undernutrition 1, 8, 15, 17, 24–25, 85–87, 90, 93, 99–101
UNHCR xi, 18, 73, 116, 131, 178
UNICEF 23, 33, 37, 52–53, 56, 59, 61, 68, 73, 78, 87, 92, 96, 135, 137, 142, 146–148, 158–160, 162–164, 166, 170, 175
urban settings 18, 20, 111, 129

Vector-borne diseases 93, 112, 138
Violence 42, 90–92, 98, 142, 153–154, 157–163, 165–166

WASH
  Access 2, 20, 23, 142–143, 146, 148
  in school 27, 70, 135–138, 141, 146, 148, 166

Programming ix–xii, 36, 48, 67–68, 70–71, 80, 121, 137, 165, 176–177, 179
Systems 34, 37, 40–42, 44–45, 48–49, 61, 99, 137, 140, 142, 144, 177, 183
Washing facilities 68, 89, 112, 125, 135, 138
Waste management 69, 89, 112, 120, 143
Wastewater 76, 143–144
Water Insecurity 36–37, 140, 161, 177–178
Wellbeing 34, 42, 75, 81, 109–113, 118, 123–125, 127–130, 135, 137, 154, 157–158, 165–166, 181
World Health Organization (WHO) 7, 12, 16, 19, 37, 67–68, 71, 73, 76, 78–79, 87, 96, 137, 139

Youth-friendly spaces 153

www.ingramcontent.com/pod-product-compliance
Ingram Content Group UK Ltd.
Pitfield, Milton Keynes, MK11 3LW, UK
UKHW060456150426
5217IPUK00028B/2092